ONWARD

ONWARD

ENGAGING THE CULTURE WITHOUT LOSING THE GOSPEL

RUSSELL MOORE

PUBLISHING GROUP

NASHVILLE, TENNESSEE

978-1-4336-8617-7

Published by B&H Publishing Group
Nashville, Tennessee

Dewey Decimal Classification: 261.1
Subject Heading: CHURCH AND SOCIAL PROBLEMS \ CHRISTIANITY
\ POPULAR CULTURE

1 2 3 4 5 6 7 8 • 19 18 17 16 15

To my son Jonah Yancey Moore.
Born on Mardi Gras, with a prophet's name,
May you carry the sign of Jonah, onward, into the future.

(Matt. 12:39–41)

By remaining faithful to its original commission, by serving its people with love, especially the poor, the lonely, and the dispossessed, and by not surrendering its doctrinal steadfastness, sometimes even the very contradiction of culture by which it serves as a sign, surely the Church serves the culture best.

—Walker Percy

CONTENTS

INTRODUCTION

He always said he'd been "born just fine the first time." This joke was his way of waving off our coffee-shop debates about the existence of God. We were both college students in Bible Belt America; I a born-again Christian, he a once-born atheist. He wasn't so much antagonistic to religion so much as he found it sort of strange and out of touch with real life, along the lines of discussing the habitat of elves. He didn't believe in God, and found the idea of heaven to be the most boring thing imaginable. At least the Muslims had virgins waiting in Paradise for sex, he said, but who would want to play a harp, at any time, much less for all eternity? And then one day, out of nowhere, he asked me to recommend a church.

"Can you find me a good Southern Baptist church?" he said. "But one that's not too, you know, Southern Baptist-y?" Surprised to find myself here in the turn-lane of someone's Damascus Road, I stammered that I didn't even know that he had become a Christian. I was waiting for his eyes to well up with tears, as he would recount how my rendition of the theistic argument for design had clinched the decision for him, saving him forever from atheism and despair. He rolled his eyes. "I don't believe any of that stuff," he said. "But I want to go into politics, and I'm never going to be elected to anything in this state if I'm not a church member. And I've looked at the numbers; there are more Southern Baptists around here than anything else, so sign me up."

I was stunned into momentary silence as he stopped to check out a girl walking past our table. He then took a swig of coffee and continued, "But seriously, nothing freaky; if anybody starts screaming about hell or pulling a snake out of a box, I'm out of there."

My atheist friend was unusually honest, but I don't think he was, honestly, all that unusual. Atheism, he realized, isn't just about what one believes or doesn't believe—it is a tribal marker, one that made him something of an exile in the culture of the Christ-haunted South. He was willing to strike a deal with an innocuous form of Christianity in order to get what he wanted out of "real life." Church membership would protect him from cultural marginalization, which was, to him, scarier than hell. Finding Jesus was his way of asking America into his heart, as his personal lord and savior. He was one of many, those who recognized that to be good citizens, to be good neighbors, to be at home in America, one needed to be a Christian. This Christianity didn't require one to carry a cross, just to say a prayer and to agree to certain values and norms.

> Church membership would protect him from cultural marginalization, which was, to him, scarier than hell.

The Collapse of the Bible Belt

Those days are changing, and fast. Increasingly, one need not be religiously identified at all, much less a regular churchgoer, to be at home in American culture. Opinion polls demonstrate this, as does the lessening of certain forms of conspicuous public piety on the part of political and cultural and business leaders. Many within the church are panicking as they see the rise of the religiously unaffiliated in America.[1] Some see it as the death knell for Christianity, and for supernatural religion of any sort. As the rest of the country becomes more like the Pacific Northwest, some would suggest that perhaps Thomas Jefferson was right after all: the Unitarians will inherit the earth. Some suggest that the church must "change or die," by jettisoning those parts of the Christian message most offensive to the ambient culture. And others would suggest that the secularizing of America is another threat, like Communism and "secular humanism" of generations past, that we should denounce angrily. Others

---

1. See http://www.pewforum.org/2015/05/12/americas-changing-religious-landscape.

still counsel that we ought to give up on American culture altogether, and retreat into our enclaves to conserve the gospel for another day.

I don't accept the narrative of progressive secularization, that religion itself will inevitably decline as humanity evolves toward more and more consistent forms of rationalism. As a matter of fact, I think the future of the church is incandescently bright. That's not because of promises made at Independence Hall, but a promise made at Caesarea Philippi—"I will build my church, and the gates of hell shall not prevail against it" (Matt. 16:18). I believe that promise because I believe the One who spoke those words is alive, and moving history toward his reign. That is not to say that the church's witness in the next generation will be the same. The secularizing forces mentioned before are real—obvious now in New England and in the Pacific Northwest but moving toward parts of the country insulated so far from such trends. One can almost track these forces as one would a tropical depression on a hurricane radar map. The Bible Belt is teetering toward collapse, and I say let it fall.

When most people analyze the changes in the American religious landscape, they tend to do so in terms of the lens of politics and culture wars. Journalists and sociologists tend to see evangelical Christianity in terms of "advance" or "retreat." For them, if Christianity doesn't operate in precisely the same patterns of partisan voter-bloc organizing, then such constitutes a "pullback" from politics. And if Christians emphasize the public nature of the gospel message, the call to work for justice and righteousness, this represents a threat to American ideals of separation of church and state. Many think this way because they view Christianity the same way my college atheist friend did, as a means to something else, something "real." For those who don't have theological convictions, the idea that others might is often incredible; these convictions must be about something else, money or power or fame. And there have always been those Christian leaders who have confirmed such suspicions because they too have acted as though those things were ultimate. At their worst, Christian efforts at cultural and political engagement have been sometimes disastrous for the mission of the church. Such attempts have too often created subcultures of "us" versus "them," that divide people up into categories of "red state" and "blue state" rather than that of church and mission field. At their best, such efforts have reminded us that all of our lives are to be framed by what is permanent and what is ultimate: the kingdom of God.

A New Era of Cultural Engagement

American culture is shifting, it seems, into a different era, an era in which religion is not necessarily seen as a social good. Christianity in its historic, apostolic form is increasingly seen as socially awkward at best, as subversive at worst. This is especially true when it comes to what, at the moment, is perhaps the most offensive aspect of such Christianity: our sexual ethic. Our understanding of human sexuality, and behind that of human meaning, is at the heart right now of virtually all of the ongoing "culture war" skirmishes, over the sanctity of human life, over the purpose of marriage and family, over religious liberty and freedom of conscience. Many of the political divisions we have come down to this: competing visions of sexuality as they relate to morality and the common good. For a long time, the church in America has assumed that its cultural conservatism was American, that most people at least ideally wanted to live up to our conception of the good life. Those with eyes to see ought to recognize that if those days ever existed, they are no more.

We must retool, then—some tell us—if we're going to reach the next generation and if we are going to maintain any influence in American society. We will lose the next generation, they say, because of our "obsession" with sexual morality. We need a more flexible ethic, they say, to adapt or else we will die. This argument is hardly new. In the early twentieth century, this was precisely the rhetoric used by the "modernists" within the mainline Protestant denominations. They were concerned, they said, for the future of Christianity. If the church was to have any future, they warned, we must get over our obsession with virginity. By that, they didn't mean the virginity of single Christians and their neighbors, but the virginity of our Lord's mother.

The younger generation wanted to be Christian, the progressives told their contemporaries, but they just couldn't accept outmoded ideas of the miraculous, such as the virgin birth of Christ. What the liberals missed is that such miracles didn't become hard to believe with the onset of the modern age. They were hard to believe from the very beginning. First-century peoples, and their forebears in ancient Israel, might not have known how the planets orbit, but they knew how children were conceived. That's why Joseph's reaction to Mary's pregnancy was not "Well, it's beginning to look a lot like Christmas." He assumed she had cheated on him, and this assumption was entirely reasonable because he knew how women get pregnant.

The Christian message isn't burdened down by the miraculous. It's inextricably linked to it. A woman conceives. The lame walk. The blind see. A dead man is resurrected, ascends to heaven, and sends the Spirit. The universe's ruler is a Jewish laborer from Nazareth, who is on his way to judge the living and the dead. Those who do away with such things are left with what modernism's dissenting prophet, J. Gresham Machen, rightly identified as a different religion, a religion as disconnected from global Christianity as the New Age religion of Wicca is from the ancient Druidic rites.[2]

The same is true with a Christian ethic. It didn't become difficult with the onset of the Sexual Revolution, or the secularizing of American culture. It always had been difficult. Walking away from our own lordship—or from the tyranny of our desires—has always been a narrow way. The rich young ruler who once encountered Jesus wanted a religion that would promise him his best life now, extended out into all eternity. But Jesus knew that such an existence isn't life at all, just the zombie corpse of the way of the flesh—always hungry but unable to die. Jesus came to do something else; he came to wreck our lives, so that he could join us to his. We cannot build Christian churches on a sub-Christian gospel. People who don't want Christianity don't want almost-Christianity.

Strangely enough, the increasing marginalization of Christianity offers an opportunity for the church to reclaim a gospel vision that has been too often obscured, even within the sectors of the church we think of as "conservative." Make no mistake: the cultural Christianity of Bible Belt civil religion kept some bad things from happening. It's possible that I may exist now due to such social realities. I may have had ancestors who stayed together long enough to form my family, because divorce would have made them outcasts in their Mississippi hamlet. The loss of the Bible Belt may be bad news for America. But it can be good news for the church.

The problem with American Christianity is that we often assumed there were more of "us" than there were of "them." And we were sometimes confused about who we meant when we said "us." The idea of the church as

---

2. J. Gresham Machen, *Christianity and Liberalism* (Grand Rapids, MI: Wm. B. Eerdmans Publishing, 1923).

part of a "moral majority" was not started, or ended, by the political movement of that name. The idea was that most Americans shared common
goals with Christianity, if not at the level of metaphysics then at the level
of morality. We could get the conversation to the metaphysics if we started
with the moral. The narrative was helped along by the fact that it was, at
least in some ways, true. Most Americans did identify with Christianity,
and with the goods of Christianity such as church-going and moral self-
restraint. These were approved of by the culture as means toward molding
good citizens, the kind that could withstand the ravages of the frontier
or the threats of global Communism. Mainstream American culture did
aspire to at least the ideal of many of the things the Christian church talked
about: healthy marriages, stable families, strong communities, bound
together by prayer.

Now, politically and socially, this is what a group is supposed to do:
attach itself to a broad coalition and speak then as part of a majority. The
problem was that, from the very beginning, Christian values were always
more popular in American culture than the Christian gospel. That's why
one could speak of "God and country" with great reception in almost any
era of the nation's history but would create cultural distance as soon as
one mentioned "Christ and him crucified." God was always welcome in
American culture. He was, after all, the Deity whose job it was to bless
America. The God who must be approached through the mediation of the
blood of Christ, however, was much more difficult to set to patriotic music
or to "Amen" in a prayer at the Rotary Club.

Now, however, it is increasingly clear that American culture doesn't
just reject the particularities of orthodox Christianity but also rejects key
aspects of "traditional values." The "wedge issues" that once benefitted
social conservatives do so no longer, and instead now benefit moral liber-
tarians—from questions of sexuality to drug laws to public expressions of
religion to the definition of the family.

Where Do We Go from Here?

This leaves American Christianity to ponder the path forward from
here. The alternative many will find is some form of a siege mentality. They
will retain the illusion of a previously Christian America, and will grow all

the angrier, thinking that we have lost something that rightly belonged to us. Moreover, there will always be those who will set up a kind of protection racket, labeling the intensity of Christian conviction on the basis of the theatrical force of expressed outrage. Others will wish to simply absorb into the larger culture in their secular lives, while carving out counter-cultures in their churches to hold fast to the gospel, not recognizing how quickly the culture often outweighs the counter.

We ought to approach the future without the clenching of our fists or the wringing of our hands. We ought to see the ongoing cultural shake-up in America as a liberation of sorts from a captivity we never even knew we were in. The closeness of American culture with the church caused many sectors of the American church to read the Bible as though the Bible were pointing us to America itself. That's why endless recitations of 2 Chronicles 7:14 focused on revival in the nation as a means to national blessing, without ever seeming to ask who the "my people" of this text actually are, and what it means, in light of the gospel, to be "blessed."

The strangeness of Christianity will force the evaporation of those who identify with the almost-gospel of Jesus as means to American normality, and it can force the church to articulate, explicitly, the otherness of the gospel. This does not lead to disengagement, but to a different form of engagement, one that is more explicitly Christian while at the same time more open to alliances with those who are not. With a clear gospel grounding, politics and culture can be important without being spiritualized into a sort of totem of personal expression.

The shaking of American culture is no sign that God has given up on American Christianity. In fact, it may be a sign that God is rescuing American Christianity from itself. We must remember that even Israel's slavery in Egypt was a sign of God's mercy. The people of God were in a strange land not because God had forgotten them, but because he was sparing them from a famine in Canaan that would have wiped out the line of Abraham, and, with it, the gospel itself. The church has an opportunity now to reclaim our witness, as those who confess that we are "strangers and exiles on earth" (Heb. 11:13). That strangeness starts in what is the most important thing that differentiates us from the rest of the world: the gospel. If our principal means of differentiation is politics or culture, then we have every reason to see those around us as our enemies, and to see ourselves as somehow morally superior. But if what differentiates us is blood poured out for our sins, then we see ourselves for what we are: hell-deserving sinners in the hands of a merciful God.

A Christianity that is without friction in the culture is a Christianity that dies. Such religion absorbs the ambient culture until it is indistinguishable from it, until, eventually, a culture asks what the point is of the whole thing. A Christianity that is walled off from the culture around it is a Christianity that dies. The gospel we have received is a missionary gospel, one that must connect to those on the outside in order to have life.

> **Our call is to an *engaged alienation*, a Christianity that preserves the distinctiveness of our gospel while not retreating from our callings as neighbors, and friends, and citizens.**

Our call is to an *engaged alienation,* a Christianity that preserves the distinctiveness of our gospel while not retreating from our callings as neighbors, and friends, and citizens.

This means our priority is a theological vision of what it means to be the church in the world, of what it means to be human in the cosmos. We must put priority where Jesus put it, on the kingdom of God. But while we are a Kingdom First people, we are not a Kingdom Only people. Jesus told us to seek both the kingdom of God "and his righteousness" (Matt. 6:33). We pursue justice and mercy and well-being for those around us, including the social and political arenas. This means that we will be considered "culture warriors." Maybe so, but let's be Christ-shaped culture warriors. Let's be those who contend for culture, but not those who are at war with the culture. We will see ourselves in a much deeper, much more intractable, much more ancient war—not against flesh and blood or even against cultural forces, but against unseen principalities and powers in the heavenly places.

We will recognize the necessity of engagement in social and political action, even as we see the limits of such action, this side of the New Jerusalem. But we will engage—not with the end goal of winning, but with the end goal of reconciliation. This means that morality and social justice, while good, are not enough. We witness to a gospel that seeks not only to reconcile people to one another but to God, by doing away with the obstacle to such communion: our sin and our guilt. That comes not by voter blocs or by policy papers but by a bloody cross and an empty tomb.

Over the past century or so, the "culture wars" could be categorized as disputes over human dignity (the pro-life movement, for example), family stability (the sexual and marriage and child-rearing debates, for example), and religious liberty. The intuitions of American Christians on these fronts have often been right, I believe, even if too often unanchored from a larger gospel vision and from a larger framework of justice. We should learn from the best impulses of such engagement, and use our articulation of our views at these points as part of an even bigger argument. These should point us back to a vision of kingdom, of culture, and of mission, rooted in the gospel and in the church, even as we work with those who disagree with us in many ways toward an approximation of justice in the public arena. As we do this, we shouldn't be ashamed of Jesus, and we shouldn't be afraid to be out of step with America. We are marching onward, toward a different kind of reign.

The church now has the opportunity to bear witness in a culture that often does not even pretend to share our "values." That is not a tragedy since we were never given a mission to promote "values" in the first place, but to speak instead of sin and of righteousness and judgment, of Christ and his kingdom. We will now have to articulate concepts we previously assumed—concepts such as "marriage" and "family" and "faith" and "religion." So much the better, since Jesus and the apostles do the same thing, defining these categories in terms of the creation and of the gospel. We should have been doing such all along. Now we will be forced to, simply to be understood at all. Our end goal is not a Christian America, either of the made-up past or the hoped-for future. Our end goal is the kingdom of Christ, made up of every tribe, tongue, nation, and language. We are, in Christ, the heirs of this kingdom. The worst thing that can happen to us is crucifixion under the curse of God, and we've already been there, in Christ. The best thing that can happen to us is freedom from death and life at the right hand of God, and that's already happened to us too, in Christ. That should free us to stand and to speak, not because we're a majority, moral or otherwise, but because we are an embassy of the future, addressing consciences designed to long for good news.

Conclusion

I thought about my unbelieving college friend a while back, as I was having another conversation with an atheist, this time a lesbian progressive activist in a major urban cultural center. She wanted to talk to me because evangelical Christianity piqued her interest, as a sociological phenomenon. She was most interested in our sexual ethic, and peppered me with questions about why we thought certain things were sinful. We had a respectful, civil conversation, though she couldn't help but laugh out loud several times when I articulated viewpoints quite commonplace not only in historic Christianity but in Judaism and, for that matter, Islam. She said I was the first person she'd ever actually talked to who believed that sexual expression ought only to take place within marriage, and that I was the only person she'd ever met in real life who thought that marriage could only happen with the union of a man to a woman. She said that if she ever met anyone who had seen someone for more than three or four weeks, without having sex, she would not first assume that this person had some sort of religious conviction, but rather that this person must bear the psychological scars of some sort of traumatic abuse. She followed this up by saying, "So do you see how strange what you're saying sounds to us, to those of us out here in normal America?"

Before I could answer, I was distracted by those two words: "normal America." How things had turned around. Most of the people in the pews of my church back home would consider themselves to be "normal America." They would view this woman—with her sexual openness and her dismissal of monogamy—as part of some freakish cultural elite, out of touch with "traditional values." But I suspect she's right. More and more, she represents the moral majority in this country, committed to "family values" of personal autonomy and sexual freedom. She is normal, now.

She snapped me out of my daydreaming by asking again, "Seriously, do you know how strange this sounds to me?" I smiled and said, "Yes, I do. It sounds strange to me too. But what you should know is, we believe even stranger things than that. We believe a previously dead man is going to show up in the sky, on a horse."

Chapter One

A BIBLE BELT NO MORE

We sang a lot in my home church about being strangers and exiles, longing for a home somewhere beyond the skies. But I never felt like a stranger or an outsider until I tried to earn my Boy Scout "God and Country" badge.

Our troop was made up, as our community was, mostly of Baptist and Catholic children, and we would gather each week at St. Mary's to talk about what it meant to be morally straight. To work on earning this badge, though, we were shuttled over to the United Methodist church for sessions on what it meant to do our part for Christian America. Afterward, we had an open question and answer session with the pastor. And that's when I discovered I was embarrassing the preacher, my troop leader, and maybe even my country.

I wanted to talk theology. My pastor was warm and welcoming, but I rarely had the opportunity to sit and ask whatever I wanted, and what was on my mind was the devil. A classmate of mine at the elementary school had watched some horror film on demonic possession, and he told me all about it, eerie voices, heads that turned all the way around, the whole thing. It shook me up. So I asked, "Can a Christian be possessed by a demon, or are we protected from that by the indwelling of the Holy Spirit?"

The Methodist minister had been ebullient to that point, in the way a county supervisor cutting a ribbon at a storefront might be. But now he seemed uncomfortable, shifting in his chair and laughing stiltedly. He hemmed and hawed about pre-modern conceptions of mental illness and about the personification of social structures, with lots of throat clearing between every clause. I had no idea what he was talking about, and there was too much at stake to let him off the hook this easily. I didn't want to risk projectile vomiting demonic ooze. My grandmother was Catholic, but could I spare the time it would take to get to her house to round up a crucifix? I asked the question again. This time he was abrupt, and clear: "There's no such thing as demons."

Now, I was really confused. "Oh, but there are," I said. "Look, right here in the Gospel of Mark, it says . . ." The pastor interrupted me to tell me he was quite familiar with Mark, and with Matthew, and with Q, whatever that was. He knew they believed in the devil, but he didn't. In this day and age, the literal existence of angels and demons wasn't tenable. This was the first time I'd ever encountered anyone, in person, who knew what the Bible said but just disagreed with it. And he was the preacher. Moreover, I picked up in the nonverbal cues there that he didn't just find the idea of angels and demons incredible; he found it embarrassing.

The "God and Country" badge wasn't really about conforming us to the gospel, or to the Bible, to any confessional Christian tradition, or even, for that matter, to the "mere Christianity" of the ancient creeds and councils. This project didn't want to immerse us (or even sprinkle us) into the strange world of the Bible, with its fiery spirits and burning bushes and empty tombs. We were here for the right kind of Christianity, the sort that was a means to an end. We were to have enough Christianity to fight the Communists and save the Republic, as long as we didn't take it all too seriously. We weren't there to carry a cross; we were there to earn a badge. We weren't to be about Christ and kingdom, just God and country. This notion of Christian America stood in the backdrop of the culture wars of the last generation.[3] If we are to engage in a new context, we must understand what we, perhaps unwittingly, embraced, and how to navigate beyond it.

Even though Moral Majority was, formally, a cultural-political organization that lasted for a fixed amount of time in the 1970s and 1980s, the

---

3. For a discussion of what "Christian America" means to evangelicals, see Christian Smith, *Christian America? What Evangelicals Really Want* (Berkeley, CA: University of California Press, 2000), 21–60.

idea of a "moral majority" transcended any particular organization because it was more of a mood than a movement, and it both predated and outlasted the organization by the name. The idea was clear. Most Americans agreed on certain traditional values: monogamous marriage, the nuclear family, the right to life, the good of prayer and church attendance, free enterprise, a strong military, and the basic goodness of the American way of life. The argument was that this consensus represented the real America, and that, for evangelical Christians, evangelical Christianity represented the best way to preserve those values and to attain those ideals.

The Times They Are A-Changin'

We tend to think of culture wars mostly in terms of the ballot box, of red states and blue states, Republicans versus Democrats, conservatives versus liberals. But before the culture war came to the ballot box, it came to the jukebox.

While the roots of the culture war long predated the 1960s, the decade brought fissures to the surface and threatened, at least in the popular imagination, to split generation from generation. The counterculture of the 1960s and 1970s cast itself almost in prophetic terms, denouncing the sins of American culture. On many points, the counterculture was right. Racism was endemic in American society, propped up by systemic injustice in the Jim Crow South and elsewhere. The Vietnam War turned out to be far more morally complicated than the clear "Allies versus Axis" of World War II or "free world versus the Iron

Before the culture war came to the ballot box, it came to the jukebox.

Curtain" of the larger Cold War. The "traditional family" structure of postwar America included the sort of misogyny that excused workplace sexual harassment and sanctioned unequal pay and opportunity for women in the marketplace. For the anti-war and hippie movements, the rapid shifts in American culture on several fronts represented more than just moral and social progress, but instead the ushering in of a new era.

Bob Dylan's lyrics framed the culture shift as a kind of Noahic flood, sweeping away the old order to make way for a fresh, new one. "If your time to you is worth saving, then you better start swimming, or you'll sink like a stone; for the times, they are a'changin'." John Lennon's "Imagine" pictured an entirely new religion, one that transcended the idea of heaven and hell. And, of course, the cloying "Age of Aquarius" was more triumphalist in its eschatology than any revival tent's gospel song. But on the other side of the radio dial were other voices. Merle Haggard's "Okie from Muskogee" was heard as an answer to the counterculture. "We don't smoke marijuana in Muskogee. We don't wear our hair down long and shaggy, like the hippies out in San Francisco do." As one music critic points out, two days after "Okie" hit the top 100 charts, President Richard Nixon delivered a speech, written by Patrick Buchanan, on the "silent majority."[4] The majority didn't protest or yell or wave signs. They were quiet and virtuous. They didn't want free love or psychedelic drugs. They didn't burn their draft cards down at the courthouse. At issue was more than just a culture war. It was a matter of dueling prophecy charts.

Historian Richard Perlstein observes: "What one side saw as liberation, the other side saw as apocalypse: and what the other saw as apocalypse, the other saw as liberation."[5] It's hard to argue with that analysis. The scenes of LSD-intoxicated college students frolicking nude in the mud of the Woodstock Festival in New York would seem akin to Armageddon to the salt-of-the-earth folk in Middle America for whom "the dawning of the Age of Aquarius" would sound like a threat. At the same time, the words "We don't smoke marijuana in Muskogee" must seem like hell, if you're in Woodstock. And yet, as Perlstein notes, they had to occupy a country together.[6] So who was the real America?

Impulses of the Religious Majority

As a child growing up in the Christian culture of the 1980s, I learned my place in American culture through Rapture movies. These films—based on a pop-dispensationalist reading of prophecy—pictured a time when the church would be suddenly ripped from the earth, sailing through

---

4. David Cantwell, *Merle Haggard: The Running Kind* (Austin, TX: University of Texas Press, 2013), 157–58.

5. Richard Perlstein, *Nixonland: The Rise of a President and the Fracturing of America* (New York, NY: Scribner, 2008), 377.

6. Ibid., 46–47.

the air to the invisible (to the onlookers) Jesus Christ. These films would always then picture the panic of those who were "left behind" and would depict the societal chaos that would emerge once the "salt and light" of the culture was out of the way. We always assumed, and never really questioned, that our unbelieving friends would panic when they saw our clothes lying on the pavement or when they passed the empty church parking lots on the way to the Sunday breakfast buffet. It wasn't just the prophecy-chart parade of horribles that would terrify them: Mark of the Beast microchips and nuclear mushroom clouds and pale horses riding through the sky. It was also, frankly, a world without us, a world with no salt, no light, no Christian presence at all. We never really considered that they might be relieved to see us gone. We never really imagined that our morality might be viewed by American culture as itself scary, like the bad side of a prophecy chart.

The story line of a silent majority was, in most ways, true. Richard Nixon was elected twice, the second time carrying forty-nine of fifty states. Ronald Reagan won two landslide victories. This wasn't simply a Republican phenomenon. Jimmy Carter was a born-again, small-town Sunday school teacher, and while Bill Clinton was hardly known as morally scrupulous, his years of campaigning among Arkansas Baptists and Pentecostals taught him how to speak to a common sense of American values.

The moral majoritarian impulse among American Christians connected with this larger sense of an America under assault by unelected, and unelectable, elites. The school prayer decisions that many conservative evangelicals found objectionable—some even characterized them as "kicking God out of the schools"—were handed down by the Supreme Court. This same Supreme Court, even more shockingly, handed down the decisions codifying abortion as a constitutional right. Most people didn't want unrestricted abortion, unraveling families, and a religiously naked public square, the Religious Right contended. And at the time, they were mostly correct in that assessment.

The overheated warnings about the Religious Right were often unfair, and ignorant of what the conservatives, themselves, believed. Contrary to the caricature, the moral majoritarian impulse was never about some sort of theocratic imposition of the Bible on the structures of this world. There were a few voices for this sort of "dominion" theology, seeking the eventual codification of the Law of Moses in the public square, but these voices were marginal and, if not completely isolated from the movement, at least kept carefully out of public view. The last generation's Religious Right activism was, to the contrary, the exact opposite, affirming and reaffirming that they were not a theological movement but a political one. The tent was broad enough to include evangelical Protestants, Roman Catholics, Latter-day Saints, Orthodox Jews, and even socially conservative agnostics and atheists.[7] The rhetoric was focused much less on the kingdom of God or on the gospel of Christ than on "traditional family values" or "our Judeo-Christian heritage."

Even the language of "reclaiming America for Christ" was hardly as ambitious as it sounded, once one investigated what those using the slogan actually wanted. They were "reclaiming" after all, implying that the order they wanted once existed. And in their sermons and speeches and writings, it was quickly evident that the past to which they looked wasn't witch-burning, pre-Revolutionary Salem, or church-establishing colonial Boston. It was about getting back to the "real" America, the time before the sexual revolution. The order they had in mind, at least for America, wasn't the sort of new order envisioned in the Sermon on the Mount or the Revelation of Patmos. It was about getting back to the vaguely Protestant civil religion of "our Judeo-Christian values."

In that, the religious conservatives, and their counterparts on the smaller but vibrant evangelical Left, were often in the best tradition of American civic concern, utilizing the motives and often the tactics of the abolitionist, temperance, suffragist, and civil rights movements. Their problem wasn't with the American people, but with the powerlessness of the American people, who shared the same values with them. We don't smoke marijuana in Muskogee, or in Wheaton, or in Nashville, or South Bend, or Salt Lake City.

But, as Dylan warned us, the times, they have changed. Real strides have been made on abortion, both legislatively and culturally, but abortion remains legal. Opinion polls routinely demonstrate, rather consistently, that younger people are more willing to identify themselves as "pro-life"

---

7. Jerry Falwell, "An Agenda for the 1980s," in *Piety and Politics: Evangelicals and Fundamentalists Confront the World,* ed. Richard John Neuhaus and Michael Cromartie (Washington, DC: Ethics and Public Policy Center, 1987), 113.

than older cohorts. This is partly due to sonogram and other technologies that make it harder and harder to maintain that the "fetus" is a clump of impersonal tissue. And it's partly due to the brave, winsome, and often prophetic voices of the pro-life movement, calling the public conscience to see in the womb a child and a vulnerable neighbor. Whenever social conservatives see polls like this, we tend to announce that we're winning. Yes and no.

Yes, it's a win just that the concept of "pro-life" is still alive and viable. Feminist leaders around the time of *Roe v. Wade* probably would have predicted that the anti-abortion movement would die out by the end of the decade, just as the prohibition movement did. The movement is still here, and gaining ground. At the same time, we must remember that the large numbers of self-identified pro-life people can, in some instances, be an indicator of just how embedded the abortion rights culture is in American life.

Moreover, the abortion debate is moving rapidly from the clinical to the chemical as abortion-causing drugs become more and more common and accessible. People will not have to schedule appointments to procure abortions but instead fill prescriptions all the more for the same result. Who knows what these technological developments will do to the abortion mentality? Real gains are being made, but we cannot pretend that we do not have a long way to go until the unborn are, as President George W. Bush put it, "protected in law and welcomed in life."

The same is true with the sexual coarsening of the American cultural ecosystem. Efforts to curb pornography were successful to some degree in the last generation by persuading and pressuring retail outlets not to sell explicit magazines and hotels to stop providing rental of "adult" films. Who could have predicted that such would largely succeed, but mostly because hotels and gas stations don't have to sell pornography anymore? Pornography is now weaponized by a digital technology that renders porn all the more dangerous by its virtual ubiquity and its illusory anonymity. I remember years ago passing a sidewalk protest, somewhere in Indiana, of an adult video store in their community. The unlikely allies of conservative Christians and activist feminists banded together to take pictures of the license plates of cars there, and post them around town. It's been a long time since I've heard of such concern. Instead, every pastor I know, without exception, is dealing with an epidemic of pornography, not from businesses in the community, but from parishioners in the pews, splintering apart marriages and families.

For a long time—indeed for a much longer time than it was in fact true—social conservatives employed a moral majoritarian stance in the marriage debate. Every state that voted on the definition of marriage, it was argued, upheld the "traditional" definition of the conjugal union of a man to a woman. The problem wasn't the people; the problem was the courts imposing this redefinition. In just a few short years, the majorities have shifted with dramatic speed. Same-sex marriage once was laughed at as a scare-tactic by conservatives arguing for ridiculously dystopian consequences for an Equal Rights Amendment. Now, even the most basic religious liberty protections for those who wish not to participate in same-sex unions are pictured by activists and journalists as bigotry akin to Jim Crow-era segregated lunch counters. Turns out, maybe they *do* smoke marijuana in Muskogee.

But the biggest problem is not that we lost the culture war; it's that we never really had one. Political scientist Alan Wolfe points out that the heated and outraged rhetoric of evangelicals in the political and media spheres is often directly related to the ineffectuality of Christian distinctiveness in our living rooms and pews. Of conservative Christians, Wolfe writes: "Their inability to use their political power to lower the abortion and divorce rates, instill a sense of obedience and respect for authority among teenagers, and urge courts and legislatures to give special recognition to Christianity's power role in American religious life creates among them a perpetual outrage machine."[8] While Wolfe might be overstating his case, he is far from wrong. If the Bible Belt had held to a truly "radical" sort of religious vitality, we ought to see regions with higher church attendance strikingly out-of-step with the rest of the country when it comes to marital harmony, divorce rates, sexual mores, domestic violence, and so on. We're not the culture warriors we think we are, unless we're fighting for the other side.

---

8. Alan Wolfe, "The Culture War That Never Came," in *Is There a Culture War? A Dialogue on Values and American Public Life* (Washington, DC: Brooking Institution Press, 2006), 56.

Is Christianity Changing?

It's not just the cultural landscape that has changed. American Christianity is changing too, though not in the ways that some in the wider culture hope and some in the older generation fear. Many recognize that younger generations of evangelical Christians, especially pastors and other leaders, seem different from their culture warrior predecessors. Because of this, many assume that this wing of the church is headed Left, especially on the contentious questions of sexual morality, which are at the root of the most contested issues of abortion, marriage/family, and even, increasingly, religious liberty and church/state relations. The standard trope I hear often from secular journalists is that the historic Christian commitment to sexual morality, in which sexual relations are limited to the marriage of a man to a woman, is a stumbling block to growth. We are losing our young, this narrative holds, and we would reclaim them if only we would soften our views on sex. If we would, the pews would be filled and the baptisteries bubbling as our leftward Christian soldiers return home.

Now, it's true that newer generations of American evangelicals are interested in more than just the culture war issues of the past. Many are actively engaged on issues of orphan care, ecological stewardship, human trafficking, racial justice, prison reform, poverty, as well as abortion, marriage, and so on. This is not repudiation but an outgrowth of very conservative cultural impulses. Those working to alleviate poverty are, first of all, in continuity with every generation of conservative Christians who have done the same thing. Even when they deviate from the talking points of the Republican business class, they are hardly repudiating their moral and gospel roots. They focus on systemic problems but also on marriage stability, family accountability, and personal responsibility. And they are as committed as ever to the sanctity of human life and to marriage as a one-flesh union between a man and a woman.

Indeed, often the "broader" agenda items reinforce the social conservatism of the next generation of conservative Christians. Those working with the urban poor and the rural underclass see firsthand the devastation of family breakdown, no-fault divorce, the drug culture, predatory gambling, and so on. Moreover, the broader vision hardly makes orthodox Christianity any more palatable to the culture. When evangelicals adopt children, the secularist Left accuses them of "stealing" children for evangelism. And, if they didn't adopt, the same voices would accuse them of caring for "fetuses" without providing homes for "unwanted" children after they're born. Regardless of how broad the concern, and regardless of where this concern sometimes overlaps with that of progressives, the question usually comes around to, "Yes, but what about sex?"

And it's here that many expect to see a culture war capitulation. The problem is that "young evangelical" is a confusing term, especially for a media culture that often defines the concept in terms of marketing rather than theology or ecclesiology. Some of this is due to professional dissidents who make a living marketing mainline Protestant shibboleths in evangelical vernacular. Often this corresponds with a set of metaphorical (and sometimes literal) "Daddy issues," striking back at some real or perceived injury from a church or family of origin. These figures typically receive a flurry of attention, usually from evangelical college audiences, by questioning (usually without outright denying) doctrines, from biblical inerrancy to the doctrine of hell. These evangelicals are usually an Episcopalian's idea of what an evangelical should be, but they rarely achieve long-term influence among the churches themselves. The "red-letter Christian" who speaks as though the Sermon on the Mount is a pretty good Galilean first draft of the 2024 Democratic Party platform isn't likely to be launching a church-planting movement or an adoption agency, soup kitchen, or halfway house for those just released from jail.

A study by one research group suggested—to much press fanfare—that a new "progressive majority" is the face of American religious life.[9] Religious progressives will soon outnumber religious conservatives, and this new "moral majority" will be a liberal one, the interpretation went. My first question was, "What is a *progressive* in this story line?" After all, William Jennings Bryan, the anti-Darwinist of Scopes trial infamy, was a progressive. But so was the biblical inerrantist Calvinist Charles Haddon Spurgeon. When it comes to religion in America at the moment, progress always boils down to sex.

> **When it comes to religion in America at the moment, progress always boils down to sex.**

---

9. See page 34 on Religious Orientation by Generation: http://publicreligion.org/site/wp-content/uploads/2013/07/2013-Economic-Values-Report-Final-.pdf.

A New Kind of Church

I'm skeptical, and here's why. The Christian religion isn't an ideology, like socialism or libertarianism, tracked by self-identification. The Christian religion is a Body. A lot of people saying to a pollster that they identify as Christians hardly represents a movement. The question is, "Who goes to church?" And, congregationally speaking, Protestant liberalism is deader than Henry VIII. If adapting to the culture were the key to ecclesial success, then where are the Presbyterian Church (USA) church-planting movements, the Unitarian megachurches?

That said, the older generations are mistaken if they assume the next generation will be more of the same, just with even more prayer for "revival" and "Great Awakening" in the land. The typical younger pastor is less partisan than his predecessor, less likely to speak from the pulpit about "mobilizing" voters and "reclaiming Judeo-Christian values" through political action and economic boycotts. This is not because he is evolving leftward. It is because he wants to keep Christianity Christian. As a matter of fact, the center of evangelical Christianity today is, theologically speaking, well to the right of the old Religious Right. It's true that the typical younger pastor of a growing urban or suburban church doesn't look like his cuff-linked or golf-shirted forefather. But that doesn't mean he's a liberal. He might have tattoos, yes, but they aren't of Che Guevara. They're of Hebrew passages from Deuteronomy.

His congregation's statement of faith isn't the generic sloganeering of the last generations' doctrinally oozy consumerist evangelical movements, but is likely a lengthy manifesto with points and subpoints and footnotes rooted in one of the great theological traditions of the historic church. This pastor might preach forty-five minutes to an hour, sometimes calling out backsliding Christians from the pulpit with all the force of hellfire-and-brimstone revivalists of yesteryear. He is pro-life and pro-marriage, although he is likely to speak of issues like homosexuality in theological and pastoral terms rather than in rhetoric warning of "the gay agenda."

Unlike the typical Bible Belt congregation of the twentieth century, the new kind of evangelical church has strict membership requirements, both in terms of what it takes to enter the believing community and what it takes to say there. There aren't likely to be four-year-olds baptized after repeating sinner's prayers in a backyard Bible club, and the unrepentant often face what their parents never seemed to notice in their red-and-black-lettered Bibles: excommunication. If this is liberalism, let's have more of it.

These churches are often deeply culturally engaged, in terms of music and the arts, with often a more theologically-rich understanding of how to analyze common grace in cultural artifacts than the Christian subcultures of Bible Belt past, which too often replicated contemporary popular culture, at a lower level of quality, affixing Jesus at the end of it all. But they are often unsure of how to think of political engagement. Again, this is not due to liberalism but to theological conservatism. They have seen social gospels of the Left and the Right try to package a transcendent message for decidedly this-worldly, and sometimes downright cynical, purposes of pulling the levers of political power.

Correct the Right Way

To understand this, one must understand that evangelical Christians, of almost all sorts, are a narrative-driven people. Our evangelism often includes personal stories of how we came to meet Christ. Our worship often includes personal "testimonies," either spoken or sung. To those outside the community, these can seem cloyingly sentimental, and sometimes even manipulative. Even so, those who emphasize the personal nature of knowing Christ often define following Christ in terms of our past, what we're leaving behind. But even without a spoken testimony, one can often read what an evangelical is walking away from based on what he's reacting, or over-reacting, to. Whenever I hear a Christian say that we shouldn't emphasize the imperatives of Scripture (the commands of God), but rather the indicatives (who we are in Christ), I can predict that, almost every time, this is someone who grew up in an oppressive and rigid legalism. By contrast, when I hear an evangelical Christian wanting to build hedges of rules around the possibility of sin, I can usually guess that this someone was converted out of a morally chaotic background. The Christian who was converted out of a dead, lifeless church often dismisses liturgy as "formalism" and contrasts "religion" with "relationship." At the same time, one who was converted despite an emotionally exuberant but theologically vacuous church will often seek out the ancient roots and structure of a more liturgically ordered church.

What's true at the personal level is also true at the movement level. We tend to ping back and forth between extremes—always seeking to avoid the last bad thing. The Religious Left of the last generation was, in many ways, a reaction from some sectors of the "Jesus People" era to the empty consumerism and racism and militarism of the post-World War II religious establishments.[10] The old Religious Right was in many ways a reaction to the awful consequences of a real or perceived pietistic withdrawal of some in the church as the country veered into Sexual Revolution and an abortion culture.[11] As we move into a new era, the church in America will seek to correct the course from some aspects of the past. We should simply make sure that we correct in the right way.

Some will see any reframing of Christian public witness as a "pull-back from politics" or a withdrawal back into the enclaves. But this is not the case, for several reasons. First of all, it will be impossible. It is one thing for Christianity to correct errors in past forays into the public square: triumphalist expectations, for example,[12] or theatrical panic and paranoia rooted in a victim-status siege mentality. It is quite another to, with silence, constrict the liberty of future generations. Total disengagement is itself a privilege of a cultural Christendom that is fast passing away. A church can avoid taking controversial stances on what it means to be human or what it means to be married only so long as the outside culture at least pretends to share the same basic ideals. A church can ignore the culture only until, as the divorce culture did in the past, that culture reshapes the church in a way that obscures the gospel itself. And a church can ignore the state only as long as the state respects the territorial boundaries of Mr. Jefferson's "wall of separation." A state that sees some aspects of Christian witness as bigoted and dangerous will not long stay on the other side of that wall.

The primary reason I think evangelicalism will not go wobbly on public engagement is the gospel. In the rising wave of evangelicals, one hears the constant refrain of "gospel focus" and "gospel centrality." Some might

---

10. David R. Swartz, *Moral Minority: The Evangelical Left in an Age of Conservatism* (Philadelphia, PA: University of Pennsylvania Press, 2012).

11. See, for instance, Francis Schaeffer, *A Christian Manifesto* (Wheaton, IL: Crossway, 2005).

12. See Ronald J. Sider, ed., *The Chicago Declaration* (Carol Stream, IL: Creation House, 1974).

dismiss this as just more evangelical faddishness and sloganeering, and perhaps some of it is. But I think it is far more than that.

The focus on the gospel is tied up with the collapse of the Bible Belt. As American culture secularizes, the most basic Christian tenets seem ever more detached from mainstream American culture. There is, for those who came and will come of age in recent years, no social utility in embracing them. Those who identify with Christianity, and who gather with the people of God, have already decided to walk out of step with the culture. These Christians have already embraced strangeness by spending Sunday morning at church rather than at brunch.

This is leading to a sort of mirror image of the Rapture that the traveling evangelists warned us about. Those who were nominally Christian are suddenly vanished from the pews. Those who wanted an almost-gospel will find that they don't need it to thrive in American culture. As a matter of fact, cultural Christianity is herded out by natural selection. That sort of nominal religion, when bearing the burden of the embarrassment of a controversial Bible, is no more equipped to survive in a secularizing America than a declawed cat released in the wild. Who then is left behind? It will be those defined not by a Christian America but by a Christian gospel.

To understand why this leads to greater engagement rather than to lesser engagement, we must understand what the slow-motion collapse of the Bible Belt is about in the first place. This changes not just the number of unbelievers, but the way that believers themselves think and relate to the outside culture. Philosopher James K. A. Smith, analyzing the work of Charles Taylor, gives the example of an evangelical church-planter relocating from the Bible Belt to a "post-Christian" urban center in the Pacific Northwest. The church planter is equipped to evangelize and make disciples by asking people diagnostic questions about what's missing in their lives. A generation or two ago, that might have been what they were trusting in to get to heaven. In more recent years, it would have been what's missing in order to grant meaning and purpose to their lives. The central issue isn't that the church planter isn't adequately trained to answer their questions; it's that they are asking *different questions.* They do not feel "lost" in the world, and they don't feel as though they need meaning or purpose. The effective evangelist must engage not only at the level of the answers, but also at the level of the questions themselves.[13]

The same will be true when it comes to the social and political witness of Christianity in a new era. Older generations could assume that the culture resonated with the same "values" and "principles." They could assume that the culture wanted to conserve their "Judeo-Christian heritage." Increasingly, the culture doesn't see Christianity as the "real America." If Christianity is a means to American values, America can get by without it, because America is learning to value other things. This is, perhaps counterintuitively, both good for the church and good for the church's engagement with the outside world. J. Gresham Machen warned the church in the 1920s not only that bartering away orthodoxy wouldn't gain the church cultural credibility, but also that the great danger for the church is to see Christianity as a means to some other end.[14] Christianity does indeed build stronger families, he argued, and it does indeed provide an alternative to Marxist ideologies. But if Christianity is embraced as a way to build strong families or assimilate people into American values or fight Communism, it is no longer Christianity but an entirely other religion, one he called "liberalism." In the last generation of Christian public engagement, there were some genuine prophets and saints, who called the church out of isolation but constantly warned against a political captivity of the church, a captivity that would tap Christianity of its righteous zeal for the sake of power but would, ultimately, drain it of what every culture finds most troublesome: the exclusivity of Christ.

As American culture changes, the scandal of Christianity is increasingly right up front, exactly where it was in the first century. The shaking of American culture will get us back to the question Jesus asked his disciples at Caesarea Philippi: "Who do you say that I am?" As the Bible Belt recedes, those left standing up for Jesus will be those who, like Simon Peter of old, know how to answer that question. Once Christianity is no longer seen as part and parcel of patriotism, the church must offer more than "What would Jesus do?" moralism and the "I vote values" populism to which we've grown accustomed. Good.

---

13. James K. A. Smith, *How (Not) to Be Secular: Reading Charles Taylor* (Grand Rapids, MI: Eerdmans, 2014), vii.

14. J. Gresham Machen, *Christianity and Liberalism* (Grand Rapids, MI: Wm. B. Eerdmans, 1923), 149–56.

A church that assumes the gospel is a church that soon loses the gospel. The church now must articulate, at every phase, the reason for our existence, because it is no longer an obvious part of the cultural ecosystem. That articulation of the gospel will mean engagement because the most pressing issues are not ancillary to the gospel, in the way some other cultural and political issues are. The temptation will be, as always, to overreact to the sins and foibles of the last generation, with a pullback altogether in an attempt to avoid culture wars and social gospels. A recalibration is called for, to be sure. We are a different people facing a different context. But if we see the cosmic contours of the gospel, we must not swing into a kind of libertarian spirituality that reduces the gospel simply to matters of personal salvation and personal morality. First of all, the culture increasingly finds personal salvation and personal morality to be themselves politically problematic. There is no cordoning them off from a culture in which the personal is the political.

More importantly, an attempt at wholesale withdrawal might exempt us from some of the hucksterism and moralism of some figures in our parents' and grandparents' generations, but it will take us back to the opposite errors of some in our great-grandparents' generation, back to divorcing the gospel from the kingdom, the love of God from the love of neighbor. We could shrug off our social witness altogether, as a defense against legalism. But we would be wrong, and we would, ironically, fall into a pharisaism of the other side, building hedges around a temptation to avoid falling into it. More than that, we would be abandoning a post to which we were assigned and from which we have no permission for leave. The test will be if we can engage the culture without losing the gospel.

Conclusion

If we ever were a moral majority, we are no longer. As the secularizing and sexualizing revolutions whir on, it is no longer possible to pretend that we represent the "real America," a majority of God-loving, hard-working, salt-of-the-earth cultural conservatives like us. Accordingly, we will engage the culture less like the chaplains of some

> **If we ever were a moral majority, we are no longer.**

idyllic Mayberry and more like the apostles in the book of Acts. We will be speaking not primarily to baptized pagans on someone's church roll, but to those who are hearing something new, maybe for the first time. We will hardly be "normal," but we should never have tried to be. Jesus promised those who overcome a crown of life. But he never said anything about a "God and Country" badge.

Chapter Two

FROM MORAL MAJORITY
TO PROPHETIC MINORITY

More than fifty years ago, Martin Luther King Jr. stood before the Lincoln Memorial and delivered one of the most iconic speeches in American history. The refrain of that address is so embedded in the national memory that most people know it simply as the "I have a dream" speech. Part of the gravity of the speech came from its location, before the monument to the Great Emancipator. Part of the gravity came from the surroundings, a mighty throng of men and women and children gathered in the nation's capital, to ask for the cashing of a metaphorical "check" of equality guaranteed in the Declaration of Independence. But most of the power of that moment came from the words themselves. In this speech, King was aiming for the conscience and for the moral imagination. He was speaking not only to his own supporters, gathered there in the National Mall, but beyond them, to his opponents. He was seeking to create a new reality, one that seemed no more real at the time than a dream. There is much that American Christians today can learn about how to maintain a social witness in a post-Christianizing America.

What Are We?

If we are not a "moral majority" in this country, then what are we? I would argue that we should see ourselves as a *prophetic minority*. Some will flinch immediately at this wording. After all, they will argue that it is a concession of defeat. For those for whom everything is politics, claiming minority status seems nonsensical. Each team is supposed to claim to represent the bigger half of the populace, which is why we hear, cyclically, of an "emerging Democratic majority" and a "permanent Republican majority," and it switches back and forth. Moreover, for those who see religious motivations in nakedly political or economic terms, the priority of the gospel will always look like a withdrawal from the public square, even when it is not. If a journalist had been present when Jesus said, "Man shall not live by bread alone," the headline the next day probably would have been, "Religious Leader Calls for Pullback from Agriculture Policy." But don't call it a pullback; we've been here for years. In fact, the call to a gospel-focused engagement is a call to a more vigorous presence in public life, because it seeks to ground such witness where it ought to be—in the larger mission of the church.

Even some sectors of religious activism chafe at the honest accounting of apostolic Christianity as a minority viewpoint in Western culture. Minorities do not exert influence, they will contend, on the culture or the systems around it. The temptation is to pretend to be a majority, even if one is not. But this is a profoundly Darwinian way of viewing the world, like a frightened animal puffing out its chest in order to seem larger and fiercer, in the hopes of scaring off predators. But such is not the way of Christ.

To say that we are a minority is not to talk, as pollsters or economists would, in terms of numbers. It is to speak in terms of a mind-set, how we view ourselves. The church of Jesus Christ is never a majority—in any fallen culture—even if we happen to outnumber everyone else around us. The Scripture speaks of a world system that is at odds with the kingdom, a world to which we are constantly tempted to pattern our own intellects and affections after, until we are interrupted by the ongoing transformation of the kingdom (Rom. 12:1). The world system around us, the cultural matrix we inhabit, is alien to the kingdom of God—with different priorities, different strategies, and a different vision of the future. If we don't see that we are walking a narrow and counterintuitive road, we will have nothing distinctive to say because we will have forgotten who we are.

The loss of a majority mind-set is hastened by cultural and political trends, and we should welcome this loss. It started with good intentions, to get out of enclaves and connect with the broader public, but it came with too high of a price. The emphasis on "values" over gospel exported throughout the nation some of the worst aspects of southern Christendom. Christianity became a totem to secure a happy marriage, a successful career, well-behaved children—all that, and eternal life too. Such a Christianity doesn't have a Galilean accent, but rather the studied clip of a telemarketer. It sought to normalize Christianity by finding a goal that the church and the culture could agree on, even if Jesus were resting comfortably in his borrowed grave. The vision was a Christian America, or a Judeo-Christian America, or a "traditional family values" America.

At the same time though, some sectors of this activist streak tolerated and encouraged hucksterism, paranoia, and even heresy. Some of the leaders of religious activism were genuine saints and heroes, but others made a living outdoing one another with outrageous comments. Too often, the race for fundraising success and media platform went to the most buffoon-ish and outlandish voices in the air. This confirmed a common secular caricature of Christianity as Elmer Gantry meets Yosemite Sam.

Walker Percy rightly pointed out in the midst of the mawkish television evangelist scandals of the 1980s, "Just because Jimmy Swaggart believes in God doesn't mean that God does not exist."[15] True enough. But, as with some television evangelists, some activists diverted untold numbers from the gospel itself with a public presence that was cartoonish and crazy. These figures are seen as strange by the culture not for their commitment to gospel supernaturalism or the ethic of the Sermon on the Mount, but because of their outrageous antics.

The church of Jesus Christ ought to be the last people to fall for hucksters and demagogues. After all, the church bears the Spirit of God, who gifts the Body with discernment and wisdom. But too often we do. We receive celebrities simply because they are "conservative," without asking what they are conserving. If you are angry with the same people we are,

---

15. Walker Percy, *Signposts in a Strange Land* (New York, NY: Farrar, Straus, and Giroux, 1991), 159.

you must be one of us. But it would be a tragedy to get the right president, the right Congress, and the wrong Christ. That's a very bad trade-off. The gospel makes us strange, but the gospel doesn't make us actually crazy. In the New Testament, Jesus and his disciples were often thought to be mad. Of course they were. They were saying insane things: bloody crosses and empty tombs and Jew/Gentile unity. But they weren't actually crazy. Jesus is the most reasonable voice in the Gospels, pointing out that his opponents' arguments don't make sense on their own terms (Mark 3:22–27; 7:14–16).

> **It would be a tragedy to get the right president, the right Congress, and the wrong Christ.**

In Agrippa's court, Paul is considered insane. But it's because he believes in the resurrection of Jesus, not because he is selling prayer cloths. Paul honored the rulers Agrippa and Felix, reasoning with them that the work of Christ had "not been done in a corner" (Acts 26:24–27). He noted that is speaking "true and rational words" (26:25). He didn't mind being seen as crazy, but he kept the scandal where it ought to be, on the gospel, not on his antics. That's because the church is built on the rock foundation of apostles and prophets, not of hucksters and outrage artists. So how did we get here?

No Longer a Majority

This is inextricably linked to a self-understanding of the church's witness as majority report. In order to keep a political power-base, some religious activists had to claim as their own whoever would help the cause. Back in the mid-twentieth century, a curmudgeonly fundamentalist said that an evangelical is one who says to a liberal, "I'll call you a Christian if you'll call me a scholar." Obviously, as an evangelical, I find that characterization unfair, but I laugh nonetheless because it does get at a certain tendency in the religious academy—really of all tribes—once academic respectability is more valued than confessional integrity. But that is even more clearly true when it comes to politics. Some sectors of religious activism are willing to receive, as Christians, heretics and demagogues, so long as they are with us politically. When that happens, we are demonstrating what we believe to be truly important, and we are embracing then a different gospel from the gospel of Jesus Christ.

If politics drives the gospel, rather than the other way around, we end up with a public witness in which Mormon talk-show hosts and serially-monogamous casino magnates and prosperity-gospel preachers are welcomed into our ranks, regardless of what violence they do to the gospel. They are, after all, "right on the issues." This sort of Christianization of useful allies isn't limited simply to those who are alive and breathing. We allow some to spin Thomas Jefferson and Benjamin Franklin and others as born-again Christians founding a "Christian America," showing that it's not just Latter-day Saints who attempt to baptize the dead. Thomas Jefferson was a great American, and one we should venerate. He was right about independence from King George, but he was quite wrong about independence from King Jesus. But, for some, the important task is building the coalition, including an artificial cloud of witnesses, more than it is about asking whether these almost-gospels and counter-gospels will save or damn. Is it any wonder that some outside our ranks cynically believe that our religion is just an opiate for our voters, to help us hang on to political power?

Moreover, seeing ourselves as a majority led at times to both a theological downgrade and a counter-productive public stance. The application of the promises to Israel to the United States of America, for example, caused many to miss, as we will see in the next chapter, the meaning of the kingdom of God, and thus to bypass Jesus Christ himself. The idea of America as a Christian nation is able to get "Amens" in the churches only as long as the churches believe America is, at least in some ways, with us and not against us. But what happens when the cultural climate starts to shift in obvious ways? If the church believes the United States is a sort of new Israel, then we become frantic when we see ourselves "losing America." We then start to speak in gloomy terms of America as, at best, Babylon, a place of hopeless exile, or, at worst, Gomorrah, slouching toward the judgment of God.

This leads to a siege mentality that seeks to catalog offenses of what's going wrong in the culture, in order to shock the faithful into action. We then castigate the culture because we start seeing the culture as something we "had" and are now "losing," rather than seeing ourselves as those who have been sent into this culture in order to reach it. A Christian public witness then becomes less of a mission of a redemptive gospel and more of an ongoing session of primal scream therapy. In terms of issues, a majoritarian mind-set led, at times, to some religious activists ignoring a rich and theologically-formed heritage on, for example, some church/state and religious liberty issues, because they bought into an understanding of America as Christian-at-heart in ways that were, as we shall see, not only doctrinally deficient but also self-defeating. Thinking of ourselves as a majority can lead to some dangerous things, especially when it is no longer true.

Cathedrals and Catacombs

Several years ago, I led a group of seminary students on a study tour of Rome, working through the book of Romans and the relevant aspects of church history there. One rainy day we spent the morning in Saint John Lateran Cathedral and the afternoon in the ruins of the ancient Christian catacombs. I spent time alone from the crowds in both places, praying. As I did so, it struck me that we Christians sometimes forget the paradoxical grace of God in giving us a legacy of both cathedrals and catacombs. The catacombs, of course, are the legacy of a tiny persecuted band of believers, meeting in their underground graveyards, to escape the all-seeing eye of imperial Rome. The cathedrals represent a very different turn, a church that not only grew in size but, in fact, outgrew and outlasted the Empire itself. The catacombs represent simplicity and earthiness; the cathedrals transcendence and wonder. We need them both.

I noticed that the American evangelicals with me on this trip were disappointed when they traveled to sites of significance in church history. They wanted them to be a theme-park-like restoration of "the early church" in a way that made it seem as though the faith went by time warp straight from a pristine golden era to the Billy Graham crusades. This sort of Christian tended to like the catacombs for the same reason some people love working on their antebellum family histories but don't like family reunions. The catacombs don't talk back. Yes, there are drawings there, but because the catacomb-dwellers lacked relative power, their sins and foibles aren't as immediately obvious to us.

But the catacombs and the cathedrals taken together remind us of two things we need to know: God's sovereignty in sending down the faith, and the frailty of humanity as stewards of that faith. We can't romanticize the early persecuted church. After all, the New Testament Scriptures are often rebuking those churches for precisely the things we lament in our churches today: sexual immorality, division, carnality, arrogance (1 Cor. 4:7–13; 5:1–8; 6:1–8). And if Christianity had remained in the catacombs, it is quite possible that you and I would never have encountered Christ.

The basilica at Saint John Lateran was planted there by the Emperor Constantine. As a Baptist committed to church/state separation, my skin crawls at the mention of Constantine. His vision of a Christian empire was, in my view, a failed experiment that led to persecution and to all sorts of nominal Christianity, which is the antithesis of my believers' church conviction. And yet, God used Constantine to end a sometimes bloody persecution and to, among other things, call together the church to put down a deadly heresy or two. In the providence of God, the Trinitarian theism and the orthodox Christology with which I critique the idea of Christian empire came down to me due to the actions of the prototypical Christian emperor. Not to recognize that would be the sin of ingratitude.

Crawling through catacombs and walking through cathedrals reminded me of the paradoxical wonder of the way Jesus spoke of the kingdom of God. One the one hand, Jesus spoke of the kingdom as tiny, a "little flock" hounded by wolves (Luke 12:32; Acts 20:29). The way is narrow, he told us, and there are few who enter therein (Matt. 7:14). On the other hand, Jesus told us the kingdom is like a tiny seed that grows into a massive tree in which all the birds of the air may rest (Mark 4:30–32). If we only see the catacombs, we could valorize smallness and persecution as equivalent to holiness. And we could ignore our responsibility to build institutions and cultures to protect future generations from persecution. If we only see the cathedrals, whether of the ancient sort or of the local suburban megachurch, we could identify godliness with bigness, and authority with so-called "influence."

There's a lot in church history that went wrong. The people who build the majestic cathedrals were sinners deserving of hell. So were the martyrs of the catacombs. So are we. Lots of bad decisions were made, and some of them persist. But the biblical story too was filled with sinful people making stupid decisions, and, in all that, God was working everything out toward the glory of Christ (Rom. 9:4–5). In the heroic episodes of the church's story (Athanasius defeats Arius! Augustine turns back Pelagius! Bonhoeffer stands down Hitler!) and in the awful parts (state churches and political preening and scandal after scandal), God is orchestrating a flow of the river of redemption, taking it from the hillsides of Judea through the bustling streets of Antioch right down to that place in Dubuque or Dubai or Buenos Aires or Little Rock, or wherever it was when you first heard the name of the Christ of God.

A Prophetic Minority

Seeing oneself as a prophetic minority does not mean retreat, and it certainly does not mean victim status. It also does not confer faithfulness. Marginalization can strip away from us the besetting sins of a majoritarian viewpoint, but it can bring others as well. We must remember our smallness but also our connectedness to a global, and indeed cosmic, reality. The kingdom of God is vast and tiny, universal and exclusive. Our story is that of a little flock and of an army, awesome with banners. Our legacy is a Christianity of persecution and proliferation, of catacombs and cathedrals. If we see ourselves as only a minority, we will be tempted to isolation. If we see ourselves only as a kingdom, we will be tempted toward triumphalism. We are, instead, a church. We are a minority with a message and a mission.

This brings us to the *prophetic* aspect of our minority report. Some chafe at the word, and I understand well their hesitancy.

In a church I served once, there was an angry man, who was always "discerning" what was wrong with the world and the church, and who could turn a Sunday school class into a verbal street fight. When confronted about his quarrelsome spirit, this man produced a "spiritual gifts inventory," almost as though it gave him diplomatic immunity for crankiness. This personality test revealed that he had the spiritual gift of "prophet." For him, this was his spiritual cover for telling everyone what was wrong with them, and with the world, no matter the collateral damage. I thought of this years later when I heard a Christian media personality defend a shrill, angry tone as "prophetic," just like Jeremiah and Isaiah and the Old Testament prophets of yesteryear.

This is a matter of being conformed, not to the Old Testament, but to the spirit of the age. Our culture often identifies conviction with intensity of feeling. And intensity of feeling is marked by theatrical outrage and

attention-getting vitriolic speech. Too often, within the Christian community, "I can't believe she said that!" has replaced "Thus saith the Lord."
Along with this, we have adopted allies on the basis of this intensity of
outrage rather than on the basis of consistency with the gospel. If you are
angry with the same people we are, you must be one of us. Jesus just never
operated this way. The Pharisees were at odds with the Sadducees; Jesus
angered them both. The zealots were at odds with the tax collectors; Jesus
redeemed them both. His ministry wasn't, first of all, anti-Pharisee or anti-
Sadducee, anti-zealot or anti-collaborator. His mission was the kingdom of
God, and that casts judgment on every rival reign.

And it's not as though Jesus' prophetic ministry was a break from the
"anger" of the Old Testament prophets. Jesus, after all, could be harsh when
need be, casting out the money-changers from the temple. And the prophets themselves were not curmudgeons. They pointed beyond the warning
of judgment toward the hope of redemption. That's why Jeremiah's prophetic call is described by God this way: "Behold, I have put my words in
your mouth. See, I have set you this day over nations and over kingdoms
to pluck up and to break down, to destroy and to overthrow, to build and
to plant" (Jer. 1:9–10). In no prophet's ministry, in either Testament, is the
prophetic calling merely one of pulling down, or of "discerning" error. The
call to repentance is itself a word of hope because the voice crying in the
wilderness is preparing the way for the revealing of the glory of the Lord
(Isa. 40:1–5). And the glory came to have a name: Jesus (John 12:41).

The problem with carnal anger and outrage is that it's one of the
easiest sins to commit while convincing oneself that one is being faithful.
The adulterer is often able to rationalize his adultery, and put it out of his
mind, but he rarely sees the adultery itself as part of his holy mission. But
how many angry, divisive, perpetually outraged Christians are convinced
that they are reincarnated Old Testament prophets, calling down fire from
heaven? Now, to be sure, there's a time to call down fire from heaven. But
you had better make sure that God has called you to direct that fire to fall.
If not, then you're acting like a prophet all right, but not a prophet of God.

The prophets of Baal called down fire from heaven too, and they
screamed and raved for fire that never fell (1 Kings 18:29). And the more
frustrated they were by their powerlessness, the louder they became. James
and John no doubt believed themselves to be well within the spirit of Elijah
when they wanted to call down fire from heaven on the Christ-rejecting

villages of Samaria. Jesus wanted nothing to do with that spirit because he saw it for what it was. They viewed Jesus as just another Baal, another personal fertility god they could use to lambaste their enemies with shock and awe.

A friend of mine told me about a "parenting fail" that I could immediately identify with. His son stubbed his toe and squealed with tears. My friend tried to toughen him up, by telling him he ought not to cry like that. The next day my friend's son came home, talking about another playground injury. The son, with pride, announced that he had found a strategy to keep from crying. He just got very angry and blamed the person standing closest to him. I saw myself in the parenting fail. How often have I tried to correct some behavior, only to have my own instruction backfire on me? But the more I thought of it, the more I identified with the son too. How often do I rage rather than lament?

The prophets announced judgment on Israel and on the nations, but never as a catharsis for the prophets themselves. Instead, the judgment always pointed to a God who "takes no pleasure in . . . the wicked," but who seeks to be merciful and redemptive (Ezek. 33:11). Anger is sometimes right. God in his holiness displays wrath. But God's anger is slow to kindle, rooted in the patience of the One who is "not willing that any should perish but that all should come to repentance" (2 Pet. 3:9 NKJV). God's anger is not a means of catharsis, and it certainly isn't the theatrical display of an out-of-control temper. That's why the Bible warns us that "the anger of man does not produce the righteousness of God" (James 1:20). The sort of witness that preaches condemnation without the offer of mercy is "prophetic" all right, but only insofar as it matches the disobedience of the prophet Jonah. He was willing to tell the city of Nineveh of its coming destruction, but actually pouted when his enemies repented. Some so-called "prophetic" authority is like this. It cannot take "yes" for an answer. Rage is no sign of authority, prophetic or otherwise.

"For the Bible Tells Me So"

I can also understand the reluctance of some with the word *prophetic* when they see how it has been sometimes used by the Religious Left in this country. For some, the endless position papers on every issue from economic boycotts of Israel to minimum fuel efficiency standards are labeled "prophetic." Sometimes they are, in the sense that they are rooted in the biblical witness and are courageous in speaking the truth to power. But, more often than not, *prophetic* is simply another word for a bureaucratic action that is unpopular with the people in the pews who pay the bills for such advocacy. For some, on the Left and on the Right, prophetic is just another way to say "consistent with every aspect of my political agenda, whatever it is." We are to be a prophetic minority in that we are to, first of all, ground our witness in authority. This is to say that our witness is shaped and formed by a Christian understanding of reality, since the prophetic witness centers on Christ himself (Deut. 18:15; Heb. 1:1–3). Christians disagree sometimes about what the gift of prophecy looks like in this post-apostolic era, but one thing we can all agree on is that we have a prophetic word in the inspired Scriptures (John 16:12–14; 2 Pet. 1:19–21). Any Christian engagement with the outside culture is shaped by the internal life of the church. And the church is formed, and shaped, by the Spirit speaking in the Scriptures. We ought not to shy away then from saying, "the Bible says."

> **We ought not to shy away then from saying, "the Bible says."**

What I do not mean by this is that the Bible speaks directly to every social, cultural, or political issue. I do not think that Jesus' telling his disciples to buy a sword is, necessarily, a manifesto against government background checks for gun purchases. I also don't think that Jesus' command to Peter to put away his sword is a manifesto against concealed carry weapons licenses. Nor do the biblical commands for Israel, necessarily, have application to the legal structure of a state not in covenant with God, after the fulfillment of Israel in the person of Jesus Christ, though, the general principles there can often tell us something of what God considers just and right. I also do not think that quoting a proof text will settle a debate for people who do not receive the authority of divine revelation.

"The Bible says" does not solve questions of policy in the public arena, and it does not bind people outside the church to an authority they do not receive. But if Christians are to be shaped and formed by the authority of Scripture, we ought to train our own consciences to see how questions facing our neighbors now intersect with God's kingdom purposes. Our public life is shaped by competing interests and overlapping consensuses, and that's how it should be. But we should be honest about why we care about the issues we address.

When we speak, for example, for the need to care for orphans around the world, we can work with those who don't agree with us on virtually anything as it relates to the gospel, as long as they want to see the well-being and protection of children and families. We appeal to their sense of mercy and compassion, grounded in the image of God, even when they don't believe in any such image. At the same time, we shape and form our own consciences and those of our churches, because, for us, the orphan crisis isn't just another issue. We know that children need mothers and fathers because we can see social science data and the history of civilization suggesting such, but, beyond that, we know that God has embedded in the creation and in the gospel the priority of children knowing the love of parents. We do not see orphaned children as just another social problem, but we recognize that we were once orphans, received into a family by the adopting grace of God. Their story is our story too. We don't expect everywhere to share the same motivations, even when we work together, but we shouldn't be embarrassed by the word that is shaping us. In our social witness, we are having a two-way conversation. We are speaking to those on the outside, and we are modeling to our own people what it means to be conformed by the gospel to the image of Christ in every aspect of our lives.

We can work with our neighbors, including those who profoundly disagree with us, because we believe that everyone is embedded with a conscience and a certain level of awareness of what is right and just. We recognize that sin and the flight from God affects every aspect of our being, but that doesn't mean that every person, or for that matter, any person, is as wicked as can be. Jesus recognized a basic human intuition of what is right and true. In his arguments with his critics, for example, he pointed out that even they could see that their assertions were nonsensical. If he were demon-possessed and casting out demons, this would mean that a devil versus devil civil war is afoot. Even they could recognize that this sort of divided kingdom couldn't long stand (Matt. 12:22–26). A father's instinct—even that of a spiritually lost father—to feed his child is in sync with the way the universe is designed (Matt. 7:9–11). We can build coalitions based on these right moral intuitions, even when we disagree about where they come from and why they matter.

Once I spoke at a secular gathering on a university campus on the issue of abortion. There were people gathered from every imaginable religious group, and many with no religious convictions at all. I spoke about why I care about the unborn, about Jesus' identification with the vulnerable, about the gospel's message of death as curse. I went on to say that even those who disagree with me on why I care about this, nonetheless, can see the wrongness of the powerful preying on the weak, on denying personhood to a neighbor based simply on her stage of development. After I finished, the next speaker was an impressive young Muslim student, who read from the Koran. My mind was wandering as I was thinking about my to-do list for the next day. I then heard this young woman say something about caring for elderly parents, and about how this should not be done with drudgery since our parents once fed us, clothed us, cleaned up after us. I said, "Amen." Suddenly, I realized that I had just said "Amen" to the Koran, and looked furtively around to see if any evangelicals there noticed, afraid they might start a conspiracy that I was a secret Muslim spy or something. But, in reality, what this young woman did was entirely appropriate. She didn't appeal to the Koran as a means of silencing debate. She was revealing why the issue was of significance to her. And in so doing, she prompted me to reflect on the same matters from my own Christian vantage point. That is not theocracy; it is consciences calling out to consciences, and we should have more of it.

The prophetic office is, after all, different from the kingly office. We do not rule in the present era as kings. We have been given no such authority as the church. We have, however, been given an assignment to bear witness. The prophets bore witness to the kings and rulers and nations, pointing to what their consciences already know, if only at the subliminal level. But the judgment was left to God.

A Christian Position on Everything

To say that our witness is to be *prophetic* is also to say that it is limited. When many in our culture think of Christians, their first thought is not of Irenaeus or Augustine or the church down the street but of a television evangelist receiving a "word of knowledge" that someone in the audience is experiencing an inflamed prostate and is in need of healing. Every time there is a national crisis or natural disaster, there is some preacher, claiming to speak for God, telling us exactly what sin God was punishing by sending that hurricane or allowing that terrorist attack. The problem with this is not that such actions gives the church a bad reputation with outsiders; the primary problem is that it is idolatry. God can, of course, reveal the meaning behind his providence, but he rarely does so, even in the pages of Scripture. Moreover, God repeatedly warns against those who speak on his behalf on the basis of a pretend authority and a feigned insight (Deut. 18:19–22). "I did not send the prophets, yet they ran; I did not speak to them, yet they prophesied" (Jer. 23:21). The people of God were to shun any so-called "prophet" who did not speak for God, either because his predictions did not come to pass or because his words were inconsistent with Scripture. Too often in our day, though, a Christian leader can peddle products fitting geopolitical events into Bible prophecy, with a different "last days" prediction every decade, complete with a new potential antichrist.

Even apart from that, Christian political engagement often devolves fast into a speaking for every aspect of our allies' political agenda as though there were a word from God on everything. The last generation often saw "voter guides" with the "Christian" position on everything from the Balanced Budget Amendment to the line item veto to the Panama Canal treaty, complete with Bible verses attached to each. I have seen Christians advocate for an end to a Senate filibuster on a president's judicial nominations, pointing to the book of Judges and the lack of any time delay between God's call of the judges and their assumption of office. This is not to say that a biblically-informed wisdom won't have implications for each of these decisions, and a myriad of others, but there is no authority from God to rule definitively on these matters of prudential judgment. And when the "Christian" position on everything just happens to line up, exactly, with the favored candidate or political party, how can we not expect cynicism from those who naturally start to suspect that "God" simply means "our team." When everything is prophetic, nothing is.

We already tend to understand this in the arena of personal ethics. There are some things in which we have a clear word of authority with which we speak directly to the conscience. Should I spend this week's paycheck on cocaine and prostitutes? No. There are other issues, though, where the biblical principles are less clear and more open to prudential application. Should I send my children to public schools or private schools?

There is no definitive word binding the conscience on that. Instead, we seek to disciple the sort of wise, gospel-shaped people who can make these decisions in ways consistent with their callings in the kingdom. That doesn't mean that we don't speak to such issues, or that we deem them unimportant. It means that we learn the difference between "Thus saith the Lord" and "It seems to me."

I have friends in a more charismatic Christian tradition, one in which at some point in the service someone steps up to offer a word of prophecy. They believe that prophecy continues into the present day, as it did in the New Testament era. While I don't share the same doctrinal stance on that, I've noticed that every time I attend their church, I find nothing objectionable about these prophecy times. They seem to be grounded in words of encouragement and rebuke found in the Scriptures. I mentioned that to the pastors and they shared a knowing look with one another. They said that this took years of training their people that the purpose of these times is not about marshaling God as a mascot for their personal agendas. They said they issued a firm rule that people were not, for example, to stand up and say that God was revealing that someone in the congregation was meant to marry the testifier and should really then start returning his calls for a date. The same principle applies to our social witness.

In its best moments, the last generation's social activism was often prophetic—in the best sense of the word. At the beginnings of the pro-life movement, for example, neither political party was interested in the issue. Most of the Protestant denominations in this country (including, shamefully, my own) were functionally pro-choice.[16] The movement persisted, though, pointing the church to the Bible's witness to the dignity of human life, to a broader theology of the human person, and then pointed the larger culture to the inconsistency of holding to the inalienable rights of life, liberty, and the pursuit of happiness when such rights don't apply to the most vulnerable among us.

And that brings us back to the example of Martin Luther King. The "I Have a Dream" speech started with a contrast between Lincoln's promised end to the injustice and the then-ongoing injustice of Jim Crow. With this was a call to urgency similar in content, though different in tone, to the

---

16. For a sketch of this history, see Daniel K Williams, *God's Own Party: The Making of the Christian Right* (New York, NY: Oxford University Press, 2010), 111–20.

"Letter from Birmingham Jail." In the letter, King explicitly called out the white so-called "moderates" who counseled "patience."[17] In the speech, King pointed out "an appalling condition," the fact that Americans were, in large numbers, still exiles in their own land. With such injustice reigning, there was no room for the "tranquilizing drug of gradualism."[18]

What was King doing here? He was doing precisely what the Old Testament prophets did with Israel and Judah—pointing out sin and judgment, warning of the justice of God. We often hear caricatures of evangelical "hellfire and brimstone" preaching. But I don't think I've heard a hellfire and brimstone sermon in years. Most churches breezily converse about sin in terms of consequences to be avoided. The same is true of much of Christian witness to public and systemic injustice and unrighteousness. In fact, most of the talk I hear on sin and judgment sounds an awful lot like my dentist telling me I should really floss more. I like my dentist, and I trust him, and I know he's right. But it hardly feels like a transcendent word, because it isn't.

King's viewpoint was a decidedly minority position at the time. Even those who believed in doing away with legal segregation often still held to remnants of implicit white supremacy. Even those who said they wanted civil rights often cautioned against moving too fast or going too far. But King spoke with authority and with persuasion. He spoke to consciences. He did not simply speak about his opponents. He could have done so easily, in African-American churches, about how awful American race relations are and about who's to blame. He did more than that. He spoke to his opponents, directly to the conscience. He preached to Americans with the words they said they believed, from Jefferson and Madison and Lincoln, of self-evident truths and unalienable rights. And he preached to Christians the words of Amos and Isaiah and Jesus. King's words were intentionally resonant with the cadence of the King James Bible. Some of that was because of who he was—raised in the church, a preacher, and the son of a preacher. But, more than that, it was because he was speaking a word of judgment to the Bible Belt, from the Bible they said they believed. Whatever King's personal doctrinal commitments were or weren't, he

---

17. Martin Luther King Jr., "Letter from Birmingham Jail," in *Why We Can't Wait* (New York, NY: Signet, 2000), 90–93.

18. Martin Luther King Jr., "I Have a Dream," (Speech given at the 1963 Washington, DC. Civil Rights March, Washington, DC, August 28, 1963).

didn't preach Fosdick or Tillich or Niebuhr in these moments. He confronted the consciences of his hearers with the word of One with authority, and not with some of the scribes.[19]

But King did not speak merely of judgment. After all, Malcolm X could preach judgment, and did, in harshly nationalist Islamic terms. King knew that his argument wouldn't resonate with Christ-haunted consciences unless he appealed to the prophetic imagination. That's why he spoke of a dream. King enabled his hearers to imagine what it would be like if the appalling condition were reversed. He challenged them not to simply see the present as "the way things are." He called them to imagine what it would be like to see freedom ring, even "from every hill and molehill in Mississippi." King dismantled gradualism not just with arguments but by causing his hearers to travel, with him, beyond the limits of their lowered expectations.

Moreover, King did not picture this future as simply liberation for African-Americans. He recognized that hatred, like injustice, is a heavy burden to bear. Those singing "Free at last!" in his oracular imagery aren't just black men and women, but all people. His future is one in which "the sons of former slaves and the sons of former slave owners will be able to sit down together at a table of brotherhood."[20]

Where did King learn to speak with fiery denunciation and with welcoming invitation, at the same time and in the same speech? He learned it in church pews, hearing the preaching of the gospel. He saw there a vision that doesn't leave sin undisturbed. Jesus, as with the prophets before him and the apostles after him, consistently called out sin, and not merely in generic, abstract terms, but by uprooting all the ways sinners creatively find to consider our sins acceptable and justified. The Pharisees didn't think they were dishonoring their parents; they'd convinced themselves that abandoning their responsibilities for support of their elderly parents just gave them more to give as offerings to God. Jesus dismantled all that (Mark 7:9–13).

But the prophetic word never left off with condemnation. Jesus presented a kingdom vision including those who would never feel themselves

---

19. For a wide-ranging analysis of the civil rights movement's appeal to the conscience, see David Chappell's *A Stone of Hope: Prophetic Religion and the Death of Jim Crow* (Chapel Hill, NC: University of North Carolina Press, 2004).

20. Martin Luther King Jr., "I Have a Dream."

to be welcomed. He asked the people to imagine what, left to ourselves, we would never imagine—that the gospel is really good news, even for us. The call to reconciliation is not just for "whosoever," but, particularly and specifically, for *you*, for *me*. I wonder how much weightier our witness would be if we remembered to thunder God's justice, while always following with God's welcome, through the vision of a God who in the crucified Christ is both just and the justifier of the one who has faith in Jesus (Rom. 3:26).

More Than a Minority

A half century after the March on Washington, the country still has a long way to go to achieve King's dream of racial justice. But there's a reason the speech lingers on minds and hearts so long after. The movement was a minority, and it prevailed for many reasons. King's prophetic imagination was joined with a sophisticated political strategy, but the politics would never have gone forward without the prophetic element. After all, those suffering the injustice could not organize themselves into a powerful voting force, since a massive part of the injustice was a system preventing them from voting in the first place. We must learn to be strange enough to have a prophetic voice, but connected enough to prophesy to those who need to hear. We need to be those who know both how to warn and to welcome, to weep and to dream.

We are, if we ever were, a moral majority no more. We are, on our best days, a prophetic minority. That doesn't mean that we should disengage, and it doesn't mean we are victims. It means that we know who we are, and where our power is.

The rebellious house of Israel once believed they could triumph over the house of Judah because of their numerical and military might. "And now you think to withstand the kingdom of the LORD in the hand of the sons of David, because you are a great multitude and have with you the golden calves that Jeroboam made you for gods," the Bible declared (2 Chron. 13:8). Multitudes and golden calves; that's what every culture values. We will always be tempted to think that we must out-number and out-calve the opposition. But as happened so many times in Scripture, the minority won, and it was "because they relied on the LORD, the God of their fathers" (2 Chron. 13:18).

More than simply reading the signs of the times, we must be able to see ourselves through multiple lenses. We are a minority in earthly terms, but we are not merely an earthly people. We are part of a great cloud of witnesses, a number that "no man can number." They are the resurrected majority. When our confidence falls, we will have to remember what the prophet Elisha said to our forebear who lost his nerve, "Do not be afraid for those who are with us are more than those who are with them" (2 Kings 6:16). That assertion cannot be verified by opinion polls or by legislative scorecards. But it never could. Our frightened ancestor could only see the overwhelming horde against him. But the old prophet Elisha prayed that he would see beyond what is visible to what is real. "And behold, the mountain was full of horses and chariots of fire all around Elisha" (2 Kings 6:17). That can only be seen by prophetic authority. And it can only be seen by a minority humbled to the point that we are blind enough to ask to see.

Conclusion

As Christianity grows strange to a secularizing culture, we are free to be prophetic. This means we will live in the tension between prophetic distance and prophetic engagement. We are prophetically distant, in that we don't become court chaplains for anybody's political or economic faction. We're prophetically engaged, in that we see the connection between gospel and justice, just as our forebears in the abolitionist and civil rights and pro-life activist communities did. The priority of the gospel doesn't mean that we shrug off injustice or unrighteousness, but it means we fight a different way. But behind all of that, and above all of that, we do what prophets are always called to do: we bear witness. That requires a different vision of who we are, and where we fit, in this time between the times, between Eden and Armageddon. That vision requires us to start where Jesus does—with the kingdom of God.

Chapter Three

KINGDOM

Every time I walk past the White House, I can't help but think of a coal miner's daughter who put the leader of the free world in his place—with a smile. Loretta Lynn was at the zenith of her fame as a singer/songwriter, charming the nation both with her songs of raw honesty about life for the working poor as well as with her up-from-nothing life story, from the coal mines of Kentucky to national fame. There she was, in Washington, invited to meet with the President of the United States. When President Richard Nixon greeted her, Lynn said, "How are you, Richard? So nice to meet you." Her handlers, and the White House personnel, were horrified. "You cannot refer to the President of the United States by his first name," someone explained to her afterward in a hushed rebuke. "You cannot call him 'Richard.'"

Lynn responded, "Well, they called Jesus 'Jesus,' didn't they?"[21]

"Joseph's Son"

The singer didn't understand White House protocol, but she hit at a point of ongoing awkwardness for Christians trying to relate their faith to

---

21. Loretta Lynn and George Vecsey, *Loretta Lynn: Coal Miner's Daughter* (New York, NY: Random House, 2010), 158.

the here and now. Jesus told us to "seek first the kingdom of God" (Matt. 6:33). He taught us to pray for God's kingdom to come, on earth as it is in heaven. The message preached both by him and by his apostles was one of a kingdom that is mysteriously both here and yet to come. But the kingdom does not seem quite as "real" as the powers around us. Most Christians don't interact with world leaders, but they do interact with earthly power, whether that's opining on the direction of the country or the world with their friends, or by maneuvering the all-too-political power struggles of the office break room, the faculty lounge, the Little League baseball field. The kingdoms of the moment, whatever they are, seem more important than the kingdom of Christ, without our ever even realizing it. That's why our blood pressure is more likely to rise when we hear someone disagree with us about our political party or our sports team or an item in the news than when we hear faulty teaching from a Christian pulpit.

> **The kingdoms of the moment, whatever they are, seem more important than the kingdom of Christ, without our ever even realizing it.**

The first step to a renewed vision of our mission is to see the kingdom of God, in its future glory and in its present reality. In the kingdom, we see how the gospel connects to culture and to mission. We start to be patterned toward what we should long for, what we should lament, and what justice looks like. And, perhaps most importantly, in the kingdom of God, we see who we are and where we are headed. That changes both the content and the tone of our witness.

Back in Nazareth, they called Jesus "Jesus," all right, at least when they didn't simply call him "Joseph's son." And he was provoking controversy among the hometown. The gossip was no doubt abuzz that he had trekked out into the wilderness where he met up with his cousin—a strange end-times preacher—and underwent some sort of ritual for sinners running from the judgment of God. And then, word was, he went even deeper out into the wild, where some say he got mixed up in the occult somehow, claiming to talk with a demon. At any rate, he lost a lot of weight, and when he came back he started saying and doing strange things in the surrounding towns. Now, he was back, and it was time to see whether these signs they'd heard about would happen among the people who had brought him up.

Anyone who has grown up in a small community, and returned, knows something of the dynamic here. I remember, as a kid in Mississippi, hearing some elderly ladies talking about someone who "went up north to Arkansas and got all sophisticated." That sort of dynamic transcends time and space. There in the town synagogue, Jesus came home. And he announced the kingdom of God.

In his hometown synagogue, Jesus was handed the scroll of the prophet Isaiah. He read the words there: "The Spirit of the Lord is upon me, because he has anointed me to proclaim good news to the poor," he read. "He has sent me to proclaim liberty to the captives and recovering of sight to the blind, to set at liberty those who are oppressed, to proclaim the year of the Lord's favor" (Luke 4:18–19). And the crowd loved it. Some said he was a prophet. Some said he was a politician. But, that day, he was a pilgrim and a preacher and a problem to be stoned.

The Kingdom Is Coming

In our context, we tend to read right over the words "kingdom of God." The idea doesn't shake us because we haven't, unlike Jesus' contemporaries, marinated in the prophetic witness of the Old Testament all of our lives, at least not in the same way. Most of us have seen "kings" and "queens" only in terms of military dictators overseas or titular figures in other governments with no real ruling authority beyond holding receptions and attending funerals. We too often assume the "kingdom of God" is just another way to say "all the Christians in the world" or "everything spiritual that's happening right now" or, worst of all, the sum of all our programs and initiatives. But Jesus' hometown understood differently. And, on that point, they were right. The kingdom of God is a declaration of war.

In this reading, Jesus pictured the future to which God was drawing his creation. This future had been pictured in the tabernacle and the temple, where God would draw close to his people. But it had also been pictured in the Year of Jubilee, a time in which debts were canceled and prisoners were freed. The Jubilee year of Israel signified that the existing power structures would not always be as they are, that God would turn all things upside down. Isaiah, writing to a people weary of war and exile, spoke of a Jubilee that wouldn't be part of the cycle of a century, but a new and lasting order. This would be ushered in by one who God would anoint. That language "anointing" is kingly talk. When God anointed David with the Spirit, David was empowered to take on the enemies of the people, to fight for their safety. In the reign of the coming anointed ruler, the prisoners would find freedom, the blind would find sight, the poor would find hope, and, most important of all, the favor of God would rest again on his people.

Jesus began with the end, with the place where God wanted to take his people, and with them the universe he had made. This is crucial, both for them and for us. If we don't know where we are going, we don't know what to want. This is more of a problem among us than we care to admit. Most Christians talk a lot about heaven. We want to know that life goes on, that love is stronger than death. We want to be reunited with loved ones we miss, and the older we get the more people we've lost and so the more we want to see them. We don't want to go to hell. No one would ever offer up a complaint about the everlasting life we've been promised. And yet, if we were to inject truth serum into the communion wine in our churches, I think we might find that many of us dread life in the kingdom of God, not because we find it terrifying but because we find it boring.

The vision of the end many Christians hold is pleasant enough—a white, antiseptic family reunion with super-powers, and calorie-free food, and singing, singing that goes on and on and on, forever. The way we fit that vision of the end into our present lives is betrayed by the way we speak of it—as an "afterlife." Think about that word for a moment—the focus is on the "life" (this present span of time), and everything beyond that is defined as "after" your life. Reflect on how it would change your view of marriage if you referred to matrimony as your "after-love."

For many Christians, then, the expectation of the eternal future is along the lines of a high school reunion that never ends. Now, to be sure, a high school reunion can be a good experience, for four or five hours. The focus of a reunion is on the past. That's what we talk about: "What ever happened to Leslie Johnson; what's she doing now?" or "Remember that time that Chad Lee commandeered the intercom, imitating the assistant principal's voice and announcing that school was letting out half-day?" All of that can be great, unless it goes on for quadrillions of years, at which point the very thought ought to fill us with existential dread. I'll just say it: if that's what we've been promised, that is boring as hell. And I mean that literally. Hell is the place where human beings are focused on the past, with no future before them (Luke 16:25). That is not the kingdom of God we are waiting for.

The kingdom of God is not a static existence, nor is it simply a return to the Edenic innocence of the old creation. From the beginning, God declared the universe to be good, but in need of cultivation, of taming. That's why God's purpose was to rule the cosmos through a human king and queen, made in his image and commissioned with his authority. They were to create, to cultivate, to see to it that all things were under their feet. In the ancient command, there was always the presupposition that life would be growing and expanding, a life filled with family and agriculture and statecraft and artisanship. God's purpose is not to condemn the world that he made, but to save it (John 3:17). And, in that saving, God is restoring the harmony between humanity and himself, between humanity and nature. That is not obliteration of what we long for in this present life, but a fulfillment that is far more than we can comprehend now, above all that we could ask or even think.

Israel was, in the last days, to be the light, drawing all the nations to her (Isa. 60:3–6). The king on David's throne would inherit not just a tract of land in the Middle East but the "ends of the earth" (2 Sam. 7:10–16; Pss. 2:8; 89:20–37). The creation itself would see peace, with animals harmoniously tamed by human rule (Isa. 11:1–9). The people of God would be triumphant over all their foes, including that last enemy, death itself (Isa. 25:6–12; Ezek. 36:24–38; Jer. 31:31–36). Jesus' kingdom preaching continued this expectation. When Jesus spoke of the kingdom of God, he told his disciples, not just that they would go to heaven, but they would share with him in the ruling authority granted to him by his Father. They would "sit on thrones judging the twelve tribes of Israel" (Luke 22:30). When the mother of James and John asked Jesus to grant that her sons would sit one on his right and one on his left, her concern was not for their view but for their level of ruling authority. Jesus did not tell her she was confused, mistaking his "spiritual" rule for a "political" one. Instead, he told them that life in the kingdom is rooted in life now, and that the last shall be first and the first last (Matt. 20:20–28).

A skewed vision of the future has consequences, both personally and socially. I often cringe when I hear Christians talk about the lists of things they want to do before they die: "I really want to go sky-diving, at least once, before I die" or "I want to, just one time, climb Mount Kilimanjaro before I'm too old to do it" or "I want to see the pyramids, before I'm gone." There's nothing wrong, of course, with wanting to do these things, but often the hidden subtext is: "You only live once." The assumption behind this is deeply un-Christian, the idea that our span of life is merely the next ten or twenty or a hundred years. But, if Jesus is telling us the truth, our life planning ought to be about the next trillion years, and beyond. If we assume that what's waiting for us beyond the grave is a postlude rather than a mission and an adventure, we will cling tenaciously to the status quo, or at least the parts of it we like. We will want to, just like the pagans, want to eat, drink, and be merry, for tomorrow we shall die. (Regardless of all this, you probably should see the pyramids, since the book of Exodus casts a little doubt as to whether Pharaoh's monuments will make it to the new earth.)

Unless corrected by a holistic vision of the kingdom, we will abstract the concerns of this stage of life from the next, because we will see no overlap between the two, except that this one is where we receive the gospel to ferry us over to the next. We will then misunderstand what the Bible means when it tells us to focus our minds on heavenly things, not on earthly things, that our citizenship is in heaven (Phil. 3:18–20). We will ignore that Paul's point is not that heaven is away from earth, but that Jesus is in heaven. Of heaven, Paul wrote: "and from it we await a Savior, the Lord Jesus Christ, who will transform our lowly body to be like his glorious body, by the power that enables him even to subject all things to himself" (Phil. 3:20–21). That's why Jesus taught on "seeking first the kingdom" in the context of worry about economic provision (Matt. 6:33). If we don't see how the "kingdom come" informs this life now, we become frantic about the things of this life, wanting to make them ultimate. Or, we act as though justice and righteousness are irrelevant since, after all, what is really waiting for us is worship, so why should we be concerned about those who have no food or clothing, those whose lives are in jeopardy? Either by frantic engagement or by disengagement with the communities around us, we become, to use a word we don't often hear these days "worldly." This means to be shaped and patterned by the world around us. This does not mean that we care about issues going on in the world around us; that's not worldliness. James simultaneously says for us to remain "unspotted from the world" and to care for widows and orphans in their distress (James 1:27 NKJV). Worldliness means that we acquiesce to the priorities and the agenda of the systems now governing the world, in many cases because we don't even question them.

The Kingdom Has Come

Jesus' declaration of the kingdom was quite different. It was not from the world; that is, it didn't emerge out of evolutionary progress. Jesus was interrupting the direction the world was going, starting with his rather disruptive conception (also a subject for gossip in Nazareth). But Jesus' message was decidedly for the world. The prophetic oracle isn't just about surviving biological death, but also about peace with God and with one another about a just society. Implicit in Jesus' preaching in the synagogue was the message he would preach everywhere else later, to seek *first* the kingdom of God, and his righteousness. Kingdom first does not mean kingdom only. Since the kingdom is a kingdom of justice and righteousness, seeking the kingdom means that we come to know what to care about in the first place.

If the kingdom is what Jesus announced it is, then what matters isn't just what we neatly classify as "spiritual" things. The natural world around us isn't just a temporary "environment," but part of our future inheritance in Christ. Our jobs—whether preaching the gospel or loading docks or picking avocados or writing legislation or herding goats—aren't accidental. Our lives now are shaping us and preparing us for a future rule, and that includes the honing of a con-

> **Our lives now are an internship for the eschaton.**

science and a sense of wisdom and prudence and justice. God is teaching us, as he taught our Lord, to learn in little things how to be in charge of great things (Luke 2; Matt. 25:14–23). Our lives now are an internship for the eschaton.

The moment you burst through the mud above your grave, you will begin an exciting new mission—one you couldn't comprehend now if someone told you. And many of the things that seem important now—whether you're attractive or famous or cancer-free—will seem irrelevant. But many of the things that matter little now will take on a cosmic new significance then.

In the kingdom of God, Jesus shows us the goal of the future—of our lives individually and congregationally, and of the galaxies and solar systems around us. Finding ourselves in his inheritance frees us from clamoring and fighting for our own glory or relevance. Seeing our lives now, and the universe around us, as precursors to the life to come, we're freed from the ingratitude that turns away from God's good gifts, from the apathy that ignores those God hears. We pour ourselves into loving, serving, and working because these things are seeds of the tasks God has for us in the next phase. We don't invest any of those things with infinite meaning. My life's meaning is not found in the brief interval between birth and grave—in a happy marriage, a satisfying job, or the kind of "success" my in-laws would recognize at the Thanksgiving table.

At the same time, my sojourn in this interval is shaping and preparing me for what is ultimate, so I cannot shirk off the person I am becoming by the habits I am learning. The goal of the kingdom is the merger of heaven and earth—when the dwelling place of God transforms creation, and the kingdoms of this world become the kingdoms of our Lord and of his Christ. We do not bring this about, which is why Jesus teaches every generation of the church to pray for the realization of God's reign on earth as it is in heaven (Matt. 6:10). Even so, as we pray for that kingdom, we can see the priorities of God. The kingdom to come includes not just worship but righteousness (ethics), communion (society), authority (politics), and "the glory and honor of the nations" (culture). We articulate then what we speak to, personally and socially, from a framework of seeking first God's kingdom, and the priorities thereof. If we are united to Christ, then his priorities become ours. And if we are being trained now for rule later, then we can't assume that social issues are merely concerns for government leaders. We are government leaders, in waiting, in a much bigger government than the one we see before us.

Jesus' hometown crowd recognized that the kingdom wasn't merely "spiritual."

None of that was new to Jesus' audience. What was new—new enough to provoke a violent riot—was Jesus' declaration that the Day of the Lord had shown up, that the kingdom was now here. Before the sermon seemed seditious, it just seemed crazy. The crowd loved the "gracious words" falling from Jesus' mouth, until he said, "This is now fulfilled in your hearing." The problem was that it seemed obviously untrue. And it still does.

Already, but Not Yet

I don't know who you are, reading this page right now, but I know this. There's a cemetery plot out there somewhere, maybe not even set aside yet, waiting for your corpse. One day, no matter who you are and what you're doing, you will be quite dead. And in 100 years, chances are no one will remember your name—including the people carrying your genes in their bloodstreams. The universe seems to be conspiring against you, in everything from the natural forces that are sapping the color from your hair to the bacteria that will eventually grind your body to a maggoty pulp. The universe, it seems, is not your friend. The universe is trying to kill you. And it will. Something has gone terribly wrong.

If we're honest, we must admit that everything the nihilists say about the world seems to be true. It does not seem, contrary to Jesus, that the meek inherit the earth. It does not seem that the peacemakers are blessed. It does not seem that the mourning are comforted. And it certainly doesn't seem as though the captives are liberated, the blind see, and the poor are welcomed with good news. It seems as though the universe is run, just like those who believe in nothing would expect it to, by and for the will to power.

Jesus' gospel of the kingdom of God reframes our witness as a sort of "intervention," shocking us into seeing what "normal" is. I once read a novelist saying that he learned he was an alcoholic from his recycling bin. When he went to take it to the curbside, he noticed it overflowing with beer cans, counted them, and realized he was the only one in the house, and the recycling only runs once a week. Something was wrong.

If we do not have a vision before us of where we are headed, we will assume that the status quo is normal, and that we and our cultures and our societies are "only human," without ever realizing that we have never seen normal humanity, in our lives.

The Hebrew people conserved for millennia a story, a counter-reading of the universe from the way things seem to be. In the biblical story, our primal problem is kinglessness, a kinglessness that has enslaved us to a tyranny we can't even see. Our ancestors were to become kings and queens of the universe, but they surrendered their rule to a dark being, a reptilian invader. When humanity joined these mysterious rebel spirits in their insurrection, the harmony of the universe was disrupted. The communion between humanity and God was broken, as was the communion between the human beings themselves. Human nature, meant to be governed by God's Word, now took on the nature of their criminal spirit overlords, and was driven along both by the craving of the appetites and the fear of accusation and judgment. Nature now bucked against humanity, sensing in it not the reign of God but the dictatorship of a foreign power (Rom. 8:19–22). And yet, from the beginning, the Creator pledged that this aggression would not stand.

Long before God began to restore the kingdom, he began a pilot project—at first from one man, then a nation of those who were to be a "light to the nations"—a model of God's rule. He kept them from absorption into the nations with a distinctive code of law, one that reminded them that their redemption was yet future, down the line from Abraham. He anointed for them a line of kings, from the house of David, who were to rule in righteousness and justice, and these kingdoms would stand or fall by the obedience of the king to the word of God. These kingdoms fell. Every one of these kings, no matter how anointed, succumbed ultimately to death, proving that each of them was at least one sin short of a Messiah. And, ultimately, the kingdom itself collapsed—into division, into captivity, into exile. By the time of Jesus' sermon in Nazareth, the once great house of David was a puppet of uncircumcised Romans. But there was always the promise. The seed of Abraham would inherit the cosmos. The son of David would build God's house, and rule from the throne as a human being. The people of God would be raised from the dead, and anointed with the Spirit. God would dwell with his people, and heaven and earth would be one.

Every civilization has imagined that life has meaning, that history is heading somewhere. Utopian and apocalyptic futures alike are imagined in cultures everywhere, regardless of religion or level of development. In the covenants to Israel, God promised a reign of restored human rule on the throne of David. Wrongs would be made right, the curse would be reversed, and the sons and daughters of God would replace the alien invaders of God's good creation. But that sure seemed, and seems, a long way off.

And that's what started the hubbub in the synagogue. Jesus' hearers understood just how insane and egomaniacal it sounded for Jesus to identify himself with the coming of God's new order. It seemed like a disappointment for Jesus to speak this word of cosmic restoration, of social reordering, and then just point to himself and say, "And here I am." They wanted the signs of the kingdom Jesus had performed in the neighboring towns. They wanted the preaching of the kingdom Jesus could deliver. What they didn't want is to hear that Jesus *is* the kingdom. They wanted the glory, power, and security of the kingdom, with Jesus as, perhaps, a means to that end. They were not, and are not, alone.

Jesus announced the kingdom throughout his ministry but always tied that kingdom to himself. The ethics of the kingdom, proclaimed in his Sermon on the Mount, were obviously unattainable by anyone but him. He demonstrated the arrival of the kingdom by turning back examples of every aspect of the curse. He lived among the wild beasts, with no harm (Mark 1:13). He spoke to the winds and the waves and they silenced immediately (Matt. 8:23–27). He spoke and diseased retreated (Matt. 8:16–17). The demonic beings not only recognized his right to rule, they begged him for mercy whenever he showed up (Mark 1:23–24). Why? This was because, as he put it, "If it is by the Spirit of God that I cast out demons, then the kingdom of God has come upon you" (Matt. 12:28). As the rightful king, Jesus reestablished human rule over the angelic and natural orders by living out the destiny our fallen ancestors forfeited. He was a wise ruler with dominion over his own appetites, with a will, affections, and conscience directed by his Father, and by the Word of his God. All this was true because he was free from the one power the evil spirits have over every other human: accusation. "The ruler of this world is coming," Jesus said. "He has no claim on me" (John 14:30).

Jesus relived the story of Israel. He was brought out of Egypt, through the waters of the Jordan. He was tested in the desert. He applied the imagery of Israel—the temple, the vine, the shepherd, the light to the nations—to himself and then to those who were united to him. He was cursed and condemned and handed over to Satan, but raised from the dead and marked out by the Spirit (Ezek. 37:1–14; Rom. 1:4). In his teachings, with stories and pictures and signs, he prepared those with ears to hear for life in his new kingdom. And then he ushered it in, as the "firstborn from the dead," the "firstfruits" of God's new creation project. Jesus was the new humanity and the new Israel. And in all this, Jesus was in a fight. He was wrestling to the ground the "strong man" who had overtaken God's creation house, and with this accusing thug tied up with the gospel, Jesus was joyfully plundering his place.

Every generation of the church has wrestled with the questions that emerged from that synagogue in Nazareth, of the tension between the "already" and the "not yet" of the kingdom. Jesus anticipated his audiences' objections by saying what they were thinking: "Physician, heal yourself." That is precisely what, years later, the onlookers would say at the place of the skull: "If you are the king of Israel, come down from that cross."

What's at Stake?

The perils of getting this tension wrong are quite real. Those who mistakenly bring the kingdom *too near* (already) fall for utopianism, unrealistic expectations, politicized gospels, or, worst of all, the persecution of those who don't yet believe or who don't see things the same way. Those who keep the kingdom *too distant* (not yet) fall for prophecy chart fixations or cultural apathy or failed attempts to withdraw from society. In his resurrection, Jesus has been granted authority over everything (Matt. 28:18). He is the rightful heir and ruler of the cosmos. But Jesus does not *yet* rule everything.

This sounds heretical, at first. After all, isn't God sovereign over everything? Yes, and the Scriptures say he always has been. But the language of the "kingdom of God" Jesus used, in continuity with the prophets, is about more than that. It is about God's will being done, Jesus prayed, on earth as it is in heaven. Jesus has been gone from us for over two millennia, and swords are still used for anything but plowshares. On virtually every ocean on the planet, storms still imperil boats—and at times entire villages— with no stilling voice from the Galilean. Jesus will one day have "all things under his feet," and will turn over his completed kingdom mission to his Father. By faith, we see his authority, crowned with power and glory (Heb. 2:9), but, by sight, all we can perceive is a bedeviled cosmos, chaotic to the core (1 John 5:19; Eph. 2:2; 2 Cor. 4:4; Rev. 12:7–17).

So how do we distinguish between the *already* of God's kingdom and what is *not yet*? Jesus summed up the answer there in the synagogue: the answer is him. The question is, "Where is Jesus ruling now, and how?" The kingdom comes in two stages, because King Jesus himself does. The kingdom doesn't come initially with the shock and awe of exploding Eastern skies, but in secret, hidden ways. It comes like yeast working its way through a loaf of bread or a seed germinating in the ground, or, in fact, like an embryo stirring in a virgin's womb.

So if Jesus does not yet rule the world, where does he rule? He rules, in the present age, over his church (Eph. 1:22–23). The church is a signpost of God's coming kingdom (Eph. 3:10), a preview to the watching world of what the reign of God in Christ is to look like, a colony of the kingdom coming. In the scroll of Isaiah from which Jesus read, there is the promise that the "ancient ruins" would be rebuilt. In the time after Jesus' resurrection, the early church saw the restoration of these ruins, the rebuilding of the "tent of David that has fallen," in a church made of reconciled humanity, with the old divisions of Jew and Gentile done away with (Acts 15:15–17). Unlike the covenant order of old Israel, the church does not have coercive, military power. We do not, the apostles tell us, presently rule over the world (2 Cor. 4:4). Instead, Jesus reigns over us by his voice, in the right preaching of the Word. He reigns over us by marking out the boundaries of our fellowship, in baptism, in the Lord's Table, and in discipline. In the church, God has created an embassy of the kingdom of Christ, appealing to the outside world to be reconciled to the coming kingdom, and modeling what this kingdom will look like. We do not live kingless lives, but we are being shaped and formed, and prepared to rule, within the life of Christ's church. At the same time, we know that we do not yet rule over those on the outside.

> The church is a signpost of God's coming kingdom (Eph. 3:10), a preview to the watching world of what the reign of God in Christ is to look like, a colony of the kingdom coming.

God anointed David as king, long before he was visibly recognized as ruler of Israel. He was marked out by the Spirit, and the years of dodging spears (literal and metaphorical) from the outgoing government prepared him for the rule God prepared for him. The same is true for the church.

God is shaping us, individually and congregationally, to rule in this government-in-waiting. By drawing the church together, Jesus is "staffing up" his kingdom with joint-heirs, who learn to rule by washing feet and changing diapers and resolving disputes over whether certain widows are being neglected in the distribution of food (Acts 6:1–7). Our lives now point us away from the moment, to the kingdom.

Kingdom First

A kingdom vision is necessary, first of all, to show us *what matters*. The kingdom future shows us the meaning of everything else. We see the alpha in light of the omega, and both Alpha and Omega are summed up in Jesus Christ (Eph. 1:10). Creation and culture have meaning because they are about more than merely natural forces. They are patterned after an unveiled "mystery" one that explains the meaning of everything else in the universe. There is truly, as some insist, a "natural law" that governs our boundaries, our possibilities, and our moral limits. But this ordering structure of the universe is a word, a pattern of wisdom, a *Logos*. That is not an impersonal force, but instead a rather forceful Person, One we have come to know as Jesus of Nazareth (John 1:1–14).

The creation then is not temporary, because God has joined the "dust of the earth" in human nature to his own nature, in the person of Jesus. That also explains why as important as "natural law" thinking can be, one cannot build a moral society by avoiding talking about what distracts and upsets people: Jesus. "Nature says" is often no more compelling to the people around us than "the Bible says" on the issues they find most controversial. That's because the light of nature and the light of the gospel are, at root, the same: the light of Christ. When fallen humanity sees that light, our first reaction is moral revulsion (John 3:19). God cares about the universe because he patterned the universe after the mystery of Christ. God cares about humanity because he patterned humanity after the mystery of Christ. God cares about family because he patterned family after the mystery of Christ. Everything that exists, apart from the parasitic barnacles of sin and curse, testifies to God's glory in the person of Jesus Christ.

Seeking first the kingdom does not dampen our concern for justice and righteousness in the social and political arenas, but heightens it. The goal of history is not, after all, escape to heaven, but the merger of heaven and earth—when the dwelling place of God transforms the material creation (Rev. 21:1–4). The new earth that awaits us is not merely an arena of worship but also of righteousness (ethics), human rule (politics), communion (society), and "the glory and honor of the nations" (culture). While our vision of the end is incomplete, we "see through a glass darkly," the goal of the kingdom frees us to some degree to prioritize our concern.

If, for example, human work and creativity is not simply a means to feed oneself between the birthing table and the morgue but is instead part of both God's original creation behind us and the new creation ahead of us, we ought then to see that human flourishing is tied to meaningful labor. If God is aiming to restore the material creation, not to scrap it, then we ought not to recklessly misuse the world around us. How can we dismiss the importance of institutions when God is preparing a kingdom—which is itself an institution—of priests? How can we dismiss order and justice, when the New Jerusalem displays these things? Those who wish to disengage altogether from culture or politics (as if that were possible) are contending that some things God cares about and intends to carry over into eternity are not worth prioritizing. The kingdom maintains priorities but with perspective.

One of the most controversial topics that I ever address among Christians is not abortion, same-sex marriage, or immigration policies as you might imagine—it's cremation. Many senior adults in churches I've served have wanted to save on costs for burials and funerals and ask about cremation. I don't bind their consciences, but I point out that Christianity, historically, has rejected cremation as a false picture of the body. Burial signifies a Christian hope, that the deceased is "sleeping" and thus will be "waked" at the coming of the Lord. Cremation signifies a perspective found in Buddhism and other religions, that the body is consumed into nothingness. I find that the first implication people draw from this is that, somehow, I am suggesting that cremated people go to hell. "Can't I be resurrected from an urn as easily as I can from a casket?" they ask.

Of course. That's not the point. God can resurrect me if my body is eaten by alligators, but I wouldn't dispose of Aunt Gladys that way, shrugging and asking, "What does it matter? See her in heaven." The way we treat the body is a sign of what we believe about the future. The women around Jesus cared for his body, anointing it with spices, because it was *him*; they knew that the body is important because it will be part of the new creation, whether that resurrection happens in a matter of days or after billions of years of decay. Christians respect the body because we believe our material bodies are part of God's goal for us and for the universe. At the same time, we don't make the body ultimate. The belly is destroyed along with its contents, Paul told the churches. The body returns to the dust. Those who make the body ultimate, as ancient Egyptians seeking to mummify themselves and carry their bodies into the next life, miss the vision of the kingdom. And those who dismiss the importance of the body misread that what matters ultimately is not just spiritual life but embodied life. That changes the way we live now. The old Christian heresies that spoke of the body as a prison from which we would one day escape didn't really lead to body-denial but to body-obsession. The heretics could fight and fornicate and carouse, because they believed the "real me" was the spiritual person within, communing sweetly with Jesus in a garden somewhere.

> **The way we treat the body is a sign of what we believe about the future.**

The future of the world, and of culture and of society, is, in many ways, analogous to the future of our bodies. Jesus, after all, is the pioneer of the new creation, with a resurrected body to which he plans to conform the rest of the redeemed universe (Phil. 3:20–21). Those who make culture or politics ultimate fail to see the discontinuity between this world and the one to come. But those who disregard such things altogether, tend to become obsessed with them anyway, just disconnected from a vision of the future that would maintain them in right perspective. The same is true, for example, with marriage. Those who make marriage ultimate do not understand the kingdom of God. This was what Jesus demolished when the Sadducees attempted to trap him with the example of a woman who was widowed, in order, by seven men. Rejecting the idea of resurrection, they wanted Jesus to embarrass himself by coming out for polygamy by and by. Jesus said that they did not understand that in the age to come there is neither marrying nor giving in marriage. At the same time, those who forbid marriage (1 Tim. 4:3) don't recognize that marriage is not just an outlet for temporal needs but points beyond itself, to something more permanent: to the wedding feast of a Lamb and his bride (Rev. 19:6–9). The same is true with our witness in the areas of culture and politics.

We do not seek to legislate the kingdom of God into existence, any more than we seek to legislate the unique covenantal order of Old Testament Israel. But the pattern of justice in Israel and, even more so, the pattern of the restored future can give us a moral framework to question the assumptions of our ambient culture. The priorities of the King, seen in the ultimate restoration of creation, become the priorities of the colony of the kingdom: the church.

Our vote for President of the United States (for those of you who are Americans) is important. We are held accountable, as we'll discuss, for the discharge of our ruling responsibilities in this life. But our vote for President is less important than our vote to receive new members for baptism into our churches. A President is term-limited and, for that matter, so is the United States (and every other nation). The reception of members into the church, however, marks out the future kings and queens of the universe. Our church membership rolls say to the people on them, and to the outside world, "These are those we believe will inherit the universe, as joint-heirs with Christ." That's a matter of priority of each, not a pullback from either.

The focal point of Christ's reign in the present era on the church makes sense of our own lives. God's purpose is to conform us into the image of Christ. So, like him, we do not arrive fully formed. Jesus, in his humanity, "learned obedience from what he suffered" (Heb. 5:8). If God is working all things together for my good, then nothing in my life is a "waste of time." Every aspect of my life, my relationships, my job, my family, my suffering, is part of an internship for the eschaton, preparing me in some way to rule with Christ. If the kingdom is what Jesus says it is, then what matters isn't simply what we neatly classify as "spiritual" things. Our callings—whether preaching the gospel or loading docks or picking avocados or filing legal briefs or writing legislation or herding goats—aren't accidental. God is teaching us, as he taught our Lord, to learn in little things how to be in charge of great things (Matt. 25:14–23).

The Gospel of the Kingdom

The kingdom of God, both now and in the age to come, is ultimately about what Paul called being "hidden with Christ in God" (Col. 3:3–4).

We find our life and mission in Jesus' own rather than fitting him into the kingdom we design for ourselves. We pour ourselves into loving, serving, and working because these things are seeds of the tasks God has for us in the next phase.

But, as the same time, we don't invest any of those things with infinite meaning. My life's meaning isn't found in the brief interval from birth to grave—in an enviable marriage, a satisfying job, or the kind of "success" my in-laws would recognize at the Thanksgiving table. And, while important, our meaning isn't bound up with the rise or fall of the United States of America, much less with a political faction or party within it. "That word above all earthly powers," Martin Luther taught us to sing, "No thanks to them abideth."

The kingdom Jesus announced also shows us that we are working within the framework of spiritual warfare, and we ought then to expect opposition and suffering. The structure of the universe, the covenants to Israel, the kings, prophets, and institutions of God's people all picture ahead of time, in varying ways, the life of Christ Jesus. The life of the church pictures the same thing, after the fact. Jesus reprises the story of the universe taking on Adam's race, Adam's mission, and Adam's curse. He reprises the story of Israel, from anointing to temptation to exile. And he tells us that we will walk the same way—from the Bethlehem of our new birth to the Jerusalem of our new reign. But in between, we will follow him to the Place of the Skull. We will carry our crosses. In order to be glorified with him later, we must suffer with him first (Rom. 8:17). Turning the other cheek often leaves you with two broken jaws, but Jesus is still King, and still right.

Years ago, I happened upon a television program of a "prosperity gospel" preacher, with perfectly coiffed mauve hair, perched on a rhinestone-spackled golden throne, talking about how wonderful it is to be a Christian. Even if Christianity proved to be untrue, she said, she would still want to be a Christian, because it's the best way to live. It occurred to me that that is an easy perspective to have, on television, from a golden throne. It's a much more difficult perspective to have if one is being crucified by one's neighbors in Sudan for refusing to repudiate the name of Christ. Then, if it turns out not to be true, it seems to be a crazy way to live. In reality, this woman's gospel—and those like it—are more akin to a Canaanite fertility religion than to the gospel of Jesus Christ. And the kingdom she announces is more like that of Pharaoh than like that of Christ. David's throne needs no rhinestone.

But the prosperity gospel proclaimed in full gaudiness in the example above is on full display in more tasteful and culturally appropriate forms. The idea of the respectability of Christian witness in a Christian America that is defined by morality and success, not by the gospel of crucifixion and resurrection, is just another example of importing Jesus to maintain one's best life now. Jesus could have remained beloved in Nazareth, by healing some people and levitating some chairs, and keeping quiet about how different his kingdom is. But Jesus persistently has to wreck everything, and the illusions of Christian America are no more immune than the illusions of Israelite Galilee. If we see the universe as the Bible sees it, we will not try to "reclaim" some lost golden age. We will see an invisible conflict of the kingdoms, a satanic horror show being invaded by the reign of Christ. This will drive us to see who our real enemies are, and they are not the cultural and sexual prisoners-of-war all around us. If we seek the kingdom, we will see the devil. And this makes us much less sophisticated, much less at home in modern America.

The vision of the kingdom, then, will not just inform us on what to care about, but also how we advocate for such things. If the kingdom is where Christ is, then we dare not assume the power of the state for the purposes of the church, and we dare not subordinate the ministries of the church to the authority of the state. The kingdom is defined by the gospel, and the gospel is defined by the kingdom. If the gospel is abstracted from the kingdom, then our mission is simply about the initial evangelism of new believers. If we abstract the kingdom from the gospel, though, then the kingdom seems to be about mere morality, and, thus, an easy client from the pretend Messiah of state power. The gospel is a gospel of the kingdom of Christ.

Because the Bible speaks of the kingdom ruling over the nations and putting enemies under the feet of the people of God, some have thought we ought to merge the church with the state and punish spiritual transgressions with the civil law. But Jesus told us that weeds would grow up along with the wheat in the field of the world, and we ought not to tear up the field uprooting things right now. The division between sheep and goats would happen at the Judgment Seat, he told us, not at the courthouse. The church is the embassy of the coming kingdom, not the fullness of that kingdom. Our mission is defined in terms of a gospel appeal to reconciliation, now, not the subjugation of our foes. That's why Jesus read the portion of the scroll about the year of God's favor, but did not read the words immediately following, about the "day of vengeance of our God" (Isa. 61:2). There is a day of judgment, but the church warns of this judgment; the church does not carry it out (1 Cor. 5:12). That's because this time-between-the-times is defined by gospel invitation. As long as it is "today," it is the "day of salvation" (2 Cor. 6:2). The gospel itself gives us a vision of the kingdom in which the swords of the Spirit and of the state are kept separate until the King himself appears to end this suspension of judgment and to make the nations his footstool.

Kingdom Warfare

This vision of kingdom warfare, then, will recalibrate our expectations. Christian attempts at social witness have often swung wildly back and forth between chest-beating optimism to withdrawal and despair. One minute we are "reclaiming America for Christ," the next we pronounce that American culture is "slouching toward Gomorrah." We lose sight both of the fact that all of human history—from Eden onward—is a war zone, and that God's kingdom triumph is proven not by our electoral success or our cultural influence—as important as that is in being obediently "salt" and "light" in our culture. Our triumph is proven in the resurrection of the world's rightful ruler.

Learning to Be Pilgrims (Again)

One of the most hilarious passages of Scripture is one I return to every Easter, and every time I cannot help but laugh with glee. After Jesus' crucifixion and burial, Pilate orders the guards to make sure the disciples don't steal the body in order to engineer the appearance of resurrection. He sends the soldiers to the grave with the words, "Go, make it as secure as you can" (Matt. 27:65). Every time I read those words, including right now as I type them, I blurt out, "Yeah, good luck with that." The kingdom's advance is set in motion by the Galilean march out of the graveyard. We should then be the last people on earth to skulk back in fear or apathy. And we ought also to be the last people on earth to uncritically laud any political leader or movement as though this were what we've been waiting for. We need leaders and allies, but we do not need a Messiah. That job is filled, and he's feeling fine. We are neither irrationally exuberant, nor fearfully isolated. We recognize that from Golgotha to Armageddon, there will be tumult—in our cultures, in our communities, and in our own psyches. We groan against this, and work to hold back the consequences of the curse. But we do not despair, as those who are the losers in history might. We are the future kings and queens of the universe.

And, at the same time, we remember that we are those who, apart from the rescue effort of the gospel, would be still exiled from God and at odds with one another. We recognize that whatever our current political and cultural skirmishes, the situation we can't see is far more dire. "Therefore, rejoice, O heavens and you who dwell in them! But woe to you, O earth and sea, for the devil has come down to you in great wrath, because he knows that his time is short!" (Rev. 12:12). We live now in this demon-haunted earth, but we wait for a demon-conqueror from heaven. We rejoice, and we groan, at the same time. In short, a kingdom-informed perspective can be summed up in the lyrics of an old Grateful Dead song: "It's even worse than it appears, but it's alright." We are warriors, yes, but joyful warriors. We are not slouching to Gomorrah; we are marching to Zion.

We are stranger and exiles in the present time, that's true. But we are not losers. There will be wars and rumors of wars, literal and cultural, but Jesus is on the move. We fight, but we fight from triumph, not from defeat. Jesus, in announcing the kingdom, declared that he was "anointed." If we are joined to him, we share that anointing (1 John 2:20). That's what it means to be Christians, to be the church.

Conclusion

This brings me back to the accidental rudeness of the singer in the White House. I imagine that part of the awkwardness of the moment was her unintentional disrespect of the President. But part of it was probably just uttering the name "Jesus" in such a context. To those accustomed to power, the word probably confirmed for them their view of her as a backward, uneducated rube from fly-over country.

Novelist Frederick Buechner wrote years ago about the effect of seeing the words "Jesus Saves" painted on a highway overpass. The words cause many of us, he said, to wince with embarrassment, reminding us of the "old time religion" of sawdust trails and altar calls. But there's more. "There's something in the name 'Jesus' itself that embarrasses us when it stands naked and alone like that, just *Jesus* with no title to soften the blow."[22]

When I first read those words, I silently argued with the author in my mind. After all, the titles "Lord" and "Christ" hardly soften any blow. The word *Christ* means kingly anointing, a title so scandalous that it took courage and revelation for Simon Peter to confess it in one of the defining moments of the Bible (Matt. 16:16–17). The crowd at Nazareth was comfortable with "Jesus," but enraged at the very suggestion, not even explicitly worded, that maybe something messianic was happening here.

But that's only the case for those who really peer into this meaning, rather than seeing it as just a last name. Buechner convinced me when he wrote: "It seems to me the words 'Christ Saves' would not bother us half so much, because they have a kind of objective, theological ring to them, whereas 'Jesus Saves' seems cringingly, painfully personal—somebody named 'Jesus' of all names, saving somebody named whatever your name happens to be."[23]

And that is indeed the point. "Christ" was inoffensive to the crowd at Nazareth too. That's what they wanted: the long-promised Messiah who would set the captives free, and deliver good news to the poor and sight to the blind. But they wanted a Christ more distant, one who delivered for them their social and political objectives, without confronting them with the truth that their problems were far deeper, far more intractable, than culture or politics alone. "Jesus," after all, is a personal name—a fairly common one at the time. But it's also a message: "Yahweh saves." Joseph is told to name this Christ "Jesus" because "he shall save his people from their sins" (Matt. 1:21). That puts us all on notice that what we need to be saved from is not just poverty or disease or cultural decay—or all those things outside of us. We also need to be saved from what's within us. The kingdom is cosmic, but the kingdom is personal too. It's so personal that

---

22. Frederick Buechner, *Secrets in the Dark: A Life in Sermons* (New York, NY: Harper Collins Publishers, 2007), 28.

23. Ibid.

when Jesus revealed himself on the road to Damascus to Saul of Tarsus, he was still tied up with his hometown. Saul said, "Who are you, Lord?" And the voice within the light answered, "I am Jesus of Nazareth" (Acts 22:8).

A prophet is not without honor, except in his hometown. But Jesus is no rootless Messiah. He has joined himself to human nature, to the life of the world. And he still bears the name given to him by a Middle Eastern day laborer and sometimes refugee. He still identifies himself with a little village no one would ever mistake for a cosmopolitan center. He is Jesus. He's from Nazareth. He's the Christ, the heir of Israel's promises. And he's Lord, the meaning and goal of the entire universe.

We can learn to be pilgrims again, uneasy in American culture, as we should have been all along. But we are not pilgrims cringing in protective silos, waiting for the sound of trumpets in the sky. We are part of a kingdom, a kingdom we see from afar (Heb. 11:13) and a kingdom we see assembling itself all around us in miniature, in these little outposts of the future called the church. By putting kingdom first, we can speak from consciences formed by the future to know how to recognize what matters, peace, justice, righteousness, and how to recognize who matters, the vulnerable, the marginalized, the poor, the captive, the powerless. As we do, we remember, like our Lord, where we came from, and where we're going. And as we do, we render to Caesar what we ought. We pledge allegiance where we can. But we never forget how to call Jesus "Jesus."

> **We can learn to be pilgrims again, uneasy in American culture, as we should have been all along.**

Chapter Four

CULTURE

Early in my ministry, I found myself suddenly in the middle of a culture war, with no idea where the trenches were. I was a youth pastor, in my hometown, just down the street from an Air Force base. Like every other evangelical youth minister, I received constant advertisements from curriculum-hawkers telling me how I could be "relevant" to "today's teenagers," usually by "connecting" with them through popular culture. I couldn't do that well, though, so I just fell back on being me, and preached the gospel the best I could.

There were two groups that divided the youth group there in Biloxi. The first group was made up of "churched" kids, those who did what was expected in the Bible Belt, and made professions of faith, followed by baptism, as young children. These kids knew the gospel, from start to last, and could rattle off the right answers at will. The gospel neither surprised nor alarmed them. They knew how to embrace just enough of an almost-gospel to stay within the tribe, without embracing so much gospel as to encounter the lordship of Christ.

But, as time went on, another group of teenagers started to trickle in to our Wednesday night Bible studies. The second group was mostly fatherless boys and girls, some of them gang members, all of them completely unfamiliar with the culture of the church and with the message of the gospel. Some of them unwittingly reversed the Protestant Reformation by persistently calling me "Father Moore," just because the only clergy they'd ever seen were Catholic priests in movies. Prayer request time often proved challenging, with one girl asking for prayer that she wouldn't get pregnant that weekend since she'd run out of birth control pills and her boyfriend didn't like to wear a condom. Some of them would show up in a cloud of marijuana. The church was so strange to them that they didn't know what to hide.

The churched kids, though, learned the dark side of Bible Belt culture—how to know the books of the Bible in order, how to answer all the right questions in small group discussion, and how to get drunk, have sex, and smoke marijuana without their parents ever knowing it. Recognizing that many of the baptized kids in my orbit were, in fact, pagan, I shared the gospel, but I kept hitting wall after wall of invincible intelligence.

The unchurched kids laughed at the Bible studies based on television shows or songs of the moment. They weren't impressed at all by the video clips provided by my denomination's publisher, or to the knockoff Christian boy bands crooning about the hotness of sexual purity. What riveted their attention wasn't what was "relatable" to them, but what wasn't. They were drawn not to our sameness but to our strangeness.

"So, like, you really believe this dead guy came back to life?" one of the unchurched fifteen-year-old boys asked me one day. "I do," I replied. He said, "Wait, for real?" I responded, "Yep. For real." He blinked and whispered, "Dude, that's crazy." But he stayed around, and he listened.

The "churched" kids, and some of their parents, were outraged. Didn't I know, they asked, that some of these adolescents were in gangs, that they smoked weed, and had sex? It was beside the point that almost all of these things (save gang membership) were going on among the "churched" kids too. The point was they knew how to behave. I explained that "how to behave" could be translated as "how to hide sin" through a cycle of Saturday decadence and Sunday repentance. But that didn't change their minds. One teenager even quoted to me, "Bad company ruins good morals" (1 Cor. 15:33). The congregation was healthy so the vast majority of the parents supported me, as did the senior pastor. But I was rattled that we had to have this argument at all.

What I was dealing with was a culture war, in miniature. The churched families saw the lost kids from the outside as "the culture," the very thing we were supposed to protect our families from. We were to be a little outpost of the Bible Belt, with pizza parties and family values, protecting our kids from teen pregnancy or drug addiction or anything else that might wreck their lives. They couldn't see that we were part of the culture too, and the culture they wanted to war against was right there, upstairs from them in their own children's bedrooms. The mission didn't make sense to them, because they had forgotten who they were. They were not the first.

Culture War Is Nothing New

In Jesus' inaugural sermon, his preaching would have remained non-controversial if he had just stayed focused on the future. The people in Nazareth would have continued to marvel "at the gracious words that were coming from his mouth" (Luke 4:22). But Jesus never seemed to know how to take "yes" for an answer. He applied the vision of Isaiah to his hearers, showing them that they weren't quite as ready for the culture of the kingdom as they supposed. They wanted, like James and John later, to sit at the epicenter of the coming kingdom. All politics is local, and they wanted Nazareth taken care of by the wonder-working power of their strange hometown prophet.

Jesus told them, though, that they weren't offended by Isaiah's vision, or by his preaching of it, only because they didn't understand it. The kingdom of God was, from the beginning, meant to be radically global. That's why the Scriptures of Israel start with Adam, the root of the whole human race. "It is too light a thing that you should be my servant to raise up the tribes of Jacob, and to bring back the preserved of Israel," Isaiah wrote, elsewhere in the scrolls. "I will make you as a light for the nations, that my salvation may reach to the end of the earth" (Isa. 49:6). The promised kingdom would cause the nations to stream to it (Isa. 49:6), to be assembled before the glory of the Lord (Isa. 60:3–4; 62:2). But among those serving as priests and Levites are the outsiders, the Gentiles from the nations (Isa. 66:20–21). Jesus said that God had not just told them this, but he had also shown it, by going outside the camp to work wonders among Gentile widows and Syrian lepers.

What Jesus pictured in proclamation in his hometown synagogue in Nazareth, he pictured by demonstration in a borrowed room in Jerusalem.

He shocked the system of God's people by rebuilding the temple of Israel with stones no one wanted. He formed a church made up of both Jew and Gentile, and then ruled over this new colony of the kingdom from David's throne. He announced the kingdom, and then he demonstrated it in reconciled communities at peace with one another, and at war with the devil. Neither the proclamation nor the demonstration was popular. The hometown crowd wanted a Nazarene to stand up for Nazarene values. They wanted him to ignite a war against the outsiders. They wanted to project Nazareth into eternity, while Jesus insisted on bringing eternity to Nazareth. Jesus applied the kingdom to the culture by showing his people they did not find the kingdom strange enough to recognize it. He showed them, and us, that every genuine culture war starts with friendly fire.

> A renewal of cultural witness starts where it started in Nazareth: with a reconsideration of who we are.

A renewal of cultural witness starts where it started in Nazareth: with a reconsideration of who we are. The culture Jesus confronted was entirely comfortable with making distinctions between moral and immoral, between inside and outside. They presumed they were heirs of the kingdom because they were the offspring of Abraham, proved by their family lines and by the markings of circumcision beneath their robes. The prophetic witness challenged this perspective though. John the Baptist warned, "And do not presume to say to yourselves 'We have Abraham as our father,' for I tell you, God is able from these stones to raise up children for Abraham" (Matt. 3:9). That's precisely the point. The genetic link to Abraham was obviously not enough, since those who died, disinherited in the wilderness, did so with Abrahamic DNA running through their bloodstreams. Circumcision obviously is not enough, since Ahab and Absalom were circumcised but were hardly heirs of the promise.

The question was never whether God would keep his promise to Israel, but rather who was in Israel in the first place. John preached exactly what the Old Testament itself had warned: Israel is a vine planted by God, and the branches that do not bear fruit are pruned off (Matt. 3:10). That's the thrust of the gospel message. The Gentiles out there among the nations, those without the Law of Moses, are guilty; their consciences tell them so (Rom. 1–2). There's no argument there, even from the Gentiles. But the gospel goes further, those among the people of Israel also are found to be sinners (Rom. 3:9). Everyone who breaks the law at even one point is a law-breaker (James 2:11).

But then there's Jesus. God keeps his promise to Abraham, to David, to Israel. The inheritance goes to Abraham's offspring, but that offspring is singular not plural (Gal. 3:16). David's son does indeed build the temple for God as the shepherd king, but he does so by gathering "other sheep, who are not of this fold" (John 10:16). Israel is indeed proven to stand in God's favor just as God promised, by the nation's resurrection from the dead and anointing with the Spirit (Ezek. 37:1–14). But, just as at the beginning, Israel is singular at first, not plural. Only one Israelite walks out of the grave. Only one Israelite bears the Spirit. That's the mystery that God has now revealed in these last days. The goal of the universe is Jesus Christ. The goal of humanity is Jesus Christ. The goal of Israel is Jesus Christ. All the promises of God find their "yes" and "Amen" in him (2 Cor. 1:20).

The Nazarenes were happy to hear of release of the captives and good news for the poor because they saw themselves as the obvious protagonists in that story line. They didn't see that the remnant of Israel was defined by those who keep God's law, and there was only one Israelite who met this definition. The kingdom invades the present by showing us what our true problem is. The nations were "separated from Christ, alienated from the commonwealth of Israel, and strangers to the covenants of promise, having no hope and without God in the world" (Eph. 2:12). But, in Christ, God has formed a new humanity, bringing peace (Eph. 2:14–16). Those who were once far off are "no longer strangers and aliens" but "fellow citizens with the saints and members of the household of God" (Eph. 2:19).

This should have come as no surprise since Israel did not emerge out of nowhere but came about through the adoption of a Gentile, Abram, who was himself "without hope and without God in the world" when God found him. The mystery of the gospel is Christ himself. Those who believe in Jesus now are organically united to him, as a head to a body (Eph. 5:29–30; 1 Cor. 12:12–31). The church is an organism, the flesh and blood of Jesus, with a head in heaven and a body on earth.

If you invite me to a dinner party, I don't ask if my fingers or kidneys are also invited. You invited me, and that means everything it means to be me. If I skip out on the dinner but send a kidney in a cooler or a severed finger, you would not view this as my simply "spreading myself around" in order to attend multiple parties at once. You would be repulsed, and rightly so. A kidney or a finger separated from my body isn't "me." That's the mystery of a church made up of every tribe, tongue, nation, and language. Christ, and Christ alone, is the heir of God's inheritance, all of it. Those joined to Christ are now part of him, and thus joint-heirs with him of everything (Rom. 8:12–17; Gal. 4:1–7). "For as many of you as were baptized into Christ have put on Christ," Paul wrote. "There is neither Jew nor Greek, there is neither slave nor free, there is no male and female, for you are all one in Christ Jesus. And if you are Christ's, then you are Abraham's offspring, heirs according to promise" (Gal. 3:27–29). This is who we are, and this changes the way we address the culture around us.

God and Country

Sometime around the Fourth of July or Memorial Day, you might see a sign advertising a "God and country" rally or prayer breakfast. I can almost guarantee that if you attend you will hear, at least once, 2 Chronicles 7:14, a text one critic called "the John 3:16 of American civil religion." For those of you who don't know it, this passage reads: "If my people who are called by my name humble themselves, and pray and seek my face and turn from their wicked ways, then I will hear from heaven and will forgive their sin and heal their land." Typically, this passage will then be applied to the United States, warning that our national wickedness is keeping back God's blessing, and that only a national revival will save the country and enable God to "bless America again."

There's no doubt that we should want to see widespread repentance and the seeking of God in our country. That's not the problem. The problem is that the application of this, and other passages, to the United States—or to any other nation, for that matter—is a confusion of the question of who "we" are. The United States, or any other modern nation, is not in a covenant with God. Second Chronicles 7:14 is not a general statement about humbling or blessing, but about the gospel. God promised Solomon that God would hear prayers offered from Solomon's temple, receive the sacrifices there, and prosper the king on David's throne, so long as the people kept covenant with him.

It's easy to see why this error is so common. Ancient Israel is often identified by modern Bible readers as a nation the way we understand nations (geopolitically defined groups of people). God, who covenanted with Israel, did so exclusively—that is, to the exclusion of other nations. But when you read the Bible as it was intended to be read you see that the exclusivity of covenant with Israel was to bless every nation (Gen. 12:2; Zech. 8:13). And, as we have already seen, the nation of Israel's covenant with God is fulfilled, not by a geopolitical treaty, but in a Person, Jesus Christ. At the crucifixion and resurrection of Jesus, a new era of the covenant between God and his people came into being. Believers from every tribe, tongue, and nation would be called sons of God.

When we apply texts like this to the nation, apart from the story of Scripture, we do precisely what the prosperity gospel preachers do. The prosperity gospel teachers are drawn, after all, to passages from Deuteronomy and elsewhere promising material and physical blessing for those who are obedient, and material and physical curses for those who are disobedient. The message is that those who obey God's Word will abound with money and health, while those who disobey will face poverty and illness. They misuse the word of God though, by abstracting the promises of God from Jesus Christ. He is the One who, obedient to God, receives God's blessing and he is the One who, bearing the sins of the people, receives God's curse (Gal. 3:13). To apply these to the people directly, bypassing Christ, is to preach a false gospel of approaching God apart from a Mediator (1 Tim. 2:5). A prosperity gospel applied to a nation is no more biblical than a prosperity gospel applied to a person.

> A prosperity gospel applied to a nation is no more biblical than a prosperity gospel applied to a person.

But the temptation to apply 2 Chronicles to the nation rather than to the church persists, for the same reasons that some insist on applying Genesis 12:3 ("I will bless those who bless you, and him who dishonors you I will curse") to foreign policy rather than to where the Bible applies it: to the gospel of Jesus Christ (Gal. 3:7–14). Why is this? It's because the first question of culture is one of identity, who are we and where do we fit in the broader culture. We too often see America as somehow more "real" than the kingdom, and our country as more important than the church. But 2 Chronicles 7:14 itself starts with the question of identity: "If my

people . . . called by my name . . ." This, or any other country, is not called
by the name of God. The kingdom of God, on the other hand, is (Isa.
62:3–5).It's not unusual that we would have difficulty seeing our primary
identity. The Old Testament persistently warns the Israelites not to assimilate into the ways of the Canaanites. And the New Testament persistently
warns the church not to slide back into the "futile ways" of our forefathers.
We must grow into who we are, even as childless, elderly Abram couldn't
see how he could be "Abraham" or "father of many nations" and unstable,
deserting Simon could hardly be described as "Peter" or "the Rock." God
names his people, and then makes the name true.

Strangers and Aliens

The changes in American culture, perhaps counterintuitively, can
make this clearer—both to the outside culture of the world and the inside
culture of the church. We are, the Bible tells us, "aliens and strangers " as it
relates to the world (1 Pet. 2:9–11 NASB) but not as it relates to the City of
God, the commonwealth of Israel, now situated in heaven (Eph. 2:13). As
historic, apostolic Christianity grows more estranged from the mainstream
of American culture, we can re-learn the distinction between the church
and the world. That doesn't mean isolation or disengagement from the
world, or from the cultures around us.

We are immigrants, the Bible tells us, in the present age. Studies have
shown that some immigrants can wall themselves up from the larger culture, reenacting simply the ways and mores of the "old country." And some
immigrants can simply assimilate into the larger society, so that there's
no longer anything distinctive about them at all. But between those two
extremes, there's a phenomenon some studies have defined as an "immigrant advantage."[24] These immigrant communities combine a drive for
freedom and self-determination (the reason they came in the first place)
with a strong social network of fellow immigrants from the same country.
These immigrants then navigate their new country with the best aspects
of both their old and new countries, individual drive with community
connection.

---

24. Anand Giridharadas, "The Immigrant Advantage," *The New York Times*, May
25, 2014.

The same could be true of the church in a secularizing America, even as it was in the first century. The church is not to be walled up from the broader culture but to speak to it (1 Pet. 2:12), but that can only happen if, as sojourners and exiles, we have something distinctive to say (1 Pet. 2:11). We are called to "proclaim the excellencies of him who called you out of darkness," but we can only do so if we remember that are "a royal priesthood, a holy nation, a people for his own possession" (1 Pet. 2:9).

A Colony of the Kingdom

This means seeing the church as itself a culture, a culture being conformed to the future. The church is not merely a voluntary society of those who share the same theology, or who want to pool their resources for a common mission. The church is an *act of war.*

As Jesus approached the cross, his band of disciples were approached by a group of Greeks who came to the camp wanting to see him. Jesus seemed to change the subject. "Now is the judgment of this world," he said. "And I, when I am lifted up from the earth, will draw all people to myself" (John 12:31–32). And that's precisely what he did. If Jesus had interviewed with the Greeks, his disciples would have been unperturbed by this. It would have been an act of kindness, of charity, to receive foreigners. Jesus had something more radical in mind. By bearing the sins of humanity, absorbing the wrath of God, Jesus turned back the accusations of the devil. In his resurrection from the dead, Jesus broke the power of the Evil One, that of death.

Jesus demonstrates his inbreaking reign by calling together a church that is hidden in his own life. The church, then, is a sign to the demonic rulers of "the manifold wisdom of God" (Eph. 3:10). When people previously at each other's throats are now united, the powers of darkness see the terrifying reality of what the new culture of the church means: "Here there is not Greek and Jew, circumcised and uncircumcised, barbarian, Scythian, slave, free; but Christ is all, and in all" (Col. 3:11). In the church, the powers-that-be see a pilot project of the kingdom of God, which is plowing aside their own empire. That's because when they see the church, they don't see a society; they see one new man. They see the vine of God, and the branches joined to him, bearing much fruit. They see the offspring of

Abraham. They see the throne of David. They see the house of Israel. They hear in the songs and sermons of the church an ancient promise of a human ruler who will crush their reptilian skulls (Gen 3:15).

That's why the culture of the church is crucial for our moral and social witness. Jesus told us that the kingdom is present where he is, and he promised to be present with his church, no matter how struggling or how small (Matt. 18:15–20). The church gathered is not merely a matter of fueling the people for a week of individual devotion. In worship, the church, mysteriously and spiritually, ascends to the heavenly Mount Zion, joining an already existing worship service (Heb. 12:18–19). Our preaching isn't just information sharing; it's the voice of Jesus clearing the way for the new regime (2 Cor. 5:20). Baptism is a sign of the future, made present now, of those who need not fear the coming flooding of the world by fire, because they have already endured it, in Christ. The Lord's Table is a sign of that future kingdom victory party, now inbreaking among us, as broken bread and poured-out wine announces that he has conquered all our accusing foes. In the taste of bread and grape, there's a voice saying to the unlovable, "You are loved." There he shows us the kind of ruler he is, and thus the kind we are to be: the kind that serves at the table (Luke 22:27).

In our life together, then, God is forming a culture, by training us for our future responsibilities as joint-heirs with Christ. The king grants to his administration-in-waiting spiritual gifts, used now within the church, magnified later in the kingdom (Eph. 4:7–13; 1 Cor. 12:4–10). These gifts are not what I would choose, were I making the decisions here. I would opt for something a bit more dramatic to the outside world, and more obviously useful to me—super-speed, perhaps, or maybe x-ray vision. But King Jesus grants gifts that demonstrate the church's mission, as a spiritual body that advances onward not by might or by power but by gospel and by Spirit.

The church as a colony of the coming kingdom is why the New Testament engages in culture wars that seem, if we're honest, trivial and sort of beside the point. After all, the culture of occupied Israel was a mess, and yet Jesus chose to address in Nazareth their attitudes toward outsiders, hardly at the top of the triage of concerns. The Greco-Roman culture was decadent, by the standards of virtually any time period, and Paul addressed such seemingly penny-ante matters as cutting in line at the Lord's Supper and believers suing one another. Who cares about lawsuits over business dealings in a culture filled with sexual anarchy, human trafficking, and imperial militarization? It mattered because the church as an embassy of the kingdom was projecting a message that wasn't true: that Jesus is incompetent to govern the world. "Do you not know that the saints will judge the world?" Paul wrote. "And if the world is to be judged by you, are you incompetent to try trivial cases?" (1 Cor. 6:2).

The bickering and lawsuits in the Corinthian church were the equivalent of a presidential candidate having to go to an outside consulting firm to pick his vice-presidential nominee since, "Decisions, like, are hard." The voters would ask, rightly, if you can't pick a running-mate, how can we trust you to decide whether to go to war? That's the issue here. If the church is to "judge angels," then how much more "matters pertaining to this life" (1 Cor. 6:3). When they went before the outside world, those with no standing in the church, they betrayed that they didn't understand what the church is.

It's the equivalent of the American embassy in Russia appealing to Moscow to negotiate a salary dispute between two diplomats. Such would signal an embassy that doesn't see that the sending company has jurisdiction in such matters, not the nation to which they have been sent. Moreover, the church signaled that it found this life to be more "real" to them than the life for which they are being prepared. "Why not rather suffer wrong?" Paul wrote. "Why not rather be defrauded?" (1 Cor. 6:7). They had forgotten who they were.

For the Bible Tells Me "No"

Moreover, with all the injustice in the world, James, the brother of our Lord, took up space in his letter to the churches, and in the canonical Scriptures of the entire Christian church, to tackle the issues of fashion and seating order. He wrote: "For if a man wearing a gold ring and fine clothing comes into your assembly, and a poor man in shabby clothing also comes in, and if you pay attention to the one who wears the fine clothing and say, 'You sit here in a good place,' while you say to the poor man, 'You stand over there,' or 'Sit down at my feet,' have you not then made distinctions among yourselves and become judges with evil thoughts?" (James 2:2–4). Let me tell you honestly: I think what the churches were doing here, that James confronts, makes perfect sense. And, I'll wager, so do you.

Imagine, for a moment, a struggling church plant in one of the least religious parts of the country, say, the Pacific Northwest. Every week, the little congregation sets up their folding chairs in a rented school auditorium, setting up the makeshift audio amplification system, the lectern, the drum set. And every week, they see their tiny flock, with their little dab in the offering plate, just enough to make the rent for another week. But one morning, a world-famous computer industry executive, one of the wealthiest corporate tycoons in the world, enters through the back doors. You see the face you've seen on business magazines and leadership manuals, the head you've seen talking about investment and economic strategy and global philanthropy on television. Wouldn't you stop what you're doing and greet him, thank him for coming? If the chairs were crowded with "regular people," wouldn't you ask someone to give up their seats for this man and his family? Wouldn't that just make sense? After all, what if he were to come to Christ?

Wouldn't that be a powerful witness to your community, that Christianity isn't for losers or for the superstitious weak? And what if this multibillionaire

> That just makes sense. This I know. But the Bible tells me "no."

learned to tithe? Think of the missionaries you could send to unreached people groups. Think of the lives you could save, in the name of Christ, through global water purification and hunger alleviation? That just makes sense. This I know. But the Bible tells me "no."

The churches thought they were politically savvy by showing partiality to the wealthy and powerful, those whose influence could give the church cultural cache and perhaps save them from persecution and marginalization. The problem wasn't that they were too politically savvy, but that they weren't politically savvy enough. They didn't have the next trillion years in view. "Has not God chosen those who are poor in the world to be rich in faith and heirs of the kingdom, which he has promised to those who love him?", he wrote (James 2:5). Notice the favor of God doesn't rest with the poor simply because they are poor. These are "rich in faith." But the heirs of the kingdom don't enter by accident but instead by the initiative and calling of God. Paul told the church in Corinth to remember that "not many of you were wise according to worldly standards, not many were powerful, not many of noble birth" (1 Cor. 1:20). Why is this important? It's because the kingdom is driven by the gospel, and the gospel is defined by strangeness. The wisdom of God and the power of God aren't defined by the way human cultures define wisdom and power. God's wisdom and power aren't things to drive human ambition; they aren't things at all. God's wisdom and God's power are personal; in fact, they are a Person: Jesus of Nazareth (1 Cor. 1:24), which is a stumbling block that crosses the cultural boundaries of Jew and Greek (1 Cor. 1:23).

I once read a leadership book by a business executive in which he pointed out the importance of always being friendly to one's company's interns. His concern was not compassion or kindness, but Machiavellian self-interest. After all, he advised, you don't know where these interns are headed. One of them just might rocket up the corporate ranks faster than you, and may be your boss one day. You want to be kind to them when they are bringing in your coffee because, for all you know, they may one day be in charge of your annual performance review.

That's kind of crass, I'll grant you. But it isn't dumb. And it's, in one sense, the argument James was making. The kingdom of God changes the culture of the church by showing us a longer view of who's important and who's in charge.

The kingdom of God turns the Darwinist narrative of the survival of the fittest upside down (Acts 17:6–7). When the church honors and cares for the vulnerable among us, we are not showing charity. We are simply recognizing the way the world really works, at least in the long run. The child with Down syndrome on the fifth row from the back in your church, he's not a "ministry project." He's a future king of the universe. The immigrant woman who scrubs toilets every day on hands and knees, and can barely speak enough English to sing along with your praise choruses, she's not a problem to be solved. She's a future queen of the cosmos, a joint-heir with Christ.

The most important cultural witness the church has is not to raise up Christian filmmakers and novelists and artists and business leaders and politicians, although we ought to work to disciple those in all sorts of callings, and encourage them. The most important cultural task we have is to crucify our incipient Darwinism, in which the leaders on the inside of the kingdom colony are the same as they would be on the outside, even if there were no God in the universe. The first step to cultural influence is not to contextualize to the present, but to contextualize to the future, and the future is awfully strange, even to us.

Many, including some people I respect, would seek to correct the errors of the past—on both the Left and the Right—by arguing that Christians should influence culture by recognizing how culture works, from the top-down, by elite "culture makers" which then filter down through the masses. They are right that this is how the world works, and they are right that Christian attempts to mimic the culture by "off-brand" Christianized imitations of the regnant culture are doing nothing to "engage" the culture. And Christian political movements have often been populist and anti-intellectual, seeking to provide slogans for "the base" rather than to persuade the culture. That's true. But too deep a fascination with engaging elite forms of cultural influence, political, economic, or cultural, can easily drive us away from the kingdom itself.

Not long ago, a Christian friend in a major urban center complained about all the church planters in his city who arrived with Southern accents. These urbanites, he argued, consider Southern accents backward, ignorant, and rube-like. That may be unfair, he said, but that's just the way it is, and we ought instead to send urbane intellectuals who can defend the gospel with a level of sophistication and cultural class that can be recognized by the people there, in order to gain a hearing.

That makes sense to me, sociologically. I have certainly seen church planters who went north and built churches by creating enclaves of the Bible Belt there, drawing together heartland expatriates to sing familiar hymns and drink sweet tea together. But, as good a sociological corrective as this might be, it's just not what Jesus does.

God does care about the great cities. As the gospel advanced, God sent the gospel into the cultural and political hub of the empire, the eternal city of Rome. But the church-planting effort in Rome was led by a small-town fisherman with the most backwater accent possible, a discernibly Galilean one (Matt. 26:73). In reaching the philosophically sophisticated and culturally xenophobic city of Athens, God did not send a Greek philosopher trained in the pre-Socratic and post-Socratic texts, but a Jewish tentmaker, trained in the monotheistic scrolls of Second Temple Judaism (Acts 17:16–24). The key here is the distinction, offered by Søren Kierkegaard, of the genius and the apostle.[25] The genius commands attention because of

---

25. Søren Kierkegaard, *The Present Age* (New York, NY: Harper Torchbooks, 1962).

his influence or his brilliance. The apostle prompts attention because he is sent, with a message that bears, on its own terms, authority.

The church is not built on the rock foundation of geniuses and influencers but of apostles and prophets. This should hardly be surprising, since the kingdom is not greater than its king, and the body is not greater than its head. When confronted by the gospel, the natural response from any culture is, "Can any good thing come out of Nazareth?" That's true, come to think of it, even in Nazareth (Luke 4:24). And the natural counter-argument from the church is, "Come and see" (John 1:46). The kingdom of God dawns in trailer parks and refugee camps. That shouldn't surprise us. The kingdom came to us not from a boardroom or a literary guild, but from a feeding trough and an execution stake.

> The kingdom came to us not from a boardroom or a literary guild, but from a feeding trough and an execution stake.

Perhaps the best way to gain influence is to lose it. The cultural mandate of Genesis (1:28) is still in effect and applies to all. We need Christians as "salt" and "light" in every aspect of art and craftsmanship and politics and thought leadership, not just in those thought to be "churchly" or "Christian." But the cultural mandate was rooted in a garden temple-sanctuary, in communion with God. That temple exists now within the Body of Christ, the church. For Christians, our consciences and thought patterns are formed together, by life together in the community of the kingdom. Our moral intuitions then ought to be formed by churches that reflect the priorities and the makeup of the kingdom of Christ.

What would it mean if our leadership structures in the church weren't as predictable as that of any other organization? What if the images in our publications and digital platforms weren't always those who meet the same standards of physical attractiveness as the reigning culture, thus subtly reinforcing the message that the supermodels shall inherit the earth, but instead featured those the world might consider fat or ugly or awkward but who bear a mantle of spiritual maturity? What if our churches weren't divided up by the same economic and racial and political and generational categories that would bind us together even if Jesus were not alive? What would it mean, in your church, if a minimum-wage janitor were mentoring the multimillionaire executive of the restaurant where he cleans toilets, because the janitor/mentor has the spiritual wisdom his boss/protégé needs?

It would look awfully strange, but it would look no stranger than a cruci-fied Nazarene governing the universe. The strangeness of that lived congre-gational reality can reshape consciences and transform us by the renewing of our minds (Rom. 12:2).

The cultural proclamation is tied to the demonstration, and vice versa. They speak, first, internally to the church, reminding us of how we have been conformed to the pattern of this age, even unwittingly. The most dangerous aspects of the culture around us are not those that are the most heated "cul-ture war" flashpoints of the moment. The more perilous questions are those we don't debate at all, because we don't think to challenge them.

The Nazarene villagers read in Isaiah's words hope for themselves, since they were the poor, the oppressed, the captive. Jesus confronted them with the reality that they were just as power-hungry as their uncir-cumcised overlords—just without the means at the moment to carry out their agenda. Our cultural witness is not merely a way to lash out at the world. We are the world. We are the people Jesus warned us about. Our gospel arrests our culture first, with a kingdom that is too strange for us to comprehend.

Kingdom-Focused Cultural Engagement

Jesus' hometown village didn't know enough about the kingdom to be alarmed by it. And neither do I. As Christians we tend to do exactly as our forefathers and foremothers did: we are alarmed by what ought to comfort us, and comforted by what ought to alarm us. The doctrine of election, for example, is a subject of great fearfulness among many Christians who wonder whether passages on "predestination" might mean that somehow they would find themselves excluded from God's promises on the last day because of some invisible, inscrutable clause in the Book of Life keeping them out. Now, Christians have argued for almost the entire history of the church about the relationship of God's sovereignty to human freedom, but whatever the doctrine of election means, we can be sure of this: God's elec-tion in Scripture is meant to make people more, not less, secure in God's faithfulness.

On the other hand, many Christians act as though the Sermon on the Mount is comforting—a list of wise sayings to be crocheted and hanged on the wall. The Sermon on the Mount ought, though, to terrify us. Jesus articulated the righteousness of the kingdom, what sort of person would be an heir to it. And it's devastating. Jesus pointed out that God's law is not about merely external obedience, but about the direction of our psyches. It's not just the furtive cheater who is an adulterer, but also the one who is enflamed with desire for those he should not have. It's not just the fugitive killer who is a murderer, but also the one who is embittered with hatred. If we really get what Jesus was saying, we ought to be undone by this.

The people then, and the people now, welcome the future, so long as the future is an extension of everything we like about our lives now, just propelled out into eternity with nothing to stop us. That, though, is precisely what the sentence of death was given to keep us from: the zombie-like extension of our spiritual death forever. The culture of the kingdom is not a means to furthering our lordship over our lives, but a means of wrecking it.

The culture of the kingdom is not a projection of our lives now onto eternity, but instead the reverse: a vision of a new creation that breaks us and prepares us for our inheritance by patterning us, now, after the life of creation's heir: Jesus himself. With a kingdom vision, we recognize that the priorities of this present world system are different from those of the age to come. That's why Jesus contrasted the way of the Roman overlords with the way of a kingdom in which the last will be first and the first will be last (Luke 22:24–27). And that's why Jesus said, incredibly, that those who are heartbroken and reviled and marginalized in this era are "blessed." This is the vision of the kingdom he laid out here in his hometown, good news for the poor, freedom for the captives, sight for the blind. If not for this telescopic view of history, we would be tempted to judge worth in terms of strength or usefulness or power. This ought then to change our priorities, to reorient them to where the universe is heading, not toward where it is now.

That's why the first step to a kingdom-focused cultural engagement is the recovery of a church that practices church discipline. The apostle Paul wrote, "For what have I do to do with judging outsiders? Is it not those inside the church whom you are to judge?" (1 Cor. 5:12). Now, to be sure, Paul did not use the word *judge* the way our contemporaries do. He did not equate "judging" with moral discernment, since even in this text he discussed what was tolerated and what was not "among the pagans" (1 Cor. 5:1). We confront outsiders with their sin, because that's what gospel preaching does. We are commanded to "take no part in the unfruitful works of darkness" but instead to "expose them" (Eph. 5:11). By "judging," Paul meant that we do not hold outsiders accountable to the discipline of the Body (1 Cor. 5:3–5). The various penalties for death found in Old Testament Israel do not translate into public policy, because the commonwealth of Israel is fulfilled not in the state but in the church, and Jesus has disarmed the church from any rule over the outside world. The same language the Old Testament applied to capital punishment, the New Testament applies to excommunication from the church, exclusion from the Lord's Table (1 Cor. 5:13; Deut. 13:5). By including one among them in unrepentant sin with the name of "brother," the church was preaching a false gospel. They were also guilty of a defective view of the future. Their membership, their fellowship, their gathering around the Lord's Table signaled the makeup of the coming kingdom, and the refusal to discipline the body proclaimed that the unrepentantly immoral would, in fact, inherit the kingdom of God (1 Cor. 6:9–10). We are to hold accountable those on the inside, and speak to those on the outside with persuasion and mission.

We tend to do the exact reverse. We rail against the culture outside, and speak in muted and ambiguous terms about what is common among us. We lambaste political and cultural heresies on the outside, but sit silently in the face of doctrinal heresies on the inside. That's because we are seeking the wrong kingdom first.

The countercultural witness of the church to the kingdom, though, does not mean that the church is merely a counterculture. The church is called to exist within a culture. Christians calling the church to cultural and social engagement have, rightly, appealed to Jesus' command that the church is to be "salt" and "light" in the world (Matt. 5:13–16), preserving that which is good and illuminating what is veiled in darkness. We often forget, though, that this imagery binds together the internal and external witness of the church, the call to both proclamation and demonstration. Israel was to be the "light of the world," sending forth a light that would draw the nations to it, and teach them to walk in the ways of the Lord (Isa. 2:2–5; 49:6; 60:3). Jesus applied this language first to himself; he is the light of the world (John 8:12; 9:5). He is the Israel to whom the nations stream, bringing with them, just as Isaiah prophesied, gold and frankincense (Isa. 60:6; Matt. 2:10–11). He is the light that shines out of darkness from Galilee of the Gentiles (Isa. 9:1–2). This light, which illuminates the City of God forever, now resides within the church. It cannot be a merely internal matter, can't be hidden under a basket, but must be shined before the outside world "so that they can see your good works and give glory to your Father who is in heaven" (Matt. 5:14–16). This bridges the internal and the external. The salt must be savory or else it is of no use to the world (Matt. 5:13). And the light from the church is anchored to a lampstand within the churches (Rev. 1:20). The internal doctrinal and moral ordering of the church is a matter of mission. Without it, the presence of Christ is gone, the lampstand removed (Rev. 2:5), and with it the light that shines out into the world. A church that loses its distinctiveness is a church that has nothing distinctive with which to engage the culture. A worldly church is of no good to the world.

> A church that loses its distinctiveness is a church that has nothing distinctive with which to engage the culture.

The church is an alternative society, a colony of the kingdom, but the church is no isolated silo. "Keep your conduct among the Gentiles honorable, so that when they speak against you as evildoers, they may see your good deed and glorify God on the day of visitation" (1 Pet. 2:12). The church is an alternative family, the household of God (1 Tim. 3:15), but this does not negate responsibility to the natural family but instead informs both the importance of the family (Eph. 5:22–6:4; 1 Tim. 5:8) and limits of family loyalty (Matt. 12:46–50; Luke 9:59–62; 12:52–53). The same is true with the church as a culture and as a city. We cultivate churches that model, always imperfectly, the kingdom of God, and from that base we speak to the outside world about the priorities of that kingdom. We do not simply advocate for the agenda of the kingdom; we embody it.

That sort of engagement necessarily creates conflict, within and without. Jesus kept preaching until his hometown moved from adulation to enragement. He then did the same thing with the rest of the nation, and then onto the rest of the world. We should not seek an angry, quarrelsome cultural presence, but neither should we seek to engage the culture with the sort of gospel that the culture would want, if they, or we, were making it up. Too many attempts at reconciling Christianity and the outside culture have to do with being seen as "relevant" by the culture on its own terms. We will never be able to do that. Culture is a rolling stone, and it waits for no band of Christians seeking to imitate it or exegete it.

Some would point to the apostle Paul's speech in Athens, before the Areopagus, in which he cited the lyrics of pagan poets and the architecture of pagan temples. Christians, they argue, should follow Paul and seek to "build a bridge" with the culture, finding "common ground" through which we can attract their interest and communicate the gospel. And yet, such efforts often ignore the context of Mars Hill. Paul did not start speaking in Athens with a "common ground" idea of a generic god and then reason along to Jesus of Nazareth. He was there because he prompted a controversy for preaching "Jesus and the resurrection" (Acts 17:18), preaching to the Greek philosophers precisely what he had preached to the Jewish rabbis. He started and finished with the guarantee that God will bring about judgment through the resurrection of Jesus from the dead (Acts 17:31).

Yes, Paul took note of the altar to the unknown and, yes, he quoted the pagan poets. But he did so in order, not to build a bridge to what they already know, but to show them that even they know their beliefs are self-contradictory. The altar to the unknown god shows that they recognized there were some boundaries to their knowledge of the divine. How can you claim that these temples house the gods, he asked, when even your own culture-makers say that the divine can't be housed in edifices made with hands?

Paul systematically unhinged key facets of Greek culture and thought, boldly challenging Greek tribal pride by pointing to the common ancestry of humanity from "one man." Moreover, he affronted the cultural underpinnings of Athenian culture by returning again and again to the bodily resurrection. Nothing was more freakish and alien to Greek thought, whether Epicurean or Stoic, both of which sought to combat the fear of death by separating the prison of the body that dies from the spirit that survives. Paul at Mars Hill was doing much the same thing Jesus was doing at his hometown synagogue. Both understood their audiences, and both sought to relevantly engage them. Jesus anticipated what they might say, and what they were thinking. Paul did the same. Both quoted sayings and proverbs recognizable to their audiences. But both did so not to forestall the crisis, but to provoke it. Both continued speaking until the full strangeness of their, and our, message was heard. Neither held back on what their audience would find most culturally freakish or odd.

What we ought to understand most about the Acts 17 encounter is the Athenian response. Luke wrote that what arrested the attention of the

Athenians was not the so-called bridges Paul built to their culture by citing Athenian cultural products. What pricked their attention at the end is what pricked their attention at the start—Jesus and the resurrection: "Now when they heard of the resurrection of the dead, some mocked. But others said, 'We will hear you again about this'" (Acts 17:32). Often at the root of much of our engagement with culture lies an embarrassment about the "oddity" of this strange biblical world of talking snakes, parting seas, emptied graves. But, without that distinctive strangeness, what's Christianity for?

Conclusion

Increasingly, I am convinced that the next generation of Christian witness will be less like the Bible Belt kids I faced at the start of my ministry, with their rehearsed professions of faith and hidden rebellions. The next generation will confront us more with that second sort of lostness, those for whom the Christian witness—right down to the basics—seems foreign and irrelevant and antiquated and freakish. Jesus didn't hide the oddity of the culture of the kingdom, and neither should we. Let's listen to what our culture is saying, hearing beneath the veneer of cool the fear of a people who know that Judgment day is coming because it's written in their hearts (Rom. 2:15–16). Let's listen beneath the cynicism to the longings there, expressed in the culture, longings that can only be fulfilled in the reign of a Nazarene carpenter-king. Let's deconstruct what they—and we—tell ourselves when it's nonsense.

But let's not stop there. Let's run toward and not away from the strangeness of an old gospel of a Messiah who was run out of his own hometown, but who, oddly enough, walked out of his own graveyard. For real.

But let's do more than talk. Let's live together in churches that call our neighbors to consider the justice and righteousness they see demonstrated among us. Let's witness (albeit imperfectly and waveringly) to what the whole universe will one day look like. Let's groan at the wreckage all around us, in this world of divorce courts and abortion clinics and gas chambers, and let's pray for the day when, as the hymn puts it, "every foe is vanquished and Christ is Lord indeed." Let's show in the makeup and ministry and witness of our congregations what matters, and who matters, in the long run. Let's confront culture with the gospel, in all its strange-ness, both inside and outside the church. And let's model what happens to a culture when the kingdom interrupts us on our way to where we would go, if we were mapping this out on our own. Let's not merely advocate for causes; let's embody a kingdom. Let's not aspire to be a moral majority but a gospel community, one that doesn't exist for itself but for the larger mission of reaching the whole world with the whole gospel. That sort of kingdom-first cultural engagement drives us not inward, but onward.

---- Chapter Five ----

MISSION

We're used to seeing evangelicals and Catholics standing together out-side of abortion clinics, praying on the sidewalks in protest. They pace those cement footpaths, which mark the way to the gallows for the voiceless—and they do so together. The pro-life movement has mobilized, thankfully, an ecumenism of the trenches, as those from differing perspec-tives work together to seek to protect human life.

But there is also a darker reality, an ecumenism of a different sort—an ecumenism of the waiting room. We don't often think about how evangelicals and Catholics are sitting together inside those same abortion clinics, waiting in the lobby to end their pregnancies. Those working in abortion clinics sometimes report that their clients usually aren't secular feminist activists, but rather young women from Saint Joseph's parish or First Baptist's youth group. They are not there arguing that the life within them is an impersonal "fetus" or "mass of tissue." They speak of this life not as an "it" but as a "he" or a "she," not as a "pregnancy" but as a baby. They probably consider themselves pro-life, and that's how they'll vote. But when pregnant and in crisis, they wait, together, for the awful solution of the abortionist's knife.

These young women, I'm told, often talk about God. The Catholic women say that they know this is a mortal sin, but that they'll go to confession. The evangelical women say that they know this is morally wrong, but they have prayed to receive Christ and so are "once saved, always saved." Despite all the differences in our understanding of salvation, stretching all the way back to the Wittenberg door, both groups share, at least in the waiting room, a common doctrine of grace: "Let us sin that grace may abound" (Rom. 6:1). And waiting for them there are those who, with medical licenses and seared consciences, are promising to "fix" their problems, so they can go on with the lives they are living—maybe even right back in the same pew. The antiseptic surgical room carries an implicit dark parody of the words, "Come unto me all you who are weary and heavy-laden, and we will give you rest."

This scenario, like a thousand others, is at the intersection of personal righteousness and public justice. Within these walls, a surgical strike targets both innocent human lives and guilty human consciences, all covered over by narratives made to seem almost like good news. In a world of violence, hatred, and oppression, an almost-gospel and a halfway mission are not enough to shape consciences strong enough to cry out with prophetic witness. The kingdom of God ought to reshape our vision of what matters and who matters, a vision embodied in the psyche-forming communities of local congregations. But this kingdom culture does not silo itself away from the wreckage outside. The kingdom culture is driven outward and onward by mission. Mission is a matter of reconciliation, the reconciliation of humanity to God and of humanity with one another. This is a matter of both gospel and justice, a matter of both personal redemption and social order. A mission of redemption that leaves untroubled our place in unjust systems is far too safe, as is a mission of social activism that leaves untroubled our guilt before a holy God. If we are followers of Christ, we go where he takes us, and that will lead us into some controversy, controversy that rises first from our own idol-protecting hearts.

A Gospel-Centered Mission

In Jesus' inaugural sermon in Nazareth, the questions were all around, both spoken and unspoken. The question, "Is not this Joseph's son?" (Luke 4:22), was behind the entire episode. In the first place, the question was one of hometown pride, "Can you believe that one of ours is able to speak in this way?" But Jesus anticipated their unarticulated questions, "Why won't you do here what you've done elsewhere, and bring blessing to your own?" Jesus answered their questions by confronting them with strangers, and with the strangeness of God. There was no shortage of widows in Israel, he said, when God sent the prophet Elijah to a widow outside the camp in Sidon, to care for her in famine and to raise her son from the dead (1 Kings 17:8–24). There was no shortage of lepers in Israel when God sent the prophet Elisha to a leper outside the camp from Syria to cleanse him of his disease (2 Kings 5:1–14). By raising these stories, from their own Scriptures, Jesus was asking some questions of his own.

The mission of Christ encountered the same sort of questioning repeatedly throughout his ministry. In one of these encounters, Jesus replayed with an individual what he had gone through with his congregation. After sending out his disciples, with the anointing of the Spirit, on a mission to the surrounding villages, Jesus placed the mission in the context of the kingdom of God. God was revealing now what had long been hidden, and the powers the disciples were seeing were the result of a larger triumph, the fall of Satan, like lightning from heaven (Luke 10:17–24). In the crowd, a lawyer stood up to interrogate the teacher. His first question was the most important: "What is the gospel?"

This lawyer, mind you, was not what we think of when we think of the word, a civil attorney seeking to adjudicate criminal or civil cases in the courts. He was instead one trained in the intricacies of the Law God handed down to Israel through Moses on Mount Sinai. He asked a question that seems, at first blush, to be a matter of simple evangelism: "What must I do to inherit eternal life?" One would expect Jesus to respond the way Paul and Silas do when asked the same question by the Philippian jailer: "Believe in the Lord Jesus, and you will be saved, you and your household" (Acts 16:31). But Jesus doesn't do that. He pressed in further on the man's point of expertise, the Law, even as he pressed, back home, on his village's point of knowledge, the prophets. The man acknowledged that the Law could be summed up as, "You shall love the Lord your God with all your heart and all your soul and with all your strength and with all your mind, and your neighbor as yourself" (Luke 10:27). Jesus essentially shrugged and said, "Right. So go do that."

The difference between this lawyer and the Philippian jailer is a quite simple one: desperation. The jailer, after an earthquake in which the power of God shook his life's work apart, the jailer reached a crisis, and cried out for deliverance. The lawyer saw the question of the gospel as a means to an end. He was, like the religious leaders around him, seeking to put Jesus "to the test" (Luke 10:25). The gospel inquiry was a means to entrap this new teacher, and thus to keep the status quo in place. At the root of this interview was the lawyer's one attempt to "justify himself" with his questions (Luke 10:29), a path that never has, and never can, lead to eternal life (Rom. 3:20). Jesus with the lawyer was doing what Jesus always does; he was provoking a crisis in order to plow through a field of idols, to get at the conscience.

The question though, at face value, is crucial. The future of Christian social witness cannot assume the gospel, but must articulate it explicitly and coherently, not simply as the tagline at the end of our activism but as the ground and underpinning of it. One reason that some gospel-focused Christians are skittish about social action and political engagement is precisely because they have seen, persistently in history, those who would replace the gospel, either with public morality or with social justice.

> The future of Christian social witness cannot assume the gospel, but must articulate it explicitly and coherently.

Some of these gospel-evading attempts at an activism of the Right or of the Left are self-consciously theological. The social gospel of pre-World War I America, for example, spoke of personal evangelism and world missions, but only as a means to the end of the "Christianization" of a locality or, of the world, for the purpose of social reform. Many progressives of the time believed that monotheistic Christianity, with its Golden Rule ethic, was the evolutionary pinnacle of human religion. By sharing the gospel, they could "civilize" the "heathen" around the world in order to make the world safe for peace, democracy, more just industrial and housing policies, and so on.

The same reasoning is present in those on the Right in recent years, expressed by those who have called for efforts to evangelize the Islamic world with appeals that focus more on making America safe from terrorism than on seeing Muslim peoples come to know Christ.

The social gospel, and the various liberation theologies that have come since, often tell us that Christianity is not merely a set of doctrinal propositions—and I agree. They insist loudly that the kingdom of God is about far more than "going to heaven when you die"—and I agree with that too.

The problem is that these theologies downplay personal guilt and conversion to the point of replacing the core of the good news of the kingdom—the announcement about Jesus that is a historical claim of incarnation, atonement, ascension, and mission. They talk about the kingdom, but they, like Nicodemus himself, want to keep concealed in the nighttime whisperings the startling claim, "Unless one is born again he cannot see the kingdom of God" (John 3:3).

Others have substituted the same sort of social and political gospel for the good news of the kingdom not by developing an alternative theology but simply by avoiding theology altogether beyond the thinnest forms needed to get by. The end result is that the left-wing Jesus starts to sound like a junta leader, and the right-wing Jesus starts to sound like a Viking. Both groups fall into the old trap of seeking a Pharaoh or a Caesar instead of a Messiah. And, in either case, those groups that embrace this distorted gospel end up, again and again, burned over shells of previously Christian conviction.

It's little wonder then that those who were drawn to Christianity, not by the security of a Bible Belt cocoon, but by the alarming strangeness of a radically transformative gospel might want to do anything possible to protect the gospel from politics and social organizing. But by sharply dividing the gospel from society and politics, they run right around the corner into what they are trying to avoid. They are akin to the man who smokes three packs of cigarettes a day to keep his lungs cleared out, so he won't get the cancer that killed his father. A gospel-focused, mission-centered American Christianity could become not only separatist and isolationist but also just as politically idolatrous, though from a different direction, all the while reassuring ourselves that we are avoiding culture wars or social gospel. That temptation shows up in the second question the lawyer asked, "And who is my neighbor?"

Both Personal and Public

The question here wasn't hairsplitting. The question emerged from a guilty conscience, wrestling mightily to justify itself. Jesus returned his conscience to the demands of the law, and no conscience can stand before an honest accounting there. The lawyer's conscience knew, after all, that the one who breaks the law at one point is a lawbreaker (James 1:10–11). He was searching here for a contract-rider, a provision that would lower the bar of God's standards of righteousness and justice to a level he could attain. What this lawyer wanted was precisely what Jesus hometown crowd wanted: for Jesus to elongate their lives, just free from the obstacles they felt in their way. But Jesus recognized that this is not "life" at all, but is instead the sort of zombie-like existence, of spiritual death plus a walking appetite with no merciful end in sight, that caused God to impose physical death for sin in the first place (Gen. 3:22–24). Both the village and the lawyer wanted to interview Jesus, to see if he could grant them the life they wanted for themselves. But Jesus had some questions of his own. Jesus hadn't come to enter their lives. He came to wreck their lives, and invite them into his life.

And Jesus did for the lawyer, precisely what he did for his hometown. He pictured God's will as represented by those from the outside, on the margins of Israel's life. Jesus answered the question of responsibilities for neighbor by telling the story of a man beaten by thieves and left by the side of the Jericho Road. Religious leaders passed by, each walking to the other side. These weren't villains, at least not obviously. They were simply showing common sense. The presence of a man beaten to near death was a sign that these murderous pirates could be anywhere in the caves around. The presenting issue probably wasn't hatred and apathy, but fear and self-protection. But then there is a Samaritan, part of a people group hated by the Israel of the day for both historical and theological reasons. The Samaritan had no reason to claim accountability for this terrorized man. Remarkably though, this stranger treated the man not as a project, but as though he were kin—caring for his physical and economic needs. He showed mercy. Make no mistake about what Jesus was doing here. He was convicting of sin.

There is the first mistake of those who talk as though personal evangelism and public justice are contradictory concerns, or at least that one is part of the mission of the church and the other is a sideline matter. If we are centered on the gospel, then that means that our mission is to expose sin with the light of Christ. Sin is not neatly marked out in silos marked "personal" and "social." The Bible shows us from the beginning that the scope of the curse is holistic in its destruction—personal, cosmic, social, vocational (Gen. 3–11), and the Bible shows us in the end that the gospel is holistic in its restoration—personal, cosmic, social, vocational (Rev. 21–22).

The Law of Moses marks out sin in similar terms. The curses the Levitical priests called out on sin includes both those things most would consider "personal," such as bowing down to a graven image or having sex with an animal, and things most would consider "social" or "political," such as moving a neighbor's land boundary marker and perverting the justice due to the sojourner, the widow, or the orphan (Deut. 27:11–26). Moreover, the prophetic witness never divided up issues of righteousness from justice, or issues of the "personal" from the "social." Societies are made up of people, after all. To make a sharp division here would be like asking whether anyone is accountable for sexual immorality since it involves not a person but a couple (at least a couple, I should say). Is Ahab's acquisition of Naboth's land a matter of personal sin or social injustice? Well, it was both. Was the sin of Sodom a matter of immorality or injustice? It was both (Gen. 18:26; Ezek. 16:49). Isaiah warned of God's judgment both on the sin of idol worship (Isa. 2:8) and the grinding of the faces of the poor (Isa. 3:14–15). The guilt pronounced on Israel by Jeremiah was because the people chased false prophecies and because, "The land is full of blood, and the city full of injustice" (Ezek. 9:9). Amos thundered against the people both for sexual immorality and for the trafficking of the poor (Amos 2:6–7). Malachi indicted the people both for divorcing their wives and for those who pay unjust wages to hired workers (Mal. 2:14–16; 3:5). As the new covenant dawned, John the Baptist did the same: speaking out both against personal immorality and against abuse of office, at least once at the very same time (Matt. 14:1–12). From the cultural mandate to the Sermon on the Mount, from the prophets to Jesus to James, a Christian ethic speaks both to those things we deem "personal," such as lying, and to those things we deem "public," such as the bearing of false witness in court (just to choose two sides of the same question).

This is why churches that try the most self-consciously to avoid social issues and political questions become, unwittingly, the most political of all. The founders of my church tradition, in concert with others, spoke much of the "spirituality of the church" as a reason for avoiding "political" issues. To some degree, they were right. The church does not bear the sword that's been given to the state; the church advances by spiritual, not carnal, means. But the "spirituality of the church" was a convenient doctrine.

My denomination was founded back in the nineteenth century by those who advocated for human slavery, and who sought to keep their consciences and their ballots and their wallets away from a transcendent word that would speak against the sinful injustice of a regime of kidnapping, rape, and human beings wickedly deigning to buy and sell other human beings created in the image of God. Slavery, they argued (to their shame), was a "political" issue that ought not distract the church from its mission: evangelism and discipleship. What such a move empowered was not just social injustice (which would have been bad enough), but also personal sin. When so-called "simple gospel preaching" churches in 1856 Alabama or 1925 Mississippi calls sinners to repentance for fornicating and gambling but not for slaveholding or lynching, those churches may be many things but they are hardly non-political. By not addressing these issues, they are addressing them, by implicitly stating that they are not worthy of the moral scrutiny of the church, that they will not be items of report at the Judgment Seat of Christ. These churches, thus, bless the status quo, with all the fealty of a court chaplain. The same is true of a church in twenty-first-century America that doesn't speak to the pressing issues of justice and righteousness around us, such as the horror of abortion and the persisting sins of racial injustice.

The truth is, the call to repentance is a necessary word in order to interrupt our headlong rush toward the way that seems right in our own eyes, a way that leads to death. That shows up both in our private actions and in our corporate decisions. It shows up in the systems we put in place to perpetuate our sin, so that we won't have to consciously think about such things. There will always be those who see a social ethic as a challenge to the gospel of justification. And there will always be those who see a personal ethic as a challenge to the gospel of justification. The gospel though does not give us faith apart from repentance. Those who have bowed down to idols will not, apart from Christ, inherit the kingdom of God. Those who have transgressed the sexual limits given by God, will not, apart from Christ, inherit the kingdom of God. And the same is true for those who have abused the poor, for those who have ripped apart marriages, for those who have mistreated the sojourner or the widow or the orphan, for those who have robbed others of land or inheritance or future. The word of God exposes the conscience in order to drive it to the goodness of the good news, even at those points where the conscience argues that the word of God ought not to have jurisdiction.

Where there is sin, no matter the form, the gospel speaks a word. This requires a "both/and" approach from the church, recognizing both vertical and horizontal aspects of our sin, both the personal and social.

A Holistic Mission

The command to love God and neighbor speaks not only to the exposing of sin, but also to what it means to please God in expressing such love. The lawyer implied that he loved both his God and his neighbor, so long as he was allowed to define the terms. And he had a point. The Scriptures used the word "neighbor" in a way that could be interpreted as similar to that of "brother," as those within the household of Israel (Lev. 19:17–18). But Jesus turned the question around. The lawyer assumed, as all of us tend to do, that he was the central figure in his life's drama, and that the others around him play supporting roles. They are, at least some of them, "neighbors." Jesus asked though, "Which of these three, do you think, proved to be a neighbor to the man who fell among the robbers?" (Luke 10:36). The lawyer is walking into someone else's life story, and the question is whether his actions there will be shaped by the mercy of God.

In doing this, Jesus defined, just as the witness of the Law and the prophets had before him, love in holistic terms. We are not merely to love our neighbor but to love the neighbor as we love ourselves. In the example Jesus gave, this was not merely a "spiritual" ministry. The Samaritan neighbor cared for the beaten man holistically, showing mercy to him physically and economically, as well as socially—transcending tribal hostilities and the ritual uncleanness of coming near blood or the dead. He acted toward this stranger the way he would act toward himself. The biblical definition of love for oneself is not experiencing affectionate feelings but active care. As the apostle Paul put it, "For no one ever hated his own flesh, but nourished it and cherishes it" (Eph. 5:29). We do not love ourselves merely in "spiritual ways" but holistically. And we do not merely love ourselves in "material" ways. Man does not, after all, live by bread alone (Deut. 8:3; Matt. 4:4). This concern for the whole person, both body and soul, is why

John does not allow the church to define love in nakedly spiritual terms: "But if anyone has the world's goods and sees his brother in need, yet closes his heart against him, how does God's love abide in him?" The apostle warned, "Little children, let us not love in word or talk but in deed and in truth" (1 John 3:17–18). James likewise warned, "If a brother or sister is poorly clothed, and lacking in daily food, and one of you says to them, 'Go in peace, be warmed and filled,' without giving them the things needed for the body, what good is that?" (James 2:15–16).

Now, some would probably want to stop at this point, in order to point out that this concern for the whole person is directed specifically toward "brothers" and "sisters," that is, those who share faith in Christ. But that is precisely the same rhetorical move the lawyer tried. Yes, there is a special obligation for the church to care for one another within the household of faith, just as there is a special obligation for one to care for one's own relatives (1 Tim. 5:8). That's why the church at Jerusalem made provision for the feeding of the destitute widows within their own ranks (Acts 6:1–7). But the point is that God has commanded love for neighbor, and the Scripture defines this love in strikingly holistic terms. Paul told the church at Galatia that our active love of neighbor starts within the church but does not stop there: "So then, as we have opportunity, let us do good to everyone, and especially to those who are of the household of faith" (Gal. 6:10).

Back in the Nazareth synagogue, Jesus spoke of this holistic understanding of neighbor love in precisely the same terms, by pointing to Elijah with the widow of Sidon and Elisha with the leper of Syria. Like the Good Samaritan, the prophets crossed boundaries with active love. Elijah provided flour and oil, which meant subsistence for the widow, and raised her son to life. Through this, the woman announced, "Now I know that you are a man of God, and that the word of the LORD in your mouth is truth" (1 Kings 17:24). Elisha approached a man with an infectious disease, in order to bring him back to physical health (2 Kings 5:1–14).

This is entirely consistent with the advance of the new covenant church. Even after the public ministry of Jesus, his church continued a message of both personal justification and interpersonal justice. James, heading up the church in Jerusalem, directed the churches of the dispersion both in terms of "personal" issues, such as the use of the tongue (James 3:1–12), and in "social" matters, such as the wages paid to workers in the fields (James 5:1–6). He defined "pure and undefiled religion" as that which both remains "unspotted from the world" and that which cares for widows and orphans in their distress (James 1:27 NKJV). Of course he did. His brother, his Lord, already had, when he taught us that the faith that saves us, knowing him, is the faith that recognizes his mysterious presence among the wounded, the weak, the vulnerable, the impoverished, the imprisoned (Matt. 25:31–46).

For those who might pit James or Jesus against Paul, the New Testament allows no such skirmish, either on personal redemption or on ministry to the vulnerable. When the pillars of the church, those who had seen and learned from the risen Christ, first encountered Paul, they were suspicious of him and of his motives. Of course they were. He had been a terrorist, seeking to violently uproot the church in Syria and to murder the believers there. When they received Paul, the apostle testifies, the disciples examined his doctrine and his experience, to see to it that he was embracing and proclaiming the correct gospel, but also that he would remember the poor. That was, Paul testified, "the very thing I was eager to do" (Gal. 2:10).

> For those who might pit James or Jesus against Paul, the New Testament allows no such skirmish, either on personal redemption or on ministry to the vulnerable.

Having defined "neighbor" and "love," Jesus then answered the implicit question behind the others, "What is our mission?" The answer to the question of who was the neighbor to the vulnerable man was obvious: "the one who showed him mercy." Jesus' response was, "You go, and do likewise" (Luke 10:37). The mission of Christ does not start with the giving of the Great Commission or with the pouring out of the Spirit at Pentecost. This is instead when the church is joined to a preexisting mission. Jesus sends the church because he has already been sent (John 20:21). The Great Commission is when Jesus sent the church into the world with the authority he already had (Matt. 28:18). And Pentecost is when Jesus bestowed on the church the power to carry this commission out, by pouring out on them the Spirit of anointing that rested on him (Acts 1:8). The content of this mission is indeed evangelism, calling sinners to repent of sin and truth in Christ through the new birth. But it is not just the making of disciples but also the teaching of them "to observe all that I have commanded you" (Matt. 28:20).

When Jesus left from Nazareth, his ministry touched on every aspect of human existence: preaching, teaching, healing, feeding, and so on. This is not to say that Christians carry out the mission of Christ in exactly the same ways that Jesus did. For that matter, we don't carry out personal evangelism in exactly the same way. Jesus, after all, knowing the content of the heart, is able often to say, "Your sins are forgiven" without a great deal of investigation. And Jesus, unlike we, pronounces forgiveness personally, since he is the one who has been sinned against (Luke 5:21–24). But we still join in Jesus' mission of announcing forgiveness of sins for those who will repent and believe. In the same way, the church does not carry out a holistic ministry in precisely the same way ("take up your bed and walk"), but our mission, if it is the one handed to us by Jesus, is concerned with what Jesus is concerned about: the whole person and the whole life.

This is because, like Jesus, we groan through the Spirit (Rom. 8:23) at the wreckage of the curse in all of its forms. When we see disease, injustice, oppression, unrighteousness, disease, hostility, family breakdown, war, genocide, slavery, spiritual alienation, our response is to recognize: "An enemy has done this" (Matt. 13:28). The gospel teaches us to differentiate between the "very good" of God's original creation along with the "even better" of his coming new creation from the pain and suffering of sin and curse.

That's why the Great Commission is not simply about what we deem adequately "spiritual," and not just about making converts, but teaching these disciples "whatsoever I have commanded you" (Matt. 28:20 kjv). In our attempts to keep the gospel from being too big, we must not end up with a gospel too small to do what Jesus commanded us to do. And that means that often what we address from a gospel framework will be things deemed "social" or "political." The modern missions movement's advance into India wasn't about dealing with the injustice of infanticide or the burning of widows on the funeral pyres of their deceased husbands. The missionaries went to reach people with the gospel. But the gospel speaks to the question of

> In our attempts to keep the gospel from being too big, we must not end up with a gospel too small to do what Jesus commanded us to do.

honoring life, and obedience to Jesus means turning from practices that are unjust and oppressive and murderous, even when those practices are embedded in culture and recognized by law.

Evangelism or Justice, Which?

Some would ask how then the church "balances" a concern for evangelism and discipleship with a concern for justice? In many ways, this question could easily have been asked by the lawyer encountering Jesus, or by the priests and Levites in Jesus' story. How do we "balance" caring for beaten persons on the side of the road with our priestly duties in keeping the law of God? Walking to the other side of the road could easily have made sense as a way of keeping priorities straight. The truth is, we already know how to balance such things, and we already do. The issue really is the same as that dealt with by the apostles Paul and James on the issue of the relationship between faith and works.

Sure, there have been churches and movements that have emphasized public justice without a clear call to personal conversion. Those churches have abandoned the gospel. But this problem is not unique to social action; there are churches that have emphasized personal righteousness without a clear emphasis on the gospel.

I remember once being approached by a woman who had become convinced that Jesus was, in fact, raised from the dead, but she had some caveats. She said she wanted "to have sex with my boyfriends, smoke weed on weekends, get drunk now and then, and still go to heaven." I wouldn't baptize her, because she wouldn't submit to Christ and, without repentance, she couldn't inherit the kingdom of God. I didn't have any negotiating room on that. My response to her though was quite different than it would have been if she had come to me pointing to her sexual morality and sobriety, expecting that somehow this law-keeping would earn her eternal life. In both cases, there would be a refusal to see the gospel, a gospel that comes to us by grace, apart from human works (Rom. 4:5), but which works itself out in trustful obedience to Christ (James 2:14–26). We do not counteract legalism in the realm of personal morality with licentiousness or vice versa. And we do not react to the persistent social and political theologies by pretending that Jesus does not call us to act on behalf of the poor, the sojourner, the fatherless, the vulnerable, the hungry, the trafficked, the unborn, the diseased. We act in the framework of the gospel—never apart from it—both in verbal proclamation and in active demonstration. We do not shrug our shoulders and conclude that half a gospel is better than none.

The short answer to how we should "balance" such things is simple: follow Jesus. We are Christians. This means that as we grow in Christlikeness, we are concerned about the things that concern him. Jesus is the king of his kingdom, and he loves whole persons, bodies as well as souls. Christ Jesus never sends away the hungry with, "Be warmed and filled" (James 2:16). He instead points us to the love of both God and neighbor, to the care of both soul and body, with the words, "You go, and do likewise" (Luke 10:37). That sounds like a mission to me.

This does not lead to a church empowered to speak to every social or political question. But that's also true in the area of personal morality.

If a man in your church mentions in prayer request time that he's thankful for the stress relief provided to him by his monthly trips to a brothel in Nevada, you have a clear word from the Lord on that. If he says he is wrestling through whether he ought to go to Las Vegas on business at all, given the temptations he experiences there, you will have a much more nuanced and person-specific counsel, along the lines of Romans 14:1–23. You would have no authority to tell the whole congregation that boycotting Nevada is what Christians do.

The same dynamic is in play when it comes to the social and political arenas. The Bible doesn't reveal a specific policy on how Christians ought to address climate change, so Christians can disagree, based on prudential judgment, on whether a cap-and-trade policy on carbon emissions is the best way to care for the earth. A church member found to be pouring cancer-causing toxic waste into his neighbor's water supply ought not to be ignored as an "environmental" matter but as a sin to be confronted. I have a position on gun control, but I don't think it's a matter of divine revelation, so I am more than happy to gather around the Lord's Table both with those with lifetime memberships in the National Rifle Association and with those who think guns ought to be licensed and restricted for public safety. Those aren't gospel arguments but prudential arguments about whether gun control works and what the Constitution guarantees. If a member of our church argued, though, that shooting innocent people is sometimes okay, we should intervene with rebuke, discipline, and, probably, counseling.

One some issues, both of personal morality and of public justice, the church speaks definitively and with clear authority, marking out the boundaries of obedience and disobedience. Other issues we speak in a way that forms consciences in a way of wisdom, but without a clear directive rooted in divine revelation.

For example, I am startled by how many Christian parents allow their young children to have technology enabling unfiltered access to the Internet. I think that is negligent parenting, given the overwhelming temptations and dangers that come along with this. I raise the issue periodically in my teaching and preaching, in order to prompt the sorts of questions that can allow families to think through these things. I wouldn't ask for excommunication, though, for a family who allowed Internet access for their pre-teen.

On the other hand, if a father took his son to a strip club for his birthday, I should immediately start the Matthew 18 process. And in reality, we follow this path all the time. The Bible rebukes those married couples who neglect conjugal intimacy with one another, but that doesn't mean that we set a sex schedule for couples with weekly quotas.

A pastor need not be an expert on hedge fund management, and he ought not to preach a series on "biblical hedge fund management," complete with investment strategies and financial targets. Instead, he preaches on integrity, honesty, love of neighbor, avoidance of theft and fraud, and so on, in ways that shape and form the conscience of the hedge fund manager in the church. If that manager is found swindling his clients, now it is a matter of direct address by the church.

A small group Bible study teacher need not be an expert on archaeology in order to teach the Bible or in order to disciple the archaeologist in her group. If that archaeologist asserts, though, that the Davidic kingdom never existed or that the bones of Jesus are located probably somewhere beneath a gas station in Jerusalem, now it becomes a matter for direct address by the church.

A church shouldn't direct the artistic creativity of a member beyond shaping her conscience on beauty and truth and wisdom. If, however, her first hit single is, "I'm Glad Jesus Is Dead So He Can't Tell Me What to Do" or "Torturing Foreigners Is a Fun Thing to Do," now the church speaks unequivocally in rebuke.

Cultural Engagement and Mission

Some would argue that we should disengage from social or political issues because the New Testament itself seems to. Unlike the prophets toward both Israel and the surrounding nations, Jesus and the apostles seem relatively unperturbed by the moral climate of the Roman Empire. The church isn't engaged on matters of outlawing slavery or gladiator-fighting or empire-building wars. Of course, they didn't. Rome, after all, was governed by an emperor, and the people of God had no say in the decisions made at the imperial heights of power. The pastoral epistles don't direct the churches politically directly for the same reason that the apostle Philip gave no directions on marriage or sexual morality to the Ethiopian eunuch. The gospel informed all of the Christian's callings and vocations. Those who were married, then, were expected to live as husbands and wives based on a gospel order. Those who were parents had their parenting informed by a Christian ethic. The early church, though, was made up primarily of those who lacked power (1 Cor. 1:26), and who thus bore no accountability for decisions made in the cultural and political spheres. Even so, we see the New Testament pointing us to callings informed by the gospel, even in what we might consider "politics."

John the Baptist called the crowds to repentance. A drunk coming to be baptized would have been told to repent of intoxication. An adulterer would have been told to walk forward in fidelity, to "go and sin no more" (John 8:11). Some responded to John's preaching, notably tax collectors and soldiers, both officers of Caesar's government. They asked the prophet, "Teacher what shall we do?" John's response was not to mark out their "personal" obedience from their "political" obedience. He said to the tax collectors: "Collect no more than you are authorized to do" (Luke 3:13). He said to the soldiers: "Do not extort money from anyone by threats or by false accusation, and be content with your wages" (Luke 3:14). These were matters both of personal repentance and of public justice.

American Christians often don't realize that we are more like the tax collectors and the soldiers—regardless of our specific occupations—than we are like the occupied peoples of the Empire. Paul wrote to the church at Rome that the sword of Caesar is given by God, to be wielded with accountability to God based on the responsibilities and limits derived from God's delegated authority. In a democratic republic, the final authority for making decisions of statecraft (sword-wielding) rests with the people themselves. In the voting booth, we are delegating to others how to swing the sword of public justice on our behalf. A church that doesn't form consciences for such a calling will only ensure that those consciences are shaped by something other than the gospel.

Contrary to what some might think, the new birth itself is not the stand-alone remedy for the work for righteousness and justice. We cannot simply assume that "changed people" will "change the world." Political structures and cultural mores are complex systems that live long past the life spans of their creators, and often shape what seems possible to those who grow up in them. Personal piety ought to alert us to questions of systemic injustice, but we cannot pretend that it always does so. If the new birth conferred immediate wisdom and insight, we wouldn't need the directives on how to live, given repeatedly in both Testaments. Even if a global awakening were to lead to the conversion of the whole world, we would still need to ask how we ought to work together—socially and politically—to steward culture and to settle disputes among us.

> A church that doesn't form consciences for such a calling will only ensure that those consciences are shaped by something other than the gospel.

Some would argue that we ought to speak only to those who are "inside" the church on such matters and not at all to the outside world. Their motivations here are at least partly right. In terms of disciplinary accountability, as we have seen, we make a sharp distinction between "inside" and "outside." But this distinction is quite wrong when it comes to bearing witness. I once heard a preacher say that it didn't matter to him if his neighbor went to hell as a policeman or a serial killer; he's still going to hell. I think the preacher is well intentioned but, frankly, lying.

It does, in fact, matter to him if his neighbor goes to hell as a serial killer, because the preacher would not react to the murder of his own children with a shrug that says, "Well, they're Christians, so they're in heaven; what does it matter?"

John the Baptist confronted political authority "outside" of the community of regeneration without hesitation. Herod's taking of his brother's wife, and his hormonally-induced vows made at the prompting of her dancing daughter, were about more than just the condition of his soul. The king was not just immorally using his private parts; he was also unjustly using his public office (Matt. 14:1–13). The Word of God speaks to both.

A Cross-Shaped Mission

Jesus not only spoke of the man beaten on the side of the road, he almost started his ministry as a man beaten by the side of the road. "When they heard these things, all in the synagogue were filled with wrath," Luke recounts. "And they rose up and drove him out of the town and brought him to the brow of the hill on which their town was built, so that they could throw him down the cliff" (Luke 4:28–29). When Jesus pressed his message with clarity, the response was murderous rage. The most surprising part of this account, though, is the anticlimactic way it ends. "But passing through their midst, he went away" (Luke 4:30). Jesus seems here like a coward, walking away from a fight, a fight he started. But Jesus wasn't walking away from danger; he was walking toward it. He was picking up a mission that would take him from the Galilean hillsides onward to Jerusalem, to the Place of the Skull. The execution this little village planned for their hometown prophet would be carried out by the Roman Empire. His hour had not yet come.

The cross-shaped nature of this mission was already evident in Jesus' refusal, right before his hometown sermon, to take from the devil the reins of the government of the universe. Satan was willing to surrender his authority over "all the kingdoms of the world" for a moment of worship. A Christ-run universe would have reflected the values and ethics of Jesus; but there would be a world-ruling Messiah and there would be no sinless sacrifice able to atone for the world. The devil recognized that his kingdom could only, ultimately, fall by the gospel. The devil did not fear bloodless moralism. He had nothing to fear but blood itself.

The gospel of historic Christianity is cosmic. In Christ, God reconciles "to himself all things, whether on earth or in heaven, making peace by the blood of his cross" (Col. 1:20). The gospel is also social, reconciling people with one another, and motivating them to care for human flourishing and human suffering. But the gospel of Jesus Christ is, first of all, personal. We love our fellow human beings, and serve them in their suffering, precisely because we believe that God loves not just "humanity" but individual humans, that Jesus died for persons, that God's wrath is propitiated against persons, and that persons will be raised, individually and collectively, body and soul, on the last day, either to everlasting life or to everlasting condemnation.

Any Christian witness that doesn't start and finish with the gospel is unspeakably cruel and, in fact, devilish. The devil works in two ways: by deception, "You will not surely die" (Gen. 3:4), and by accusation, "who accuses them day and night before our God" (Rev. 12:10). The devil wishes to assure some people that there's no need for repentance, and others that there's no hope for mercy. Some people are deceived into thinking they are too good for the gospel while others are accused into thinking they are too bad for the gospel. No one is more pro-choice than the devil on the way into the abortion clinic, and no one is more pro-life than the devil on the way out of the abortion clinic. The gospel of Jesus Christ tears down both strategies.

The fact that gospel clearly calls us to repentance is hated by the outside world. And the gospel clearly calls us to mercy by faith in the blood of Christ, even when we can't believe that we'd ever be received. In our day, that personal aspect of the gospel is probably most controversial when it comes to issues of sexual morality. Some would suggest that we do precisely what the universalists of old did on the question of God's judgment of sin. Instead of a blanket universalism though, they counsel a targeted universalism, which leaves unperturbed one area of sin. But this not only is unfaithful to God; it is unloving to neighbor, leaving those in need of mercy terrorized by their own consciences. We empower darkness when we refuse to warn of judgment. The gospel brings our sin out into the open, but not in the way the devil does. The gospel does not expose sin in order to condemn but in order to reconcile.

The gospel also informs the tone of our engagement. We are not prosecuting attorneys, seeking to indict our opponents with their sin. The devil does that just fine on his own. We are defense attorneys, or as the Bible puts it, "ambassadors of reconciliation" (2 Cor. 5:20). A defense attorney has to be just as precise about the evidence for guilt, in order to persuade a client he needs representation in the first place and to help that client throw himself rightly on the mercy of the court. We speak of sin, and we warn of judgment, but in order to see persons made right with God, not in order to vent our spleens. We are not standing athwart history, yelling "Repent!"

We are, like John before us, pointing to Christ and announcing, "Behold, the Lamb of God who takes away the sins of the world."

Any "gospel" that evacuates the cross of judgment against sin, that alienates the gospel from personal reconciliation with God and with others, is something other than the gospel of Jesus Christ. And any Christianity that turns us away from the truths handed down to us about Jesus—his deity, his humanity, his miracles, his atoning death, his bodily resurrection, his future return, his authority in Scripture, his building of his church—is pointing us to some different Messiah.

Conclusion

Whether in a story from a Jericho ditch, or in a letter from a Birmingham jail, we must be reminded that we serve a God of both justice and justification, and we must not pit the two against each other. Our mission is rooted in a gospel that tells us honestly of the bad news of our sin and the good news of God's grace. Our mission reconciles sinners to God, but also reconciles person to person, community to community, humanity to nature. We must speak truth to power, even as John the Baptist did to King Herod (and sometimes with the same results). Let's feed the poor, house the homeless, shelter the widow, adopt the orphan, advocate for the unborn, and steward the environment. But, as we do, let's, most importantly, preach peace and justice, for individuals and for the whole world, found in the bloody cross and empty tomb of Jesus. As the culture finds Christianity stranger and stranger, we will find that the strangest thing we have to say is, "Jesus saves."

> **Whether in a story from a Jericho ditch, or in a letter from a Birmingham jail, we must be reminded that we serve a God of both justice and justification, and we must not pit the two against each other.**

Chapter Six

HUMAN DIGNITY

On a shelf near me right now stands one of my favorite pictures. It's a black-and-white photograph of a line of civil rights workers, protesting in the heat of the Jim Crow era. They are standing shoulder-to-shoulder, all of them bearing the same sign. Placarded in large letters on the sign are the words, "I Am a Man." I love this picture for its simplicity, and for the courage and truth telling represented there. At the same time, the picture makes me tremble that such things ever needed, and still need, to be said.

I didn't grow up in the time of segregation. By the time I was born, the schools were integrated, and the most significant civil rights and voting rights legislation had been implemented. But I remember Sunday school.

Like most churches in my tradition, at the time, we children would go to church each week bearing little envelopes with our offerings for world missions. One week, when I was perhaps four or five, I was fidgeting through the Bible lesson, and pulled a quarter out of my envelope. Somehow it ended up in my mouth. The lady who was teaching us that day noticed, and, I'm sure, didn't want me to choke on the coin, so she tried to motivate me never to do something like that again. She said, in a memory that stays with me to this day, "That's filthy; why, you don't know whether a black man may have held that coin."

Now, this lady was not a Klansman. She probably didn't think of herself as a proponent of white supremacy. The point is that she didn't think at all. She didn't see that her statement was precisely the culture the civil rights movement confronted: the idea that her African-American neighbors were unclean, were something not quite human.

It might be my imagination playing tricks on me, but it seems to me that she followed up this statement by gathering the children together to sing "Jesus Loves the Little Children." Her words, moments before, probably didn't sound to her, or to us, contradictory to our singing, "Red and yellow, black and white, they are precious in his sight; Jesus loves the little children of the world." Jesus loves black people; that's why we brought our dimes and quarters to send missionaries to Africa. But what they touched might make us unclean. She couldn't see that these were two very different gospels, and that only one of them could be true. I suppose if you had asked her why she was perpetuating bigotry in her class, she might have said you were being "political." Her job wasn't to talk about racial tensions or civil rights matters. Her job was to teach children the Bible, and to motivate them to share the gospel around the world. She might have dismissed the whole conversation as a matter of social policy, a diversion from our mission. She would have been wrong.

An Ancient Threat

The threats to human dignity are with us always, from racism and slavery to abortion and torture. Over the past half-century, many Christians have mobilized around the pro-life movement in response to the legalization of abortion by Supreme Court action in 1973. The pro-life movement, however, was not a merely reactionary posture, fueled by culture wars. Abortion was not simply a "wedge issue" to distinguish social conservatives from the sexual revolution. The pro-life movement was connected intrinsically to the church's witness to human dignity going back all the way to the church's emergence in Jerusalem in the first century. Christians who object to the violence of abortion are in continuity with a long tradition of Christian teaching against the oppression of the vulnerable and against the disposability of human life. The church, made up of fallen sinners, has done so imperfectly, and some bearing the name of Christ have sometimes stood on the wrong side of human dignity, but the great movements against bloodshed and slavery and exploitation have often come with the prophetic, moral grounding of the gospel of Jesus Christ.

Moreover, the pro-life movement, like the abolitionist and civil rights movements, is much more than a political movement (though it is nothing less). The pro-life movement has, of all the recent Christian forays into public engagement, been the most holistic in its work, seeing the need for laws to protect unborn children but also a cultural witness to persuade women not to abort, men not to abandon their children, and society to see the goodness and value of every person, even when shielded from sight in the womb or when sick or diseased or developmentally challenged. With that has come also ministry, rooted in churches and in community organizations, to equip mothers to choose life for their children, often offering job-training, counseling, and shelter from situations of domestic abuse. Seeing the horror of abortion jolted many churches toward our James 1:27 duty to care for widows and orphans in their distress, as the church mobilizes for adoption of children who need families, foster care for those in the system in need of support, and the welcoming of pregnant women in crisis. At the same time, the abortion issue has awakened in many a Christian conscience to hear the cries of the "least of these," whether in or out of the womb—leading to justice and mercy ministries toward the poor, the homeless, the trafficked, the addicted. While a pro-life, whole-life witness has a long way to go yet, the church does not live up to its caricature as those who, in the words of one critic, believe that life "begins at conception and ends at birth."

At the same time, the pro-life movement, like the abolitionist and civil rights movements, necessarily entailed a theological vision. The central question behind the abortion debate, after all, was, "Is the fetus my neighbor?" A Christian articulation of reality had to, by necessity, lay out an accounting for what it means to be a person, and why this matters. That's especially true when the issues related to human dignity have become, due to technology, much more complex, as they move into questions of embryonic research, reproductive technologies, genetic screening, and human cloning. The theological vision behind these questions though is applicable to issues far removed from the petri dish or the nursery crib. Those who develop a sense of how human dignity fits in the larger meaning of the universe have consciences that can be trained to see related issues of racial reconciliation, euthanasia, war and peace, treatment of migrants and workers, capital punishment and prison conditions, as well as the rapidly changing challenges to human uniqueness proposed by technologies that promise life-extension and even artificial intelligence.

These questions are not simply about equipping Christians to do the right thing in the arenas of statecraft and public culture. A Christianity that doesn't prophetically speak for human dignity is a Christianity that has lost anything distinctive to say. The gospel is, after all, grounded in the uniqueness of humanity in creation, redemption, and consummation. Behind the questions of whether we should abort babies or torture prisoners or harass immigrants or buy slaves is a larger question: "Who is the Christ, the Son of the Living God?" If Jesus shares humanity with us, and if the goal of the kingdom is humanity in Christ, then life must matter to the church. The church must proclaim in its teaching and embody in its practices love and justice for those the outside world would wish to silence or to kill. And the mission of the church must be to proclaim everlasting life, and to work to honor every life made in the image of God, whether inside or outside the people of God. A vision of human dignity can exist within the common grace structures of the world, but a distinctively Christian vision of why humanity should be protected must emerge from a larger framework of kingdom and culture and mission.

> A Christianity that doesn't prophetically speak for human dignity is a Christianity that has lost anything distinctive to say.

On a Sunday this January, probably of whatever year it is when you read this (at least as long as I'm living), I will probably be preaching somewhere in a church on "Sanctity of Human Life Sunday." Here's a confession: *I hate it.*

Don't get me wrong. I love to preach the Bible. And I love to talk about the image of God and the protection of all human life. I hate this Sunday not because of what we have to say, but that we have to say it at all. The idea of aborting an unborn child or abusing a born child or starving an elderly person or torturing an enemy combatant or screaming at an immigrant family, these ought all to be so self-evidently wrong that a "Sanctity of Human Life Sunday" ought to be as unnecessary as a "Reality of Gravity Sunday." We shouldn't have to say that parents shouldn't abort their children, or their fathers shouldn't abandon the mothers of their babies, or that no human life is worthless regardless of age, skin color, disability, or economic status. Part of my thinking here is, I hope, a sign of God's grace, a groaning by the Spirit at this world of abortion clinics and torture chambers (Rom. 8:22–23). But part of it is my own inability to see the spiritual combat zone that the world is, and has been from Eden onward. This dark present reality didn't begin with the antebellum South or with the modern warfare state, and it certainly didn't begin with the *Roe v. Wade* Supreme Court decision. Human dignity is about the kingdom of God, and that means that in every place and every culture human dignity is contested.

Even those who reject Christian doctrine, or even any religious teaching at all, can acknowledge that something seems wrong with the world. Cruelty and violence and injustice seem to be about more than just our learned behaviors but something almost hardwired into human nature itself. People would see the timing and the reasons behind this "fall" in different ways—whether it's the rise of the industrial economy or the end of some prehistoric matriarchy or a thousand other scenarios. But the Christian accounting of humanity, in continuity with the Hebrew Scriptures, teaches that at some point in our primal past, humanity came into contact with a dark, mysterious, personal reality that was wild, intelligent, powerful, and in a state of insurrection against the Creator. These intelligences have been identified by different names in various cultures—spirits or watchers or powers or devils or demons. But whatever they are called, these forces seemed to have a special interest in humanity, and in reframing for humanity how we should see ourselves.

The demonic elements of the universe wish for us to see ourselves as either more than we are or as less than we are. They wish for us to see ourselves as beasts, animals driven along only by our appetites and our instincts, and thus unaccountable morally to God, or as gods ourselves, those with no ethical boundaries other than those we impose on ourselves, and thus morally unaccountable to God. The quest to deify humanity, to unshackle ourselves from creatureliness, always leads not to the exaltation of the human but to the degradation of the human. This is why the apocalyptic vision of the Bible is of a humanity that demands to be worshipped as a god and that arises as a Beast out of the sea (Rev. 13:1).

A Human-Centered Universe

In order to understand why human dignity matters, and why human dignity is always contested, we must understand that the kingdom of God is centered on humanity. The universe is human-centered. I can imagine as I write this the bristling of some of you, especially those of you who are the most theologically orthodox and articulate. To say that the universe is human-centered, you might think, sounds like the sort of heresy we often hear from those who wish to redefine God or his works in terms of human expectations or categories. What I mean, though, is that the universe was created to be governed, under God, by human image-bearers. The universe was called into existence as an inheritance for Jesus, that in all things he might have the preeminence (Col. 1:18).

The Old Testament tells us that the universe was not called together arbitrarily but by the Word of God (Gen. 1:3), a Word the New Testament tells us is not a thing but a person (John 1:1). The Scriptures affirm that the meaning of all reality is encoded in something

> **The universe was called into existence as an inheritance for Jesus, that in all things he might have the preeminence (Col. 1:18).**

the apostle Paul called "the mystery of Christ" (Eph. 3:4). This mystery is that in Christ there is a "summing up" of everything—not simply the aggregate of all souls but "things in heaven and things on earth" (Eph. 1:10) in the person of the incarnate, crucified, and resurrected Jesus. The order and harmony of the universe are described in the Genesis account of, for example, the regularity of times and seasons. This order is described in terms of a manifold wisdom of God, by the Psalms and elsewhere in the Hebrew Scriptures, and is grasped by non-Hebraic thought in the concept of the *Logos* or the *Tao* ordering the harmony of the cosmos. In the mystery of Christ, the mud of the earth—the substance from which humanity is formed—is joined to the eternal nature of God himself so that the material world is now connected, without confusion but also without separation, to God himself.

In Christ Jesus, God joins deity to humanity, permanently, in the human heir of the universe. It is not that Jesus *was* human, but rather that Jesus *is* human. God's purposes in Christ, then, explain why the Scriptures take so seriously the dignity of humanity as created in the image of God

(Gen. 1:27). Humanity, from the very beginning, is distinct from the rest of nature, including the rest of the living creatures, because of this mysterious image bearing. The image is debated among Christians, and has been for thousands of years.

Is the image primarily rationality (though the angels are certainly rational, and they do not bear God's image)?

Is it primarily moral accountability (although, again, the angels are morally accountable)? Is it primarily the function of humanity in carrying out God's will?

Such debates seem, to me, to be beside the point. The image of God, biblically speaking, is a mysterious reality in which the invisible world and even inanimate nature seems to recognize in humanity the distinctive mark of our Creator (Rom. 8:19–23). This image is about who we are—not just about what we do—but clearly the image of God defines and equips us to carry out God's mission, ruling beneath and for him over the rest of the creation. This is the end-result of redemption—a humanity once again, under God, on the throne of the cosmos.

Warfare and the Image of God

That's why the skirmishes over human dignity are, long before they are cultural or political, part of an ancient clash of the kingdoms. The exploitation and murder of innocent human life is one of the very first wicked manifestations of a fallen universe, unloosed from the protection of Word-directed human headship. The fall of humanity is followed immediately by fratricide (Gen. 4:8–16), and by vigilante murder celebrated in song. The covenant of God with creation after the Noahic flood includes a warning against bloodshed, set in the context of human dignity as bearers of God's image (Gen. 9:6–7). As the children of Abraham move toward the initial down payment on our inheritance, God forbade them from pursuing Canaanite idolatry, specifically denouncing by name the god Moloch, who demanded the violent sacrifices of human babies (Lev. 20:1–8). The Israelites themselves are threatened with death, as Pharaoh seeks to strangle the people of promise in the cradle with mass murder. This same spirit is at work in the dawning of a new covenant as another king sought to destroy innocent infant life, when threatened by the prophesied rule of a baby from the House of David (Matt. 2:1–18). At every place in between, God mandated not only the saving of life from murder but also the protection of the vulnerable—the poor, the sojourner, the widow, the fatherless, the diseased.

This threat through Scripture is not incidental. It is not just Pharaoh and Herod who are slaughtering the innocents. The gospel is opposed by an ongoing spirit of antichrist (1 John 2:18), which rages against the kingdom and seeks to set up its own mirror-image empire.

This anti-gospel rage is murderous (John 8:44; 1 John 3:8, 11–15). The ascended Christ explained this historical trail of blood metaphorically in a vision to the apostle John as an ongoing war between the Serpent and the people of the Messiah (Rev. 12:1–12). It should not surprise us then that, in every age, there is a clash between Christ and the powers of this age. It should not surprise us that human appetites, when unrestrained by their creation purposes, can turn murderous (James 4:2). And it should not surprise us that the spirit of every age seeks to define human worth in terms of power and usefulness, while the gospel of the kingdom defines human dignity in strikingly different terms, as Christ himself identifies himself not with the powerful but with the vulnerable. A fallen universe seeks to wipe out vulnerable human life precisely because such life bears the unmistakable imprint of the one who overcomes not by might nor by power but by his blood. Behind the hostility to the weak there is a far more mysterious, far more ancient guerilla insurgency against the human child who, as promised, will crush the old reptile's head (Gen. 3:15).

Several years ago, I heard a lecturer talking about church ministries of mercy to the poor and the vulnerable. The crowd in the room, evangelical Christians all, seemed to be in agreement with the lecturer because—as one respondent put it—social ministries give us the opportunity to share the gospel and to give credibility to our verbal proclamation. The lecturer agreed that this was true, but then he stopped and talked about a group home near his congregation, filled with severely cognitively disabled children. This man's church went to this home every day, to brush the hair of these children, to sing to them, and sometimes just to sit quietly and hold their hands. The children, he said, are probably not even aware of their presence. "They can't hear or respond to the gospel," he said. "So is our ministry to them worth it?" Of course it is. This ministry is "worth it" for the same reason it was "worth it" for Jesus' friends to wash and to anoint his body with spices after his crucifixion. It was honoring him, loving him, recognizing him. He tells us when we stand with those who are marginalized—the poor, the unborn, the orphaned, the widowed, the diseased, the abandoned, the disabled, the poor, the elderly—we are standing with the "least of these," my brothers (Matt. 25:45). And when we care for his brothers, Jesus tells us, we will recognize him there too.

The presence of the weak, the vulnerable, and the dependent is a matter of spiritual warfare. The womb reminds us that we are not self-existent. None of us are "viable" apart from others and from the ecosystem God has built around us. The infant in the womb is dependent indeed upon his or her mother, and cannot survive without her. But that is not unique to the fetal stage of development. A newborn is just as dependent upon a mother's care, which is why the psalmist speaks of learning to trust God at his mother's breast (Ps. 22:9). Jesus quoted a line from this same psalm as he was being crucified, with his own mother looking

> The presence of the weak, the vulnerable, and the dependent is a matter of spiritual warfare.

on, from whom he had nursed as an infant. We aren't self-existent gods. Caring for those who don't seem to "matter" takes a kind of compassion that tells us that life is not about instinct and gene-preservation and the will to power. We aren't animals.

Abortion, torture, euthanasia, unjust war, racial injustice, the harassment of immigrants, these things aren't simply "mean" (although they are that too). They are part of an ongoing guerilla insurgency against the image of God himself, as summed up in Jesus of Nazareth. Jesus identified himself with humanity—in all of our weakness and fragility. He did not arrive fully mature, on a white horse in Jerusalem. He took on a human nature at every stage of development—from "embryo" to "fetus" to infant to child to man. He was conceived as an orphan—without initially a human father—and was dependent for his very life on an adopting father who was willing to sacrifice his own life-plan to protect him and to provide for him (Matt. 2:13–15). He lived as a migrant refugee in a foreign land, a land long hostile to his own. He died helplessly convulsing on a cross, dependent on others for hydration. Even in death, Jesus counted himself with thieves, and was laid in a borrowed grave. Jesus, in his humanity, wasn't "viable" on his own either.

The Culture of Death and the Kingdom of God

As we seek the kingdom of God, our intuitions are shaped to long for the ultimate triumph of life over death (Isa. 25:7–8; 1 Cor. 15:26). The kingdom tells us what matters and who matters, and that the criteria for that is sharply different from the social Darwinist values of success, power, utility, or strength. If the messianic kingdom is ruled by joint-heirs, whose "worth" is not determined by fleeting concepts of power, then the church ought to recognize the same. If the kingdom of Christ is distinguished by "pity on the weak and the needy" whose lives are threatened by "oppression and violence" (Ps. 72:13–14), then the people of the kingdom cannot ignore the silent cries of "embryos" frozen in fertility clinics, "fetuses" dismembered in antiseptic hospitals, "unwanted children" languishing in institutions, "illegal immigrants" exploited by cartels and businesses, or "invalids" wasting away in lonely nursing homes. If the kingdom is ruled by those from every tribe and nation (Rev. 5:9–10), then how can the believing community stand by while some of the cosmos's future rulers are denied justice because of the pigment of their skin? We ought to be listening to see who the world-system wants to devalue and degrade, most often first with words, so that we can know for whom we should be speaking and standing.

Pope John Paul II rightly spoke of the issues of human dignity before as a "culture of death" sparring with a "culture of life." He was right. These questions aren't ultimately about public policy and politics—although they manifest themselves there. The base-level issue is a cultural framing of what matters and who matters, a framing that is rooted in a theological counter-story to the one God is telling. Sometimes that is explicit, as with the noxious and heretical twisting of the Bible to attempt to support black inferiority by white supremacists. Sometimes this culture is much more implicit, allowing people to degrade human dignity without ever knowing what they are doing at all. Our task as the people of God is to recognize this culture where we see it, to know where this comes from, and to speak a different story.

The culture of death seeks to disconnect humanity from nature and body from soul. The disconnect between humanity and nature is seen in our concept of human dominion. Now, some would suggest that a Christian concept of "dominion" found in the early biblical texts of Genesis is dangerous and subversive, conjuring up the idea of theocratic

Christians seeking to impose their will on society or earth-destroying Christians who believe that paving over every last inch of ground is God's will. While there have been some identified with Christianity who have held such views, they do not represent the teaching of the Bible or the framework of the kingdom of Christ.

Dominion isn't a Caesar-like rapaciousness, but a Christ-like stewardship. Dominion is in the context biblically of cultivation of land, which takes conservation and care, and the mandate to be "fruitful and multiply." Dominion is about inheritance, about stewarding with future generations in mind. Human dominion, then, is not predatory. Human uniqueness is not about harming other creatures, or about mishandling nature, but about cultivating it, a cultivation that includes rest for the land and protection of other creatures. Humanity is not separate from the rest of nature. We are not made of ether but of Spirit-enlivened mud. We come from the earth, and we must receive from the earth what we need to survive and to flourish. We have dominion over the world around us, but we do not have dominion over other human beings, to make decisions of whether they can live or die, live freely or be exploited for the appetite of other human persons. Every person recognizes some aspect of human dominion—even those who would suggest that human beings are just another species or a parasite on the planet. These people, after all, direct their advocacy in moral terms, not to flies or dogs or even other primates—but to human beings, of whom they recognize there is something unique in the world.

The culture of death also reveals itself in the unnatural and unbiblical disconnect of body from soul. Christians in my tradition, tragically, did not initially oppose the abortion culture, for the same reason some of them did not initially oppose the slavery culture or the Jim Crow culture. They saw the "soul" as the "part" of humanity with which the gospel is concerned. The child could be biologically present in the womb, but somehow be human without a soul. This flawed theology was also present in those who thought they could evangelize the "souls" of slaves while they simultaneously thought they could "own" their bodies to do their labor. Such a way always ends in death.

The threats to human dignity often do not start with a feeling of hatred, but with an attempt to "fix" what is wrong with humanity. Once abstract data and reason replace the mystery of human existence, then the result of such rationalism is not cool detachment but hedonism and violence.

If enslaved persons are valued for their economic power, then they are "worth" more to the powers-that-be in slavery than out of it.

If infants are not conscious of themselves, and if self-consciousness and reason are what it means to be human, then what are they? It turns out that if one doesn't know what it means to be a person, one can kill without ever feeling bloodthirsty. In fact, you can feel as though you are saving the world.

The ethical anarchy around us is the result of a society that thinks it can divide the life of the body from the life of the soul (if, in fact, there is a soul). It is the result of a society that thinks it can medicate away the fear of death, because it thinks that human existence is only the sum total of neurons firing. This is why advocates for legal abortion and euthanasia no longer argue that unborn life isn't human. One need only argue that such life isn't happy, and there are always those who can "fix" unhappiness if not with a pill then with a scalpel.

Power and the Powerless

Joined to this cultural confusion about the meaning of humanity is something else: cold, hard cash. The slaveholders' wicked regime was about trafficking persons for their own economic benefit. Jim Crow likewise was built off of a planter regime that wanted to use persons for economic power. The trafficking of girls and women around the world is motivated by the profits of pornographers and prostitution cartels. Militarism is driven, often, by the profits that can be attained by weapons manufacturers and others. And the abortion culture uses the thoroughly American consumerist language of "choice" and "empowerment," but what's at stake are billions of dollars. The culture of death is sustained by more than simply the penumbra and emanations of an old Supreme Court decision. That's why, despite their talk of adoption as a "choice," the abortion industry hardly ever leads women through an adoption process relative to how often they promise them the "fix" of a "terminated pregnancy."

We shouldn't be surprised by any of this. Money and power, abstracted from the kingship of Christ, always lead to violence. Pharaoh ordered the execution of the Hebrew children because they threatened his pyramid-scheme economy in the elite "1 percent" of the ancient world. Herod carried out the same decree because he wanted to protect his kingship, a kingship that carried with it the generous financial support of the Roman Empire. No one, Jesus told us, can serve both God and Mammon. In saying this, Jesus personalized money in a disturbing way. When capital becomes god, it is no longer merely some*thing* but some*one*. The demonic force of rapaciousness so distorts the soul that, when it is threatened, someone is going to be exploited and someone is going to die.

Human Dignity and the Church

A church culture informed by the kingdom of God must start there. If we are to be a pro-life people, we must first cast aside our idols. The marginalization of the church in a secularizing society can give us an opening to do this. After a generation of Christian churches emphasizing, sometimes explicitly and sometimes implicitly, financial and social and political prosperity, is it any wonder that when being pro-life moves from voting for candidates to dealing with an unwanted pregnancy, so many church members slip off into the darkness of the nearest large city with a guilty conscience and an envelope full of cash? Mammon is a jealous god, and he's armed to the teeth. We need to create the kind of kingdom-shaped culture within our churches that constantly shines the light of Christ wherever these false gods exist in our own affections. And then we need to demonstrate what it means to believe that a person's life consists in more than the abundance of his possessions.

We do that, first, by recognizing that the struggle for life isn't a matter simply of the church versus the world, but of Christ versus the church. We must repent of the way that we, sometimes without even knowing it, have prized the powerful over the powerless. Let's stop highlighting in our church testimonies and publications how God "blesses" the millionaire who tithes. Let's stop trumpeting the celebrity athletes and beauty queens as evidence of God's blessing. Let's show that God has blessed us in a Christ who never had a successful career or a balanced bank account but who was blessed by God with life, and with children that no one can number, from every tribe, tongue, nation, and language. What would it mean for your pro-life witness if your local congregation were served by a deacon or a worship leader with Down syndrome? What would it mean for your pro-life witness if the person reading Scripture this next Sunday isn't polished for performance but instead is the stammering voice of an elderly woman in the beginning stages of dementia? It would signal that life is about more than perceived usefulness.

We ought to equip churches to counsel families through ethical decisions that are difficult and often hidden. Is abortion moral in the case of an ectopic pregnancy? Should an infertile couple sever reproduction from the one-

> **We must repent of the way that we, sometimes without even knowing it, have prized the powerful over the powerless.**

flesh union through advanced reproductive technologies? Is it ever ethical to authorize doctors to "pull the plug" on a loved one who is dying? How should churches respond to undocumented immigrants in their congregations? How do affluent families find relationships with those who are poor—not out of "community service" but out of a need to connect with the rest of the body of Christ? Before these questions can be addressed socially or politically, there must be consciences shaped by teaching and, beyond that, by intuitions formed by seeing the lived reality of such all around them in the church.

When it comes to issues of the right-to-life and of civil rights, we assume that we are "winning" or that we have "won." This is a dangerous assumption. Yes, great strides have been made toward racial justice, but the idea that this struggle has been "won" and we can now move toward the benign neglect of a "color-blind" society ignores the ongoing problems of racial injustice faced in this country and around the world. Likewise, on the abortion issue, it is true that opinion polls indicate that more and more people identify themselves as "pro-life." But this does not mean we are winning.

I remember once having a coffee-shop discussion with friends about where we would have stood on the Vietnam War, had we been alive in the 1960s. Such was an almost useless dialogue because we have no way of knowing the answer. None of us have a draft notice in the mail. None of us are sitting in the Situation Room wondering if the fall of Saigon would mean the advance of the Soviet Union toward world domination and nuclear holocaust. None of us are Cambodian farmers or South

Vietnamese shrimpers in danger of being murdered by the Khmer Rouge or the Vietcong. A feminist leader once said that most people are pro-life with three exceptions: rape, incest, and "my situation." I fear she is all too right. Pharaoh was pro-immigrant until the Israelites threatened the economy. The first Herod Administration was pro-Messiah until the actual Messiah showed up. The second Herod Administration had no problem with desert prophets until one meddled with his "adult entertainment." Lots of people are pro-life and pro-child until the lives of children become personally inconvenient.

Our congregations must be cultures of human dignity and human flourishing, workshops of kingdom reconciliation where people of different skin colors, income levels, national backgrounds, and ranges of ability and disability love and serve one another. A congregation that excludes people from the baptistery because of that person's ethnicity (and don't be deceived into thinking that doesn't still happen) isn't just a "backward" church, but an antichrist church with a missing lampstand. We ought to have the spine to say so—and to call those churches to repentance or to exit from fellowship with us. The next century will offer challenges to human dignity in the public square, and in our churches. These will test our resolve perhaps in ways not seen since the culture wars of slavery and segregation—wars in which too many conservative Protestants were on the wrong side of the kingdom of Christ.

Our churches must embody a culture of human dignity because we see bound up in that the gospel itself. Our pro-life witness ought to be seen in pews filled with unwed mothers who are welcomed, not shamed. Our pro-life witness ought to be seen in Sunday schools filled with children with fetal alcohol syndrome and autism and cerebral palsy and AIDS who are hugged and loved and received because we see in them Jesus and because we embrace a gospel that told us a long time ago that life is better than death. Our churches must embody the reconciliation of the gospel not by doing more "ethnic" ministry, whose very nomenclature assumes that there are "regular" people and "ethnic" people. We're all ethnic. The "white" church doesn't "do ministry" to those "ethnic" churches dependent upon it. We assume often without thinking that the church is white, American Protestants doing missionary work for the benefit of everyone else. But the church isn't white or American; the church is headed by a Middle Eastern Jewish man who never spoke a word of English. We do not need more "ministry" to the poor or racial minorities or immigrant communities. We need to be led by the poor and by racial "minorities" and by immigrant communities.

Cultures shaped by the kingdom vision of human dignity and human limits are especially important as we move into a time when the central question is not, first of all, when does life begin or when does life end, but what the meaning of human life is at all. Technologies are moving rapidly toward the integration of the machine into the human person, toward the quest for the extension of life indefinitely through the "download-ing" of the "self" into machines, and toward the endless manipulation of human life through cloning, genetic screening, and even human/animal hybridization. The questions we may face in the future are whether or not artificially intelligent cyborgs can be saved, and whether we should baptize robots equipped with functioning human brains, or whether the church should bless the marriage of a human being with an artificially intelligent computer system. We may soon see a world in which only Christians have disabled babies in their strollers, only Christians have bald little girls fighting through chemotherapy, only Christians have little boys in "husky" size pants as they struggle with childhood obesity. How will we then talk with our neighbors about the miracle of the new birth, when their old birth was something engineered by others? How will talk with our neighbors about the unconditional love of God as a Father for his children, no matter what, if the concepts of begetting and fatherhood are only distant cultural memories?

These are new scenarios, but they are not new questions. Wendell Berry warned that "the next great division of the world will be between people who wish to live as creatures and people who wish to live as machines."[26] And that might be a more literal question than what even he imagined. Only a vision of what people are for, and what it means to bear the image of God, can start to address such questions. These won't be answered by syllogisms but by people with consciences trained to know what humanity is for, by life together around the Table, in the singing of hymns, in the serving of one another with basin and towel.

---

26. Wendell Berry, *Life Is a Miracle: An Essay Against Modern Superstition* (Washington, DC: Counterpoint, 2000), 55.

A Pro-Life, Whole-Life People

In terms of mission, the pro-life movement of the last generation is perhaps one of the most hopeful signs of the future—of a vital, gospel-driven social witness of the church in the public arena. The pro-life movement, after all, was not merely reactive, not simply a "culture war" in search of "wedge" issues to exploit. While Christians are always vulnerable to cynical exploitation by political parties, the pro-life cause predated the abortion platforms of either political party, and persists even when politicians of every ideology would rather see it quietly die.

On its best days, the pro-life movement was animated by a holistic ethic of caring both for vulnerable unborn children and for the women damaged by abortion. It has thus engaged in a multi-pronged strategy that addresses, simultaneously, the need for laws to outlaw abortion, ministry (including job-training and childcare and housing and financially-accessible healthcare) for pregnant women in crisis, adoption and foster care for children who need families, and a persuasive cultural witness about why life matters. Moreover, the pro-life movement has kept both an internal focus—showing the people of God theologically why the image of God matters—and an external focus. The external focus, unlike other aspects of the culture wars, has remained (with some exceptions and outliers) marked by kindness and civility, often in the face of vitriolic mischaracterization. This was by necessity since the goal was not label good guys and bad guys in order to assemble electoral coalitions. The goal was also to persuade people not to abort their children or euthanize their parents. One cannot accomplish that goal by demonizing and screaming at the people one wishes to persuade. This is why the pro-life movement persists. While I am, as I said, made nervous by triumphal claims that we are "winning" based on opinion polls, still it's a win that the pro-life issue is still alive. The abortion rights movement probably assumed that forty years after the Supreme Court decision legalizing abortion that the issue would be as settled as school integration or women's suffrage. It's still a controversy, though, and the pro-life side hasn't been sidelined by history. That's a win.

Consciences awakened by the abortion issue ought to then be formed to understand the deeper and broader questions of human dignity and human limits too. Abortion does not and cannot stand alone, just as abolition and civil rights did not stand alone. We should be pro-life and whole-life, and the principles of human dignity and sanctity of human life we have reemphasized against the abortion culture ought to be applied to all those who are marginalized (orphans, widows, immigrant communities, the poor, and so on). It ought to prompt us to a wider view of neighbor-love and human flourishing. That being said, we ought to be careful about the way that we speak of a comprehensive ethic of human life in order to keep such comprehensiveness from evaporating the very framework from which we are speaking.

Take for example, the charge that the pro-life witness of the church is compromised if the church does not support extensive gun-control measures. Some ask, "Is gun violence not a pro-life issue?" Of course, gun violence is a pro-life issue. Murder is evil and is a violation of the dignity of the person and of the right to life. That said, what people mean typically when they speak of gun violence as a pro-life issue is not gun violence, directly, but about gun control measures. Many Christians and other pro-lifers support gun control measures, of course, and some support very extensive measures. But the gun control debate isn't between people who support the right to shoot innocent people and those who don't. It's instead a debate about what works in solving the common goal of ending violent criminal behavior. That's why orange-vested, deer-hunting gun control opponents and sandal-wearing, vegan gun control advocates can exist in the same church without excommunicating one another. Whatever one thinks of gun control, no one in the debate today supports selling guns to those who intend to kill. The question is instead how to prevent guns from being used criminally. Some think gun control measures are a necessary way to do this; others think such laws are ineffective and counterproductive, that we should be enforcing better the laws we already have. That's a very different question from whether the child in the womb is a person bearing the right to legal protection from direct killing.

Because I am pro-life, I oppose the use of nuclear weapons. The indiscriminate killing of civilian noncombatants is inconsistent with a Christian vision of just war and with the sanctity of human life. That doesn't mean, therefore, that unilateral nuclear disarmament is the pro-life answer. The question is whether unilaterally disarming would be provocative enough to actually make nuclear warfare more rather than less likely. We can debate this, but it isn't a debate between pro-lifers and anti-lifers. It would be such if there were those who believed in using nuclear weapons against civilian populations because those populations weren't "viable" and thus lacked human rights. Then this would be a direct parallel with the abortion question.

When I served, as a very young man, as an intern and then a campaign aide to a United States congressman (who was and is strongly pro-life), our only real disagreements came over mandated family medical leave and foreign aid. I was for both, and he was opposed to both. I thought family medical leave, for example, would help to ensure that mothers would be better able to keep their babies, and thus discourage abortion. He thought legislating this federally would prevent small businesses from employing as many people. The single mother I was worried about would, he was afraid, be laid off from her job and be just as vulnerable to the abortion-mongers. I disagreed with him (and I still think I was right), but our disagreement wasn't about the value of human life. We had a difference on the prudential means to get to a common goal.

Is the cause of civil rights bigger than simply ending segregation and barriers to voting? Of course. But what happens if the term "civil rights activist" were applied to segregationists who supported better funding for "separate but equal" schools or to white supremacists who opposed the Vietnam War? The fundamental threshold question for civil rights is whether all Americans, white and black, should be equal in the sight of the law. Is the pro-life issue bigger than abortion? Yes, indeed. But in order to be pro-life, we must first deal with the question, contested in our time, of whether children are persons or property, based simply on whether they are existing inside or outside the biosphere of the womb.

> **We must first deal with the question, contested in our time, of whether children are persons or property, based simply on whether they are existing inside or outside the biosphere of the womb.**

That said, convictions about human dignity, forged in our time in the abortion controversy, ought to have implications for how the church, and how Christians, view other questions as well. Abortion-rights advocates are wrong to insist that it is hypocritical for one to be both pro-life on abortion and not oppose the death penalty or all wars. Whatever one thinks of capital punishment, there is a difference between the debate over whether the state has the authority to punish murderers with the ultimate penalty and whether innocent human beings should be offered no legal protection. Moreover, while some Christians in the history of the church have been pacifists, there is a strong tradition, rooted in Scripture, that some wars, when meeting very strict criteria, may be just. Nonetheless, our pro-life convictions ought to inform how we see such issues, even those of us who support some instances of war or capital punishment.

Christians, and other pro-life persons, ought to have consciences shaped in such a way that we are the first to ask whether a military action is necessary, whether it will imperil innocent civilian lives. We ought to be the first to question the sort of unbridled militarism that bristles for war at the first provocation. We ought not to hold to an "any means necessary" understanding of winning wars, as those whose consciences are shaped by social Darwinist or nihilist assumptions might.

As such, we must oppose torturing human beings for the same reason we oppose "choice" in abortion rights, because torture dehumanizes both the tortured and the torturer. We ought to be those insisting that capital punishment, where it exists, is not discriminatory against the poor or racial minorities and that it not exist as part of a system in which innocent persons are mistakenly executed. A death penalty that exempts the white and the affluent, while putting to death those without the power to evade such justice, is hardly what God set forth in the covenant with Noah or in the sword-wielding delegated authority to Caesar to punish evildoers. And, even short of the death penalty, we should care about impartiality before the law, in the making and in the enforcement of laws for all persons, regardless of race or ethnicity or background.

We should work for justice for orphans and for widows, by empowering people of good will to fight the root causes of fatherlessness (war, disease, genocide, famine, poverty, divorce cultures), and by incentivizing adoption and foster-care. At the same time, we ought to oppose those efforts of technology or commerce that would seek to turn children into commodities to be bought and sold, at home or abroad. We ought to call for respect for human dignity in our prisons—working against prison rape, for example, and against unfair sentencing. We ought to recognize assaults on the dignity of women—through domestic violence, for example, and through sex trafficking in all of its forms—including the form of prostitution we euphemistically call the "pornography industry."

We ought to recognize the darkness of the culture of death when it shows up in our own voices. I am startled when I hear those who claim the name of Christ, and who loudly profess to be pro-life, speaking of immigrants with disdain as "those people" who are "draining our health care and welfare resources." Can we not see the same dehumanizing strategies at work in the abortion-rights activism that speaks of the "product of conception" and the angry nativism that calls the child of an immigrant mother an "anchor baby"? At root, this is a failure to see who we are.

We are united to a Christ who was himself a sojourner, fleeing political oppression (Matt. 2:13–23), and our ancestors in Israel were themselves a migrant people (Exod. 1:1–14; 1 Chron. 16:19; Acts. 7:6). Moreover, our God sees the plight of the fatherless and the blood of the innocent, but he also tells us that because he loves the sojourner and cares for him so should we, "for you were sojourners in the land of Egypt" (Deut. 10:18–19). We might disagree on the basis of prudence about what specific policies should be in place to balance border security with compassion for the immigrants among us, but a pro-life people have no option to respond with loathing or disgust at persons made in the image of God. We might or might not be natural-born Americans, but we are, all of us, immigrants to the kingdom of God (Eph. 2:12–14). Whatever our disagreements on immigration as policy, we must not disagree on whether immigrants are persons. No matter how important the United States of America is, there will come a day when the United States will no longer exist. But the sons and daughters of God will be revealed. Some of them are undocumented farm-workers and elementary-school janitors now. They will be kings and queens then. They are our brothers and sisters forever. We need to stand up against bigotry and harassment and exploitation, even when such could be politically profitable to those who stand with us on other issues. The image of God cannot be bartered away, at the abortion clinic counter or anywhere else.

A pro-life, whole-life people will also share with Christ Jesus a focus on the poor. The unborn child is most vulnerable because he or she is invisible, hidden with the body of the mother. The child doesn't seem to matter. The act of abortion and other like injustices are justified by those who carry them out not only by this invisibility, but also by the perceived anonymity of their actions. They say in security, "No one sees me" (Isa. 47:10). As the psalmist puts it, "They kill the widow and the sojourner, and murder the fatherless; and they say, 'The LORD does not see; the God of Jacob does not perceive'" (Ps. 94:6–7).

The same is true, often, with those who are economically vulnerable. Their situation is not just that they are without resources, but that their lives are precarious. Global economic realities are complex, no doubt, and Christians will have debates about which prudential means are the best ways to help the poor, without unintended consequences that actually salve the conscience but harm the poor. We have no mandate to replicate the structures of Old Testament Israel, a covenant nation, on a state outside of such a covenant. But these structures do show us that systems to keep the poor from exploitation and starvation are both good in the sight of God and possible in the ordering of a society. Even more than that, a pro-life people ought to be those constantly uncloaking the invisibility behind which the poor are often covered in the systems around us, and asking how they are being exploited, both economically and culturally. We cannot surrender to the social Darwinist idea that the poor are "takers" and "losers," which is itself simply a republication of the "pro-choice" arguments about the unviable unborn child.

We should also remember that human dignity is not just a matter of rights, but of responsibility. Christians in this country of the most orthodox and evangelical stripe sometimes roll our eyes at questions of ecology. This is because we tend to equate such questions with the most caricatured extremes of the environmentalist movement (much like, come to think of it, many people do with us in terms of the lunatic fringes of American religion). We reject the theological and political assumptions of some of those most ardent about environmental protection so we feel as though this is someone else's issue. Moreover, the people who tend to agree with us on issues of life and family and culture tend not to talk much about these issues so we, once again, baptize the entire agenda of our allies and ignore the entire agenda of everyone else. The conservation and stewardship of natural resources is part of the dominion mandate God gave to humanity, to cultivate and to pass on. Every human culture is formed in a tie with the natural environment. In my hometown, that's the father passing down his shrimping boat to his son or the community gathering for the Blessing of the Fleet at the harbor every year. In your town, it might be the traditions of farming or whaling or the frontier or the mountains. When the natural environment is used up, made unsustainable for future generations, cultures die. And what's left in the places of these cultures and traditions is an individualism that is defined simply by the appetites, for sex or for violence or for the piling up of stuff. That's hardly "conservative" and it's certainly not Christian.

This does not mean that we will agree on a specific set of policies in many cases to conserve and steward the earth. Many of these questions will again be prudential decisions made by those who are weighing options against one another. But just because these are matters of wisdom and prudence, that does not mean the church plays no role. The church disciples her members into wisdom and prudence. The church shouldn't have a biblical blueprint on carbon offsets or wind power subsidies or each family's recycling strategy, but that doesn't mean the conversation is left in the secular wildness of everyone doing what is right in his own eyes, with no king in Israel. It means the church does the hard work of cultivating generations of people with consciences awake to their dependence on land and water and air, and their responsibilities to generations yet unborn. This means cultivating the instincts of the people of the kingdom to the meaning of creational stewardship, of human dominion, of the limits of the appetite, and of cross-generational responsibility. When some see the earth as merely raw material for the appetite, we dissent, and see the arena of God's present glory and God's future kingdom. When others see humanity as a "parasite" on the earth, to be capped through population control, we dissent there too, and see humanity as the joint-heirs of Christ. When some tell us that we should choose between caring for the earth and welcoming new life, we stand with our mandate from Eden, which gives us both. Procreation is pro-creation.

The Gospel Itself

The most important aspect of our mission, as it relates to human dignity, isn't our social action or our responsibilities as citizens or as culture-makers. The most important aspect of our mission for human dignity is the gospel itself. When we recognize that human dignity is contested by spiritual warfare, we understand that politics is indeed downstream from culture, and that culture is downstream from conscience, and that conscience is downstream from the kingdom of God. We cannot combat a culture of death merely with appeals to abstract human dignity based on natural law (not that there's anything wrong with that). In every assault on human life, there's not only a life left for dead but also a conscience left for hell. The gospel addresses both.

On the abortion question, for example, the sheer numbers of children aborted each year ought to prompt us to realize that perhaps as many as one out of every three women in our congregations has aborted. With her is typically a man who approved of or paid for or pressured her to this act. Many of them sit silently, in the fear that God can forgive any sin but this one. They try to forget it, and secretly wonder if they are included in the "whosoever will" of our gospel invitations. When we preach both of justice and of justification, God breaks the power of condemnation. He uncovers sin and judgment. The cries of the oppressed, the orphaned, the murdered are heard, and their Redeemer is strong. The gospel doesn't wave away such judgment. The gospel says that those found in Christ are joined to the judgment he endured to the cross, and they stand with him in the new creation of an empty tomb. The repentant woman who had an abortion, the repentant man who empowered an abortion, and indeed the repentant abortionist who committed the abortion, are not beyond the grace of God. Every accusation against them, and against you and me, is true. But in Christ, we have been through the scrutiny of the tribunal of God. We have already been through the justice of hell. And in Christ, God declares what he thinks of us, "You are my beloved child, and in you I am well pleased." We warn of justice, but we always, this side of the grave, offer mercy.

This gospel, then, grounds human dignity since in it Christ Jesus offers himself not to spirits or angels but to the sons and daughters of Adam. We have to be reminded of that or else we will always be pulled back to seeing ourselves in terms of "the flesh"—who we think we are apart from our union by the Spirit to Christ. We start then to divide ourselves against one another as Jew and Gentile, black and white, rich and poor, First World and Third World, healthy and disabled, young or elderly, documented or undocumented, born or unborn. But the gospel cuts across the boundaries, and indeed crucifies them all. If we come to God, it will be through one Jewish mediator-king, or it will not be at all. Our call to remember human dignity is, before anything else, a call to remember who we are.

The pro-life movement of the present, like the abolitionist and civil rights movements, is not, and never was, a "moral majority" issue. Left to ourselves, the majority will always protect the powerful, and forget the weak. That's especially true when the weak at issue are not only powerless but invisible. As technology advances, our advocacy for human life has become in many cases stranger and stranger to the world around us, as we advocate not only for late-term infants in the womb but for those "embryos" who are sacrificed for medical research or for fertility treatments. We argue not only against abortion "for birth control," but for the sacrificing of human life for what seem to be heroic causes: the curing of diseases, the providing of children to infertile families, the advance of the human race into new vistas of evolutionary progress. But as Walker Percy put it a generation ago to the abortion-rights movement of his day: "According to the opinion polls, it looks as if you might get your way. But you're not going to have it both ways. You're going to be told what you're doing."[27] That's called bearing witness, and it's not a matter of politics or power but of gospel and of mission.

The kingdom tells us what matters—and it's not raw power and force of will. The kingdom tells us who matters—and that's not defined by power and force of will. The church is to embody these realities, and the mission sets out to teach and persuade the outside world of a gospel that honors and protects life. To deny human dignity, then, is to kick against Christ himself, since he brings with him nothing of the sort of power or wisdom the present age craves. When we care for the vulnerable—the unborn, the aged, the poor, the diseased, the disabled, the abused, the orphaned—such is not "charity." These are not "the disadvantaged," at least not in the long run. These are the sorts of people God delights in exalting as the future rulers of the universe. It takes more than American values to see that.

Conclusion

Those signs of the civil rights activists in the picture on my shelf were words of hope, but they were also words of judgment. Those bravely bearing those signs were declaring that they'd decided not to believe the rhetoric used against them. They refused to believe that they were a lesser

---

27. Walker Percy, *Signposts in a Strange Land* (New York, NY: Farrar, Straus, Giroux, 1991), 342.

race, or even a different race. They were persons, bearing the image of God. They bore then a dignity that could not be extinguished by custom or legislation. But those signs also pointed out the reverse. Those who oppressed them were not gods; they were just men and, as such, would be subject to the judgment of nature's God. The words "I Am a Man" were another way of saying, "I Am Not Afraid of You."

The gospel that reconciles the sons of slaveholders with the sons of slaves today is the same gospel that reconciled the sons of Amalek with the sons of Abraham. It's a gospel that reclaims the dignity of humanity and the lordship of God, because it is rooted in the One who shares deity with his Father and who shares humanity with us, and is thus in his own person bringing heaven and earth together. Our mission then is defined not just by precepts and principles and priorities but by a person. And that person is Jesus of Nazareth, who defiantly and triumphantly steps out of history and declares, with us, "I Am a Man."

> **Our mission then is defined not just by precepts and principles and priorities but by a person.**

Chapter Seven

RELIGIOUS LIBERTY

Every once in a while, I hear about a church embroiled in controversy over a flag. Usually this is not because the youth pastor burned the Stars and Stripes in protest on the church lawn, but rather because there's a fight about whether to have an American flag in the sanctuary. The most memorable case for me was a pastor who wanted to do away with the flag, but didn't want to be seen as un-American, so he devised a plan to secret the flag away in the middle of a Saturday night, hoping the congregation just wouldn't notice the next day. This game of "Rapture the Flag" didn't work, of course. By dawn's early light, they saw that the flag was not there. And that's when the metaphorical bombs started bursting in air.

There's a reason why this debate was about more than just pulpit architecture. Both sides of the dispute were trying to hold on to something commendable. Those who wanted the flag there on the platform, right across from the Christian flag, probably weren't trying to turn the national emblem into an Asherah pole. Patriotism—the love of one's country—is a natural affection. Saluting the flag is a sign of gratitude, for the freedoms purchased through the sacrifices of others. It's also a sign of humility; a recognition that we are not atomized vapors but rather that we exist in a context, in a place, and in a culture. When rightly applied, patriotism is akin to what God commands us to do in showing honor to mother and father.

At the same time, the pastor in this case wasn't a political revolutionary. He wanted to maintain the priority of the gospel and of the kingdom. He knew that American identity came easy for his congregants. The sense of national belonging is all around them in the culture, from their educations to the advertisements they see to the symbols of national heritage all around them. That's why some of them welled up with tears much more readily at a stirring rendition of "The Battle Hymn of the Republic" than they did at the Doxology. He knew that their rootedness was important but not ultimate, and that the flag can be a perilous thing for a people already prone to forgetting who we are. He knew that sometimes patriotism for one's country seems easier than patriotism for the New Jerusalem because it's so experientially immediate.

Religious Liberty and the Kingdom of God

The conflict in this church is a microcosm of a much bigger question, that of the complicated and perilous relationship between the church and the state. The "culture wars" of the last half-century have often centered on this relationship, on questions of what the meaning of religious liberty and separation of church and state is and should be. These conflicts aren't merely confined to an American context, where religious liberty is encapsulated in the Constitution's Bill of Rights as our First Freedom but is relevant to the larger picture of the global church, as the body of Christ faces, in some places, persecution and, in other places, the temptation to be persecutors. The church's witness on these matters has sometimes proven incoherent at best, and counter-Christian at worst; and this tendency grew more pronounced wherever Christianity was assumed to be the default posture of American culture. As the illusion of a Christian America dissipates, the church has the opportunity to reclaim a broad vision of religious liberty for all, rooted in kingdom and culture and mission.

The question of religious liberty is, first and foremost, a question of the kingdom of God. That question starts, first of all, with the imagery of kingship itself, imagery that points to God's approval of order and government. Sometimes Christians argue that the state is a post-Fall necessity, that only the family and the church are part of the creation order as God designed it. Usually this argument is made in order to demonstrate the primacy of the family and the church, or the individual, over against the state overstepping its bounds. This argument is especially persuasive in times when people are frustrated by the overreach of the government in military or tax or other matters. It seems cathartic to see government itself as the problem not just in the short-term but permanently.

But such an argument is neither necessary nor true. Governance is present from the beginning, both in God's reign over the universe he creates and the reign of the primal humanity over the creation. James Madison was partly right when he said in the *Federalist Papers*, "If men were angels, no government would be necessary." Certainly, without a doctrine of sin there would be no need for the coercive, penal force of the law—no need for prisons or armies or police forces. But this is not to say that there would be, apart from sin, no need for government. Indeed, even angels seem to have a government—with an order and hierarchy reflected in the biblical witness.

That government is more than merely a necessary evil is also seen in the end goal of the cosmos: the kingdom of Christ. The universe is not hurtling toward anarchy or toward tyranny but toward the servant kingship of a rule in which Jesus refers to his joint-heirs not as his servants but as his friends (John 15:15). As I mentioned earlier in this book, however, a vision of the kingdom of God without an understanding of how to distinguish the "already" and the "not yet" is dangerous—both to people and to the gospel. The kingdom of God, after all, in its consummation is all-encompassing.

Those who would pretend to enforce the kingdom with tanks or guns or laws or edicts do not understand the nature of the kingdom Jesus preached. The risen Christ promised that the "one who conquers" will be given "authority over the nations and he will rule them as with a rod of iron" just as, Jesus said, "I have received authority from my Father" (Rev. 2:27). The "conquering" here though is not about subduing enemies on the outside, but about holding fast to the gospel and following the discipleship of Jesus to the end (Rev. 2:25–26). We are not yet kings over the world (1 Cor. 4:8), but are instead ambassadors bearing persuasive witness to the kingdom we have entered (2 Cor. 5:11, 20). This is not the time of rule, but the time of preparation to rule, as we, within the church, are formed and shaped into the kind of Christlike people who, at resurrection, can sit with him upon the thrones of the cosmos (Luke

22:24–28; Rev. 3:21). The kingdom is not fully come until the last enemy, death, is fully conquered (1 Cor. 15:24–28), and every occupied cemetery plot testifies that this moment has not yet come.

Our vision of the kingdom then drives us to see who "we" are, and the answers are different in terms of the church and in terms of the state or the tribe or the culture. The church at Philippi is identified as just that, those who live in Philippi. The flag is still there. And yet, as part of the church, the Body of Christ, they are not a colony of Rome but a colony of heaven (Phil. 3:20). The covenant with Israel included vast measures of state power enforcing the law of God on the Israelite nation, awaiting the age of the Messiah. Now that this age has arrived, Jesus has disarmed the church, rebuking Peter for the use of the sword at Jesus' arrest (Matt. 26:52–53). The wheat and the tares are to grow together in the field of the world, with no authority by church or by state to uproot them (Matt. 13:24–30). At the same time, the church is to distinguish, internally, between believers and unbelievers, saints and strangers, with no authority to enforce such distinctions on the outside culture (1 Cor. 5:10–12).

Reclaiming Separation of Church and State

This understanding of the kingdom means a separation of church and state. Some conservative Christians reflexively recoil at such language, because they associate with the sort of state-enforced secularization that the late Richard John Neuhaus famously called "the naked public square."[28] But the separation of church and state wasn't invented by secularist progressives, but by orthodox believers who didn't want the state empowered to dictate, or to suppress, doctrine and practice. A government in the business of running the church, or claiming the church as a mascot of the state, invariably persecutes and drives out genuine religion. It's a good old phrase that we ought to reclaim.

> **A government in the business of running the church, or claiming the church as a mascot of the state, invariably persecutes and drives out genuine religion.**

28. Richard John Neuhaus, *The Naked Public Square: Religion and Democracy in America* (Grand Rapids, MI: Wm. B. Eerdmans, 1984).

Church/state separation does not mean the division of religious people from citizenship. Citizens come to decision-making, and culture-makers come to culture-making, with their consciences formed somewhere and by something. A Buddhist may point to his Buddhist principles of the destructiveness of the unrestrained appetites in her reasons for why she is concerned about environmental policy. And a Christian is well within the bounds of public discourse to point to the Bible as the reason why she cares about human dignity enough to oppose racially-discriminatory voter suppression or a lowering of penalties for child pornography. Church/state separation means that the church does not bear Caesar's sword in enforcing the gospel, and that Caesar's sword is not to be wielded against the free consciences of persons made in the image of God. The spheres of authority, in the present age, are quite different. An axe-murderer who comes to faith in Christ is completely forgiven of his sins, by virtue of his union with Christ. But he is not therefore released from prison; such would be a dereliction of the state's justice. At the same time, the church should not withhold welcoming him until his sentence is served; such would be a dereliction of the church's gospel. That's the separation of church and state. The state should not be in the tare-pulling business—or even in the tare-inspecting business—but should only work for public order, safety, and well-being.

The separation of church and state clearly bounds in the authority of both, both of which are potentially abused. Every crooked or power-hungry politician would love access to the "keys of the kingdom" in order to get and maintain power. If you can control whether or not people go to hell, after all, you can accomplish nearly anything in the court of public opinion. As one Baptist leader of the last generation put it, "Everybody wants a theocracy, and everybody wants to be Theo."

The Scriptures do teach that the "powers-that-be" have legitimate authority, but this is not an unlimited authority. The apostle Paul bounds in the power of Caesar's sword to the punishing of "wrongdoers" (Rom. 13:4). The apostle wrote that taxes are to be paid, along with honor and respect, to those to whom such things are due (Rom. 13:7). Such is in continuity with Jesus' oft-quoted teaching to "Render to Caesar the things that are Caesar's, and to God the things that are God's" (Mark 12:13–17). Taxes are within the proper realm of Caesar's authority, but the clear implication is that not everything is. The coins bear Caesar's image; not everything does.

On the opposite side of the spectrum from Romans 13 is Revelation 13, also written within the context of the Roman Empire and the questions of Caesar's authority. The "minister of God's wrath" in the one context is a "beast rising out of the sea" in the other. What's the difference?

The Beast state oversteps its bounds, sets itself up as a god, and seeks to regulate worship through threat of violence or economic intimidation (Rev. 13:15–17). Every authority, under God, is limited. The Israelites are obedient to the authority of Pharaoh, but God blessed the Hebrew midwives for refusing to obey his decree to slaughter the male children, precisely because Pharaoh did not have the right to snuff out innocent life (Exod. 1:15–22). Daniel honored King Nebuchadnezzar, until the king decreed the bounds of Daniel's conscience-informed diet and his prayers. Peter and John were obedient to the temple authorities—authorities Jesus said were legitimate (Matt. 23:3)—until they were told how and what to preach, at which time they defy such authority (Acts 4:19–20).

The limits on the power of the state demonstrate that there is a moral law behind expressions of human law, so that the voting majority is not always right. That's the ancient truth Rosa Parks was affirming when she refused to give up her seat, launching the Montgomery bus boycott against Jim Crow repression. She, and other civil rights activists, never argued that these laws weren't supported by the majority; they were. She, and those with her, argued that these laws were wrong—and not simply wrong, but that they overstepped the legitimate limits on state power. The civil law can maintain order—can promote the common good—only if it is grounded in something other than the arbitrary will of a ruler or of a mob. We can render unto Caesar and we can render unto God only if we know the difference between the two.

The state, then, does not bear the "keys to the kingdom," and thus cannot rule over the spiritual mission of the kingdom colony. Nor can the church, in this time before Judgment Day, rule over the civil state. Jesus himself refused to do this. When someone "in the crowd" cried out for Jesus to "tell my brother to divide the inheritance with me," Jesus' response was sharp: "Man, who made me a judge or arbitrator over you?" (Luke 12:13–14). Jesus turned and immediately addressed the issue in terms of the man's moral character and his accountability before God at Judgment

Day (Luke 12:15–21), but he refused to act as an agent of the state in judging between disputes of those outside of the church.

The distinction between the temporal government and the kingdom of Christ, expressed now in the church, means that not everything that is wrong should be criminalized. The state carries out justice against "wrongdoers," Paul tells us (Rom. 13:4). Clearly, "wrongdoers" here is not equated with "sinners." Since all of us are sinners (Rom. 3:23), the jails would be full and the streets empty because there would be none left unprosecuted, no not one. The police power of the state is set up to maintain public safety and order according to the principles of public justice. Everywhere in the New Testament, the mission of confronting personal sin is given to the church, not to the state. Even in the worst case of sexual immorality, the ultimate step is excommunication, not the setting up of a police state to execute (1 Cor. 5:1–13).

Any and every sin leads to personal death and judgment, but not every sin is a matter of public injustice. Murder is a personal sin against God and neighbor, yes, but it is also an act of injustice and violence in the public sphere, in a way that anger in one's heart against a neighbor is not. Is adultery in the interest of the state? In some ways, "Yes," if the state is assigned to determine who is responsible for the breakup of a marriage covenant, in the divvying up of household resources, or in the determining of child custody. But the state has no interest in punishing adultery in terms of its effects on the moral or eschatological well-being of the adulterer. The state is incompetent to judge such things.

> **Any and every sin leads to personal death and judgment, but not every sin is a matter of public injustice.**

Liberty and Justice for All

One of the primary issues of human rights in the world today is that of blasphemy laws. These usually exist in the Islamic world, at the moment, and are used against Christians, Jews, and other religious minorities. Virtually every Western Christian would oppose such state persecution, and would stand in solidarity with persecuted brothers and sisters in Christ. But it's worth asking why. If we had a Christian majority (in fact, not just in self-reported identification), with the will to pass all the laws it could, would we be justified to seek to outlaw Islam or atheism or Wicca or Santeria? No. The passing of such laws is a repudiation of the beliefs held by those who seek to pass them. A religion that needs state power to enforce obedience to its beliefs is a religion that has lost confidence in the power of its Deity.

Christians should fight for the liberty of Muslims to be Muslims, to worship in mosques and to freely seek to persuade others that the Koran is a true revelation of God. This isn't because we believe Islamic claims, but precisely because we don't. If we really believe the gospel is the power of God unto salvation, we don't need bureaucrats to herd people into cowering before it. Christians haven't always perceived this very well. Some have tried to advance the kingdom by law and by force. But that doesn't lead to the triumph of Christianity; it only covers paganism in Christian veneer. The places where Christianity was once "official" and "state-established" are the very places that are now as burned over and as secular as they can get. This is not a coincidence.

Religious liberty for everyone and pluralism in the public square does not mean that truth is relative or that all religions are equal pathways to God. Nor does it mean that religious truth claims don't matter. Quite the opposite is the case. The gospel drives us to an understanding that the ultimate accounting of justice doesn't rest with the state, or with ourselves, but with the Judgment Seat of the kingdom of God. No government bureaucrat can stand with a person before that tribunal. We stand there one-by-one, either with a Mediator in Christ Jesus or alone with our own sins.

The conscience, then, cannot be put in a blind trust, by or for anyone. The gospel goes forward not through manipulation or coercion, but through the open and persuasive proclamation of the gospel as a conscience to a conscience (2 Cor. 4:2). The Spirit convicts of sin. One cannot coerce faith into being, or out of being, regardless of whether one is a theocratic ayatollah or a secularist parliament.

The gospel is big enough to fight for itself. And the gospel fights not with the invincible sword of Caesar but with the invisible sword of the Spirit. When we seek to freely persuade our neighbors, and not to coerce them, we are confessing that the Spirit of God is mighty enough to convict of sin, to pull down strongholds and fortresses of the mind and conscience. The kingdom of God cannot be entered into by the way of the flesh, Jesus tells us, only by the supernatural work of the new birth. No one is born again by Caesarian section. We share the gospel with everyone, but the gospel comes with persuasive witness, which requires a freeness of either receiving or rejecting. We believe therefore in liberty and Jesus for all.

My wife will sometimes nudge me if she sees me rolling my eyes in a worship service. It's entirely involuntary, and sometimes I don't even know I'm doing it. But there's only one or two things that can cause it. The first is when a worship leader changes an old hymn to remove perfectly good biblical words. I am convinced that every time a worship leader deletes "Ebenezer" from "Come Thou Fount," an archangel sharpens his sword. I know, I know; they tell me that most people don't know what "Ebenezer" is, so it is "vain repetition" if we sing it anyway. I argue that most people don't know what "grace" is either or what "Israel" is or who "Jesus" is, until we teach such things, and that the singing of the people of God is a key part of that teaching. Nonetheless, I'm just a curmudgeon on that one, and that probably won't change. My other tendency to eye-rolling happens whenever I hear an "announcement prayer." I define this as any public prayer that is designed to communicate information to the hearers more than to lead the people into communication with God. Such prayers go along something like this: "Lord, as you know we have our men's breakfast coming up this Saturday at eight o'clock in the morning, in the fellowship hall. And Lord, you know, that reservations can be made up until noon Friday in the church office, and Lord, you know that there are limited seats available . . ." That's an announcement, not a prayer, and we'd all be better off if we just called it what it is. Call me curmudgeon. But, the more I think of it these days, the more I think that the "announcement prayer" is a key facet of the culture behind some of our disputes over religious liberty, in North America and around the world.

Most of the people seeking to restrict religious liberty aren't villains, scheming in a remote lair to uproot Christianity in order to replace it with secularism. All of us recognize that there are some limits to every right—including those natural rights we are endowed with by nature and nature's God. Many of them genuinely don't "get" religious motivations, because they have never experienced such motivations. They are, then, perplexed when they see, for example, nuns who wish not to be forced by the government to pay for contraception or Muslim schoolchildren who wish to be allowed to wear headscarves to school or Jewish families who wish not to have government bans on circumcision. Many assume these must really be about something else, such as political power or economic gain.

What many do understand are other real or illusory transcendent motivations, which is why many of the conflicts over religious liberty now are clustered around issues of sexual liberation. This is why those who care about religious liberty must resist the temptation to speak only to these issues using the "neutral" common grace public language of rights and the common good (although this is an important part of it). We must speak also of why we are motivated the way we are, which will require open discussion of the distinctiveness of our convictions. Such does not require the larger society to accept our convictions, of course, but they do help to explain why some religious liberty incursions aren't simply civic nuisances to us, or to others in similar situations, but do genuine violence to the one of the deepest mysteries of human life: the conscience.

Religious Liberty and Civil Religion

Understanding the culture around us also means that we recognize that secularization, at least in some forms, brings with it, not the lessening of the temptation toward the establishment of religion, but in some cases, the heightening of it. The problem, of course, is that as philosophers from Charles Taylor[29] onward have pointed out, "secular" means different things. If by "secular," we mean not "holy" or set apart for the work of the kingdom, then, yes, the state and the world in which it exists is indeed "secular"—and should be.

But if by "secularization" we mean the loss of the ability to comprehend religious motivations or religious people, we have an entirely different set of problems, problems involving a state empowering itself to be theologian-in-chief.

For example, sometimes groups will call on the military to ensure that chaplains pray "inclusive" and "nonsectarian" prayers in public. This is especially problematic for evangelical Christians ending their prayer "in Jesus' name." I once had a chaplain tell me that someone in the chain of his command told him simply to pray "in your name" or "in God's name"

---

29. Charles Taylor, *A Secular Age* (Cambridge, MA: Belknap Press of Harvard University Press, 2007).

since this would be less offensive to those hearing the prayer and, after all, "What difference does it make?" Now, from the military's point of view, it probably doesn't seem to be too much to ask for a chaplain to pray a sensitive prayer to a generically identified God. But, for many Christians, especially evangelicals, "in Jesus' name" isn't just a common prayer trope, like the word "just" before every request or the "lead, guide, and direct us" or "bless the gift and the giver." They instead recognize that "there is one God, and there is one mediator between God and men, the man Christ Jesus" (1 Tim. 2:5). We can come before God only because we share the Spirit of Christ through whom we cry "Abba, Father!" (Rom. 8:15).

"What difference does it make?" is a perfectly legitimate question if prayer is merely a civic function, but it cannot be that for one who believes there is a God addressed. The very question is the equivalent of asking a Roman Catholic chaplain to serve the Eucharist to soldiers of all religions since "bread is bread." Who is the military to decide such matters? Chaplains do not serve a uniformly civic function. They serve both God and Caesar, set apart by their religious institutions and placed in the military in order to empower military personnel to exercise their religious convictions. If the only chaplains who are allowed to pray are those willing to pray like Unitarians in public, we do not have genuine religious pluralism in the military any more. We have instead the state establishment of various forms of Unitarianism.

The same happens in contexts outside of the military, wherever prayers are offered there is the pressure, whether cultural or legal, to conform to a "nonsectarian" prayer. But what is a "nonsectarian" prayer?

Would it be a prayer that is offered to God but doesn't mention Jesus? How is that prayer not exclusionary of polytheists?

More to the point, how does the government decide what is an appropriate level of "sectarian" content?

Does the government allow one to say "God" or "heaven" or "Ground of Being," but rule one out of bounds for mentioning "Allah" or "Krishna" or the Bible or the Torah or the Bhagavad-Gita?

If so, then we have an establishment of a religion, a state-enforced generic civil religion. Prayer is not the place to spar among religions or to make apologetic points; to do so would be one more form of an "announcement prayer" (maybe a "sermon prayer"). But the idea that all the religions are basically one is itself a religious claim, a claim that many religions reject. Our various differences often show up in the ways we pray. Those differences should be the subject for debate among ourselves, but not for the government to referee by pretending they don't exist or by choosing a side among them.

Such conflicts over accommodation of religion will no doubt become even more pronounced in the years to come as the culture secularizes while, at the same time, religious communities become even more defined by their distinctiveness. This is not necessarily bad news for the church.

Again, it gives us an opportunity to correct ways our communions have become more American than Christian. The concept of Christianity as a cultural majority often has done violence to a Christian understanding of the relationship between church and state, between the kingdom and the world. I'm surprised by how often I hear professing Christians suggest that the United States should, for example, deport all Muslims or that their local City Councils should zone mosques out of existence. Behind all of this is the assumption that "we" are a Christian commonwealth, with the power of the sword given to punish spiritual disobedience. This is a misreading both of the Scriptures and of the world around us. Does one really believe that handing the "keys of the kingdom" of spiritual discernment to Caesar is either right or in the best interest of the Christian gospel?

The state may tolerate a vague, generic, nonthreatening religion, but there is, as one Revolutionary-era preacher put it, "nothing more obnoxious to an established religion than the gospel of Jesus Christ." In the fullness of time, a spiritually-empowered Caesar will decide that gospel preaching shouldn't happen, if it disturbs the commerce of the silversmiths of Artemis (Acts 19:21–41), and it always does. The kind of religion the state, any state, will support will always be a "God and country" civil religion that supports the agenda of the politicians. That's true if we hand over the power to outlaw religious convictions and practices or if we expect the government to write prayers for our schools. Do we really believe that unregenerate people can approach God, without a Mediator, to pray? If not, why would we ask the government to force people to pretend to do so?

This sort of agenda can only exist in the illusion of an America that is itself born-again, through and through. That illusion is over, and happily so. Once a religion has become a means to an end, of national unity or public morality or anything else, it is no longer a supernatural encounter with God and is just another program. That's why we ought to always be wary of government seeking to "bless" us with state-written "nondenominational" prayers or with direct funding for our religious initiatives (which inevitably cut out the gospel-centered heart of these initiatives). A Christless civil religion of ceremonial Deism freezes the witness of the church into something useless at best, pagan at worst. Government-run doxology cannot regenerate a soul, or resurrect a corpse.

Christianity under Siege?

The opposite temptation from a cultural majority illusion though is that of a siege mentality. Religious liberty is genuinely imperiled, perhaps more than at any time since the revolutionary era, but we will not be able to articulate our commitments in this arena if we don't know how to differentiate between state persecution and cultural marginalization, between public oppression and personal offense.

Several years ago, I was flipping through magazines on an airplane when I came across a couple of pages that spiked my blood pressure. A beer advertisement was tagged with the headline, "Silent Nights Are Overrated." A few minutes later, in a second publication, there was an advertisement for an outdoor grill which read: "Who Says It's Better to Give Than to Receive?" My first reaction was a personal, if not tribal, offense. "Would they advertise in Saudi Arabia during Ramadan with the line 'Fasting Is Overrated,'" I fumed, "or by asking in India, 'Who Says Everything Is One with the Universe?'" I was missing the point.

The truth is, these companies were trying to sell products, not offend constituencies. Taking shots at any group's religious beliefs isn't good economics. I'm willing to bet whoever dreamed up these ad campaigns didn't "get" that they might be making fun of Jesus Christ. The slick Madison Avenue ad agency probably didn't reflect together in a brainstorming session about how the song "Silent Night" is about the holy awe of the dawning Incarnation in Bethlehem. To them, it probably seemed like just another Christmas song, part of the background music of the culture during this season. Saying it's "overrated" probably didn't feel any more insensitive to these copy writers than making a joke about decking the halls or reindeer games. The writers probably never thought about that the statement "It is better to give than to receive" is a quotation from Jesus, via the apostle Paul (Acts 20:35). It probably just seemed to them like a Benjamin Franklin-type aphorism, along the lines of when someone says, "scarlet letter" without recognizing Hawthorne or, "to be or not to be" while not knowing the difference between Hamlet and Huckleberry Finn.

We ought not fume about such things, as though we are a protected class of victims. We ought to see that our culture is less and less connected with the roots of basic knowledge about Christianity. Many, especially, in the culture-making wing of American life, see Christmas the same way they see Hanukkah. They know about menorahs and dreidels, but not about the Maccabean fight. That ought not make us outraged, but prompt us to see how our neighbors see us—sometimes more in terms of our trivialities than in terms of the depths of meaning of Incarnation, blood atonement, and the kingdom of Christ. This means we need to spend more time engaging our neighbors with the sort of news that shocks angels and redirects stargazers and knocks sheep-herders to the ground. That will seem strange, and that's all the better, because it is strange.

> **Not everything that offends us should offend us, and not everything that offends us is persecution.**

An Incarnation safe enough to sell beer and barbecue grills is a gospel that is too safe to make blessings flow, far as the curse is found. Not everything that offends us should offend us, and not everything that offends us is persecution.

But there is genuine persecution, in every era, and we ought to work for congregational cultures that recognize this. In one sense, many of our congregations are already on the way at this point, those churches with a culture of strong missions advocacy. These congregations may spend time praying for different people groups around the world, and may even visibly signify their concern for the nations with flags of various countries positioned throughout the church. Part of our missions focus should be concern about religious persecution and violence, and not just of Christians. After all, how can we love the world with the gospel if we are apathetic to, for example, global anti-Semitism, or the burning of houses of worship of religious minorities? We should pray for human rights and religious freedom for everyone, everywhere—not just for those who believe our gospel.

That being said, our congregations also should cultivate a special focus on those within the Body of Christ who are hounded and beaten and imprisoned and jailed around the world, just as the Scriptures call us to do (Heb. 10:33–34). This is not a matter, really, of the "strong" standing up for our "weak" brothers and sisters around the world.

In one sense, of course, it is. We have relative freedom, and we can pressure the State Department to act, we can send relief to communities in peril, and we can use technology to alert the global community to what is happening to religious minorities persecuted around the world. But our remembering of those persecuted is not only so that we can advocate for our brothers and sisters, but also so that we can learn from them how to live as Christians. When we encounter those persecuted Christians around the world, we see a glimpse of what Jesus has called us to do. We see the sort of faith that isn't a means to an end. We see the sort of faith that joins the global Body of Christ across time and space, in the confession of a different sort of reign. We see a gospel that isn't: "American affluence, with heaven at the end."

When we pray for those in prison for their faith, we remember that the gospel came to us in letters written from jail. When we plead for those whose churches are burned in Egypt, we remember that our hope isn't in building religious empires but in a New Jerusalem we've never seen. When we weep for those who are (sometimes literally) crucified in the Middle East, we are reminded that our Lord isn't a life coach or a guru but a crucified Messiah. That can remind us of the gospel we signed up for in the first place, and free us from our fat, affluent, almost-gospels, which could never save in the first place. And we can be reminded that the persecuted Christians for whom we pray and advocate very well may be those who will send missionaries to carry the gospel to a future post-Christian Europe or North America.

The most important thing the church can do to protect religious liberty and freedom of conscience is to hold to the gospel itself. Many Christians in the history of the church have gone to jail, from the book of Acts to right now. We ought to work diligently to keep Christians, and others, out of jail for religious convictions.

But there are worse things than going to jail. After all, one can maintain freedom by simply accommodating to the spirit of the age. The prophet Daniel's cohorts, those who prayed to the king's statue, never saw the inside of a lion's cave. Pontius Pilate lived to a relatively ripe old age, untroubled by the sort of state harassment that did away with the apostles.

Judas Iscariot was never arrested for anything, collaborating as he did with the state to carry out their dark mission. Those who fell away from the early church escaped the Colosseum with their lives. All it cost them was a pinch of incense, a momentary mumbling of "Caesar is Lord," and their souls. God forbid. We should protect our legacy of a free church in a free state. We ought to pray and work for a "quiet and peaceable life in all godliness and honesty" (1 Tim. 2:2 KJV). But that is not the ultimate sign of our success. It is better for our future generations to be willing to go to jail—for the right reasons—than to exchange the gospel of the kingdom for a mess of Esau's pottage. Sometimes jails filled with hymn-singing, letter-writing, gospel-preaching Christians can do extraordinary things.

Religious Liberty and Mission

This means that religious liberty is as much about children's Sunday school as it is about the Supreme Court—indeed more so. If we're going to claim a future for liberty, we must remember why we have it: for the gospel and for the advance of the mission. If our descendants love this gospel, and see themselves first as citizens of the kingdom, they won't flinch when a terrorist group threatens to cut off their heads, since they know Christ. If they have to choose between thriving in the marketplace and following Christ, they are willing to hunger, for a time, to be filled at the Table of the Lord. If soldiers line them up against their church walls, wherever they may be, they will still march on to Zion, singing the promises of a triumphant and resurrected Christ. They won't do that raised up on a weekly diet of prosperity gospel and how-to moralism. They won't do that for a political party or a family tradition or a Bible Belt culture. They will do it for the same gospel that drove our ancestors to be beheaded and burned and drowned while maintaining, all the while, to the powers-that-be, that there is, in fact, "another king, Jesus" (Acts 17:7). A church can only stand for religious liberty if it knows that the Judgment Seat of Christ is more ultimate than the state.

Moreover, the culture of the church should shape the consciences of a new generation on issues of religious liberty on the basis and limits of genuine authority not only by our proclamation but also by our demonstration. The Bible commands us, for example, to pray for "kings and all who are in high positions" (1 Tim. 2:2), and to show submission and honor to those in such positions (1 Pet. 2:13–14). Now, this is, of course, easy to do when the elected official is popular within the congregation, or happens to line up politically with the church's leaders. But when the opposite is the case, that's when we really see whether we are ultimately in submission to God or to our political tribes. It's here that our tendency toward the "announcement prayer" of civil religion is perhaps most obvious: we pray in laudatory terms for wisdom and blessing for leaders we agree with and for repentance, through gritted teeth, for those with whom disagree. Our command to honor and to pray for authorities does not mean blanket agreement, but it does mean a posture of respect.

I am always amazed by those Christians who will dispute God's command to honor, arguing that "kings" in our system are the people. And, so their argument goes, we're called to honor the Constitution, but not elected officials. They are right that the people are the more ultimate authority in our system (although the ultimate authority is God, in any case), but this doesn't change the nature of the command. Humanly speaking, the ultimate political authority in the New Testament context was the emperor. And yet, the apostle Peter specifically called the people of Christ not only to show submission "to the emperor as supreme" but also to "governors" (1 Pet. 2:13–14). Paul called on the churches to pray and to show thanksgiving for "kings" (plural) and for "all who are in high positions" (1 Tim. 2:1–2). Behind that is a more general command to "honor everyone" (1 Pet. 2:17), to pray for "all people" (1 Tim. 2:1), to show "respect to whom respect is owed, honor to whom honor is owed" (Rom. 13:7). As the apostle Paul urges us to obey and honor the "governing authorities" we must remember that he is not speaking of a political system consistent with "traditional values." He was speaking of a bloodthirsty and pagan Caesar, a government directly responsible for the crucifixion of Jesus. We demonstrate to the next generation what it means to dissent when we show them that we do so, not as some political performance art, but out of obedience to God—obedience we are willing to follow in honor and prayer as well as, when necessary, in dissent. Because we know that we will as believers eternally say, "Jesus is Lord," we can as citizens temporally say, "Hail to the chief."

Furthermore, the church should actively demonstrate what it means to recognize the legitimate authority of the civil state by "rendering unto

Caesar" in matters of violation of the law. In the case of physical or sexual abuse by a church member, for example, the church should move through the process of disciplining the guilty party, but church discipline and accountability is not enough. The offender has not only violated God's law, after all, but also the law of the City of Man. The church should move to address the sin and spiritual issues involved immediately but should just as immediately notify the civil authorities to investigate and, where necessary, to prosecute.

The church should also teach the proper limits of authority by teaching the same about the limits of our own authority. The church has accountability to God to proclaim the truth, and to shepherd the souls of the people of God, but that authority is not unlimited and is not invested in any individual church or church official. We can cultivate the consciences of a new generation by showing them how to recognize when a church has overstepped its bounds, by, for example, binding consciences where the Scripture has not done so. This does not necessitate a skeptical people, always second-guessing the preaching and teaching of the church. But it does mean a people who know that even the church is just one apostasy away from a removed lampstand (Rev. 2:5), and that any church leader this side of Jesus can be in error and in need of rebuke (Gal. 2:11–14). The church can show this by speaking with unequivocal conviction where the Bible does, but in different terms where consciences are to be left free to come to their own conclusions. Not even the apostles themselves resolved, for example, the differences between believers over whether to eat meat or only vegetables but instead called for unity and for each to act according to his own light on the matter (Rom. 14:1–23). A congregation demonstrates the bounded nature of any authority when it refuses to use its teaching authority to bind consciences on matters best left to conscience, such as whether or not to trick-or-treat at Halloween or whether or not to send one's children to public schools. A church discipled to see this in the context of their own community is better able to recognize it when Caesar has overstepped his bounds.

So how should religious liberty fit in the mission of the church in a new era? As with other issues, the first is to recognize that it does, in fact, fit within our mission. Perhaps especially with issues of religious liberty I often encounter those who would deem it gospel-centered to simply shrug off these matters. "We shouldn't fight for a place at the table," I heard one

Christian say, of laws coercing believers to violate their consciences. "Let's just give up the table." At first blush, this sounds quite right. The Lord Jesus, after all, did not clamor for his own "rights" but freely sacrificed them for us. When we are struck on the cheek, we are to turn the other one. When someone takes our tunic, we are to give up our cloak as well (Matt. 5:40–41). That assumes though that we, in this scenario, are merely the victims. Those with police power are not to ignore assaults on others, based on a "they should turn the cheek anyway" rule. Such is decried biblically as public injustice. Giving up one's cloak is a far different endeavor than if one is a soldier forcibly collecting cloaks because "you ought to be giving those up anyway."

In a democratic republic, the people are the ultimate ground of authority (under God). As citizens, we bear responsibility for electing officials, for the laws that are made in our name, for the setting of precedents by our actions. We are not, in questions of religious liberty, simply standing where Jesus stood, before Pilate. We are standing also where Pilate stood. Shrugging off questions of religious liberty that will bind other people and future generations is the equivalent of Pilate washing his hands over his own actions. The question of religious liberty for the next generation is not merely whether we will be persecuted, but, more importantly, whether we will be persecutors. Caesar's coin, adjusted for inflation, sometimes adds up to thirty pieces of silver.

> Shrugging off questions of religious liberty that will bind other people and future generations is the equivalent of Pilate washing his hands over his own actions.

That's why the apostle Paul actively fights the legal authorities over his arrests in the book of Acts, pointing to his Roman citizenship and appealing all the way up the process. This is not because Paul was enamored with his own "rights." He clearly was not—counting everything as "rubbish" for the sake of the gospel (Phil. 3:8), willing to go without pay and to endure hardship for the sake of the churches. Paul stands before Felix and before Agrippa, pleading his case, for the same reason he does everything else—for the advance of the mission of Christ. That mission requires being at peace, so far as is possible with us, with all people. Paul therefore articulated his case, showing honor and respect for the ruling authorities, always and at every point proclaiming the gospel as he did so (Acts 23:23—26:32). At times, the apostle even defied the authorities in order to defend principles at stake.

Most Christians are familiar with the encounter of Paul and Silas with the Philippian jailer, who, after the followers of Christ were freed from the prison by an earthquake, cried out for salvation. We tend, though, to stop with his conversion (and then long enough to argue about whether or not the salvation of "his household" means anything for our debates about baptism). But the story goes on from there. The officials sent police to tell Paul and Silas they were now free to go. Paul's response is surprising. "They have beaten us publicly, uncondemned, men who are Roman citizens, and have thrown us into prison; and do they now throw us out secretly? No! Let them come themselves and take us out" (Acts 16:37). Paul appealed to the laws of the regime in which he lived, in order to work for justice, justice that would benefit not just him but those who would come behind him.

For American Christians, we exist in a republic in which the free exercise of religious convictions is guaranteed by the Constitution, not as a government grant, but as a natural right. When Christians work for religious liberty, for everyone, we are not simply acting in our own best interests, but for the common good. The conscience and the carrying out of one's religious duties are of no legal interest to the state because these matters are deep motivations that hit at the very core of our humanity. When we advocate for religious liberty, we are acknowledging that there are important issues that are not resolved by the state or by the market. A state that can pave over the conscience—anyone's conscience—without a compelling interest in doing so, is a state that is unfettered to do virtually anything. We are citizens of the state, yes, but the state isn't ultimate.

Most of us agree, of whatever religion and of no religion at all, that the state doesn't exist simply by the will to power, but on transcendent principles that are independent of the state. We often disagree on what the ultimate Reality is. But the fact that the state isn't the ultimate ground of reality serves to make better citizens of us all. With this in view, we can seek justice rather than the tyranny of the majority. A government that arbitrarily silences religious convictions or exercise is not a government that is creating true unity, but is instead a government that severs us one from another by silencing proper pluralism, replacing the quest for truth with one more layer of bureaucracy, implicitly at the barrel of a gun. That is morally wrong, and counterproductive, whether attempted by theocrats or neocrats.

Moving Forward, by Looking Back

As we move forward into the future, we must go backward a bit for a model of how to advocate for religious liberty without sacrificing either the religion or the liberty. The Body of Christ is wide and broad and deep, and each tradition brings with it some aspects that bless the others, and the wider world, even when we disagree on much else. I am not a Roman Catholic, but I wouldn't for a moment want to be without Augustine's *City of God* or the apologetics of Thomas Aquinas or G. K. Chesterton. I'm not Eastern Orthodox, but my life every day is shaped by the Nicene Creed, by the teachings of Athanasius and Irenaeus. I'm not Anglican, but I would be impoverished without the Book of Common Prayer and the writings of C. S. Lewis. I'm not Lutheran or Presbyterian, but Martin Luther and John Calvin speak to all of us, not just to those who agree with them right down to the details. The Pentecostals are teaching us all, at the moment, about serving the poor, about holding to a supernatural religion, about being a truly global church. And the list goes on and on. When it comes to my own tradition—the Baptists—I think there is a model for the future that contributes even to those who'll never know their way around a baptistery.

The early English and American Baptists show us what can happen when a state applies the Old Testament Mosaic Code—a code designed to mark out the nation of Israel in redemptive history until the coming of the Messiah—and bypasses Christ and the church with it, applying it directly to the civil state. Many of these believers were whipped, beaten, and exiled, from Old England and from New, for refusing to christen their children, or for paying taxes for Anglican churches. Their consciences would not allow such. Some of them pointed out that the king was but a mortal man—not God, with lordship over the conscience. Others pointed out that laws should deal only with matters related to our horizontal relationships with one another, not with our relationship to God, which is outside the purview and the competency of the state. They didn't want Caesar's coin for the work of the kingdom, and they also wanted no state standing between God and the conscience. This was true for everyone, of all religions and of none, with some mentioning freedom for minority religions few had ever yet even encountered—such as Muslims—in the places where they lived. This wasn't because they were leftist pluralists. They were what people today would call "fundamentalists." They believed in a Judgment Seat, and that the gospel addressed each conscience and that, because of this, religion couldn't be dispensed like a driver's license or restricted like factory pollution emissions.

Many of them were irritants and pests. They wouldn't leave sinners alone in their sin but called them to repentance toward God and faith in Jesus Christ. They didn't settle for "trust us" from the politicians, with some in the Founding Era insisting on a First Amendment because they didn't trust the "accommodations" promised by politicians. At the same time, they were often willing to form alliances with people with whom they sharply disagreed in order to guarantee religious liberty. The American Baptists worked enthusiastically with freethinking sorts such as Thomas Jefferson who never would have been able to get membership in a Baptist church without a lot of time spent repenting at an altar call. They didn't need spiritual leaders out of their politicians in order to work with them for justice and freedom, and they weren't willing to bestow spiritual recognition in exchange for political favors. They worked together where they could, and reminded the politicians that on their best days they might aspire to Mount Rushmore, but they'll never belong on Mount Olympus. This is because they believed that the church is a flock called together by the voice of the Shepherd, and must not be gathered or scattered by any other voice. Whatever your church tradition, that's a pretty good place to start, for all of us.

I'm no wide-eyed triumphalist for my own tradition. We have more than our share of our problems (don't get me started). The Baptists began hounded by power, and standing for liberty, that's true. But they didn't always stay there. They, and others, ultimately became "established" in their own right—not by the state, but by the culture. And, as we've mentioned before, the culture's approval of the church can be just as dangerous to the gospel as the state's, when the culture calls the tune. The shifting of American culture, toward a view of apostolic Christianity as stranger and more distant from a "normal American life," will bring with it increasing challenges to religious liberty. The state and the culture will wonder why it matters whether people are mandated to participate in actions they believe would imperil their consciences, when spiritual realities seem so distant and other matters—such as sexual freedom or economic advancement—seem so paramount. This will require a new focus on religious liberty in a way that can drive us back to why we believe in it at all: the kingdom of God revealed in the gospel. It can help us to reshape our congregational cultures to reflect a kingdom that comes now not with force of law but with the power of Spirit. And it can enable us to fight for freedom of conscience not as a matter of self-interested pleading but on behalf of our neighbors, even as we seek to evangelize them.

Conclusion

I'm conflicted about whether or not we ought to worry about the flag in the corner there in some of our church sanctuaries. Removing a flag doesn't remove with it the tendency to idolatry or triumphalism; it often just leaves such things unaddressed and untroubled. If the flag is already there, perhaps it can prompt the church to pray for and honor leaders, and to rightly order our patriotism. But regardless we ought to remember what a shifting culture might force us to remember, what we never should have forgotten in the first place: that national identity is important but transitory. There will come a day when Old Glory yields to an older glory, when the new republic succumbs to a new creation. We must not shirk our callings as citizens, but we also must not see our citizenship of the moment as the final word. We are Americans best when we are not Americans first.

> **We are Americans best when we are not Americans first.**

Chapter Eight

FAMILY STABILITY

More than twenty years ago now, I was waiting in a hallway right next to the baptistery where I was immersed as a twelve-year-old, just a decade before. I was waiting for the organ to start playing music, signaling that I would walk in front of my home church to greet my bride, Maria, and to pledge to her before God and those witnesses my love and my life. Today, I look back in wonder at what all we've learned in these twenty years together. The main thing is that I'm glad we didn't wait until we were ready to get married.

I knew on our first date that I loved her and wanted to spend my life with her. But many told us, "Wait until you can afford it before you get married." It's true. We had nothing. I was a first-year seminary student, and she a freshman in college. I worked and reworked budget scenarios, and never could find one that would suggest that we could pay our bills. That's why I kept delaying asking her to marry me, even after I knew she was "the one." I thought I needed stability and a put-together life before I could ask her into it.

My grandmother put an end to all that. One night she asked when I was going to finally marry "that girl from Ocean Springs." I said, "When I can afford it." She laughed. "Honey, I married your grandpa in the middle of a Great Depression," she said. "We made it work. Nobody can afford to get married. You just marry and make it work." Apart from the gospel, those were, and remain, the most liberating words I ever heard. I bought a ring that wouldn't impress anyone, then or now, but we were headed for the altar. My only regret is that we didn't marry even earlier than we did.

In one sense, I was quite right to look for stability. I was trying to be responsible. But part of the stability we needed was right there, a multigenerational church made up of those who could testify that marriage is about more than the merger of bank accounts and careers. Moreover, I needed the stability that would come from the kind of church that would hold us accountable to our vows, to give us a stable place when family life became, as it always does, difficult.

In the neighborhood I live in today, most of the couples are quite "stable," in the way I defined it as a worried single man. Their bills are paid, and their kids' college funds are stocked up. But often these families are hurting for the lack of that second kind of stability. Not long ago, my sons had invited a neighbor boy over to see our new dog. This boy had been moody and erratic, sometimes crying and screaming at the other children in the neighborhood. His parents were going through a divorce, and it was now clear with his father's impending remarriage to somebody else, that they weren't going to get back together. He said that his dog had only three legs. "Was it born that way?" asked one of my sons. The neighbor said that it wasn't, but that when the dog was a puppy, its mother and father got in a fight, and he was between them. "They tore his leg off," he said. "I guess you could say it was a divorce. That's what happens in a divorce. A mom and a dad fight, and they tear the kids apart."

When I heard this, I was shaken out of all of my sociological studies and Bible studies on marriage and "the Family." This wasn't a set of competing cultures, or dueling statistics. This hurting child revealed, without every looking up from our pet, what the family was for him. It wasn't a set of values, or a haven in a heartless world. The family was a dogfight, and he was a limping, wounded survivor.

Identifying the Problem

This child is not alone. Family life is indeed too often a dogfight, a tearing-apart of people as appetites and interests go to war, and as homes splinter apart, sometimes suddenly, sometimes gradually. Walking through the midst of this is difficult, maybe even especially as it relates to the family. Our family structures, after all, imprint and shape us more than anything else in the realm of nature, as any psychiatrist can attest. Marriage and parenting and sexuality aren't just social relationships but have a much deeper hold on us, hitting right at the core of how we see ourselves and our place in the world. Perhaps this is why the "culture wars" of the past fifty years have centered so closely on the family, from sexuality to marriage to parenting. All of us—whatever our religious or political affiliations—seem to agree that family life is both crucial and imperiled, and even fallen, although we would disagree on where this fallenness is.

For some, it is the patriarchy (which is to be smashed), or the "repressive" norms of "bourgeois" sexuality and the nuclear family. For others of us, the Sexual Revolution and the fracturing of the family represent the problem. We disagree on where the problem is, and how to fix it, but we agree that our deepest differences show up in our skirmishes over the family room and the bedroom, and what one should have to do with the other.

The language of the past generation, though, has sometimes skirted the real issues. We speak of "traditional family values" in ways that have sometimes cordoned these issues off from questions of the gospel. In some ways, this was strategic. After all, we agree sometimes on "family issues" with many, with whom we disagree on gospel matters. One need not affirm the Nicene Creed to affirm that divorce hurts children, or that promiscuity harms people, or that pornography degrades human sexuality.

At the same time, though, as the church we recognize that family matters precisely because it is more than "tradition," more than "values," more than a "culture" to war about. Family points us away from itself to the kingdom of God, to the gospel of that kingdom, and, behind all of that, to the triune God himself. We ought to make alliances with those with whom we disagree, but we ought also to make sure that we shape and form congregations to see the family as more than just natural. And, simultaneously, we ought to see that when it comes to the family, we are not the culture warriors we have pretended to be.

> **We are not the culture warriors we have pretended to be.**

Some would chalk up Christian concern about "pro-family" issues to nostalgia, a sort of longing for the way things used to be, when men were men, and women were women, and families stayed together and prayed together, in an attempt to recreate a mythical 1950s family of shiny, happy people. To some degree, there's some truth behind this claim. One respected evangelical leader once remarked that what he wished to see in American culture is a return to the 1950s, but without the sexism and racism. And, beyond that, it is easy, to contrast previous generations of family stability with the rates of divorce and of pornography, of the unhinging of sexuality from marriage, of marriage from a definition rooted in sexuality, of sex from procreation and of procreation from sex.

As Christians, with a strong sense of human depravity, we ought to agree—at least on this point—that the gauzy, sentimental view of an idyllic era of "normal" families is "the way we never were." It's hard to imagine, after all, the 1950s' family without the sexism and racism, since one can hardly quantify the damage done to families by slavery of the century before or the police-state terror of Jim Crow. And one can hardly quantify the damage done to families by, for example, domestic and sexual abuse often kept hidden under cover of darkness. The "crisis in the American family" isn't downstream from Woodstock or the Pill—whatever factors cultural trends may have played—but downstream from the wreckage of Eden. Skirmishes over the family are not the product of blind cultural or historical trends, but instead we must recognize that the family is under assault in every generation, albeit sometimes in craftily veiled ways. And the antidote to our myopic vision of the family—whether myopically nostalgic or myopically apathetic—is not just to focus on the family, but to focus on what's beyond the family: on the mystery of the kingdom of Christ.

Family in the Biblical Story Line

Those who wish to redefine historic Christian concepts of the family—whether related to gender or sexuality or marital permanence or whatever—typically seek to do so by suggesting that individual proof-texts on these issues ought to be placed within the proper context, within the overall trajectory of Scripture's story line. They are quite right. Those who hold to "traditional family values" within the church ought not to fear this, except insofar as it exposes our own timidity and inconsistency and cultural accommodation. When the goal of the trajectory of Scripture is seen in its proper context—the context it sets for itself—as the unfolding of the mystery of Christ against the opposition of the hostile cosmic powers, we see why the family is so significant and significant for reasons far more important than "saving America" or "preserving Western civilization." The family is more than a "haven in a heartless world," but is an embedded pattern of icons of Christ Jesus, his church, and the gospel of his kingdom.

When the Pharisees tried to trap Jesus with a question about divorce, Jesus knew that the issue was really about him. This was true in terms both of the immediate situation and also of the macroscopic view of the whole Bible and the whole universe. They wanted, as they often did, to put Jesus in a difficult situation with the crowds, in which he would seem to be "exposed" as outside of God's revelation to Moses. This wasn't an honest question about views on marital permanence; it was a language-game trap. Jesus volleyed back that they missed the alpha-point of the Bible's story line: God's purposes in creation. By pointing to the Mosaic era's provisions for divorce, they were missing that such things were not so "from the beginning" (Matt. 19:1–12). When the Sadducees—the opposing "party" of religious leaders from the Pharisees—tried a similar trap with a question about a woman who is widowed seven times in a row, Jesus volleyed back that they were missing the omega-point of the Bible's story line: the meaning of the kingdom of God in the age to come (Mark 12:18–27). In both sets of questions, there's a similar besetting sin. One group took too low a view of the family—failing to see its grounding in creation. The other group took too high a view of the family—idolizing it into an eternal existence apart from the resurrection goal of a new creation. In both instances, they were abstracting the family from God's purposes in Christ as the Alpha and Omega of the creation. Unwilling to recognize Jesus as the Christ, they were unable to see where God's creational structures fit into the universe, whether the structures at hand involved the Sabbath (Matt. 12:1–14) or worship (John 2:13–22) or dominion over angels (Matt. 12:22–32) or the family.

Those who wished to avoid the question of the kingship of Jesus found themselves in error at all points on the family, according to Jesus, be it through divorce or the refusal to honor fathers and mothers with financial provision. Veiled to the kingdom, they were veiled to the family order—all the while surrounding both concepts with out-of-context Scripture references and human traditions that would self-justify them, they supposed, before God. This is precisely what the apostle Paul is referring to in Romans 1:18–32 when he noted that those who refused to give thanks as creatures ultimately turn to the creation itself. Of course we do. I write the word "we" intentionally, because Romans 1 is not about some sinners, but about all of the nations outside of Israel who are in revolt against the revelation of God. According to the argument of the book of Romans, that's all of us. Such has been the case since (almost) the beginning, when the primal humanity bows down to a creature (the serpent of Eden) in distinguishing between good and evil, and then hides from God's voice in the creation, the vegetation that God had made. The downward spiral results in our being handed over to our own rebellion—rebellion with direct implications for family order, including misdirected sexuality and disobedience to parents (Rom. 1:26–27). But what is this creation order against which humanity rebels, and why did Paul fit this in the context of a discussion about his lack of shame about the gospel of the resurrected Son of David (Rom. 1:1–17)?

This is because, in the apostle's message, the gospel of Christ is the key to understanding all reality. Ephesians chapters five and six are often preached in churches in talking about issues of marriage and childrearing. But too often these chapters are treated as though they are standalone messages, perhaps written for the church of Ephesus's equivalent of Mother's Day. They are not. Rather, these chapters are the continuation of an ongoing argument. The book, after all, is a letter, to be read to the gathered congregation.

The argument in chapter 1 begins with the unveiling of the mystery of Christ and continues, demonstrating how this mystery explains our redemption (Eph. 1–2), the makeup of the church (Eph. 2–3), the ministry of the church (Eph. 4–5), and then our callings in our families (Eph. 5–6). In Christ, God achieves unity in one new man, for a humanity fractured by the Fall since Babel (Eph. 2:1–6). One key aspect of this unveiled mystery is that the family structure is not an arbitrary expression of the will of God, but is an icon of God's purpose of the universe in Christ.

The mystery of Christ, then, is why God did not design Adam to subdivide like an amoeba, but instead declared it "not good" that he was alone (Gen. 2:18). The Genesis 2 mandate to leave father and mother, to cleave to one another, to become one flesh, is accessible to all people everywhere, even without the Christian gospel or the Scriptures. Human civilizations have died out in world history for various reasons—famine, warfare, environmental calamity—but no human civilization has ever died out because the people forgot to have sex. The drive toward sexual union, the starting point of the formation of family, is a powerful pull, wild enough, and with potential consequences dangerous enough, that every human society has had to find ways to differentiate between positive and destructive aspects of sexuality. And, while cultures differ on what culturally expresses masculinity and femininity, every culture has recognized that there is distinction between the two. The gospel recognizes these universal, creational truths, and explains why they exist.

Ephesians 5 is not a collection of tips for a happier, healthier marriage. Paul wrote that he was declaring that marriage is a "great mystery," the mystery of Christ and his church. In Christ and the church, Paul was not searching for metaphors for human love. Marriage is itself the metaphor, the embodied image of the pattern God has already set. The man and the woman are alike, both formed from the same creation materials, both made in the image of God, and yet they are different. We are not genderless persons who happen to have been placed in arbitrary male and female bodies. Sexual differentiation isn't simply a matter of genital architecture. From the very beginning, Jesus taught, humanity is created "male and female."

Sometimes Christians will argue (though never consistently) that male and female distinctions are obliterated by the new covenant. Doesn't the apostle Paul teach us that there is neither "male nor female" in Christ (Gal. 3:28)? Certainly in terms of the issue addressed there—that of inheritance—there is no distinction. Men and women alike—not just firstborn sons—share in Jesus' identity, and thus, in his inheritance of the universe. The same was true from the beginning, when both men and women, were given the image-bearing rule over the rest of creation (Gen. 1:27). But this equality of inheritance doesn't mean that good differences between men and women are gone. Thus, the Scripture applies some commands to all persons without distinction, and makes some commands with particular reference to men and to women. Masculinity and femininity are not aspects of the fallen order to be overcome but are instead part of what God declared from the beginning to be "very good" (Gen. 1:31).

In marriage, humanity is joined together to form an organic union, as a head with a body, so that what belongs to him belongs to her, and vice versa. The concepts of "headship" and "submission" often rankle people, and often provoke controversy even among Christians as to what these concepts mean. Sometimes this is due to the examples of those who have used the biblical pattern to baptize unbiblical stereotypes of masculinity or femininity or to turn the argument of Ephesians 5 into the equivalent of a business model or a corporate flow chart of who's "in charge." The pattern of marriage is no such thing though. It speaks of an organic unity in which the more the husband and wife are sanctified together by Word and Spirit, the more they—like the nervous system of your body—move and operate smoothly, effortlessly, holistically. They are one flesh. Marriage is not about domineering or dominance, but about cooperation through complementarity. When Scripture speaks of "headship," the issue is not privilege but the exact reverse.

A husband's leadership is to picture the gospel. Jesus is inseparable from his bride, as a human head is from a human body. Paul himself heard this truth directly on the road to Damascus where he was headed to arrest and disrupt the church in Syria. The Galilean voice did not say to him, "Saul, Saul, why do you persecute a gathering of people who believe in the things I taught," but rather "Saul, Saul, why do you persecute *me*" (Acts 9:4). The husband then pictures Christ by crucifying his own privileges and plans and pouring out his life for his family (Eph. 5:26; Ezek. 16:9). The "headship" here is self-sacrificial and other-directed. In the same way, the "submission" the Scripture speaks of is not that of a mousy codependent or a cowering supplicant. God forbid, when the Scripture speaks of women as daughters of Sarah, who was in her most faithful moments far from that (1 Pet. 3). The submission is that of the church, which is spoken of in the gospel as joint-heirs with Christ himself. Jesus says to his church, in its original twelve foundation stones, "No longer do I call you servants, for the servant does not know what his master is doing; but I have called you friends, for all that I have heard from my Father I have made known to you" (John 15:15).

Marriage is not meant to be isolated into a cocoon of the love of the man and woman alone, but exists in the context of the extended family, the community, and the next generation. Marriage is, from the very beginning, set within the context of the future, as the love of the man and the woman takes on flesh in the newness of life of children. Again, this is pointing not just to the original creation structures but also to their kingdom fulfillment. The command to be fruitful and multiply, to fill the earth, is fulfilled by the Christ who stands triumphant before his Father, not hiding in the vegetation as did the first shamed Adam, but announcing, "Behold, I and the children God has given me" (Heb. 2:13). The love between Christ and the church leads to life and community, as new generations are born through the Spirit (John 3:3). This reality is embedded in the life cycle, as each generation gives way to the next.

> **Marriage is not meant to be isolated into a cocoon of the love of the man and woman alone, but exists in the context of the extended family, the community, and the next generation.**

As children, we learn the patterns that we will know most fully when we join the dynamic at the heart of the universe by praying, with Jesus, "Our Father" for protection, for provision, for participation in the life of the household. We learn, within the home, what it is to be loved, and what it means to be trained for greater responsibilities later on (Heb. 12:5–11). This is why the command to honor father and mother is part of the foundational set of words from God about how to live rightly before him. That's why trusting obedience to parents, and faithful rearing of children, is tied to inheritance of the land of promise (Eph. 6:1–4). And this is why those who will not care for their own households are spoken of in Scripture as "worse than an unbeliever" and as those who have "denied the faith" (1 Tim. 5:8). The household is not just a "relationship," but an economy, an economy where we learn something of what it means to be the children of God. Disharmony between parents and children is not simply a cultural problem; it implicitly pictures a false gospel of a Father who does not hear his Son, a Son who does not honor his Father, a church that is not mother to those of the faith.

The kingdom mystery behind the family is why there is no "golden age" of "family values," this side of Eden. The Fall led to a disruption not only of the peace between God and humanity, but between the man and the woman in marriage. And almost immediately after the Fall, the fracturing of the family began, from violence between brothers, to polygamy, to sexual immorality, to sexual violence, and almost every other imaginable deviation from the Genesis mandate. No generation of humanity is exempt from this tension.

Throughout the canon of Scripture, there's a close tie between family breakdown and spiritual breakdown. That's why idolatry and immorality are linked repeatedly in the Old Testament. The mystery of the Christ/church pattern itself was revealed, it should be remembered, to a congregation in the shadow of a fertility goddess (Acts 19:21–41). In forbidding the "unequal yoke" between believers and unbelievers, the apostle Paul echoed the Old Testament tie between paganism and marriages that are not rooted in common submission to God. Paul does not warn of marriage to unbelievers simply in terms of a lack of intimacy or of confusion for the children, but of spiritual consequences: "What accord has Christ with Belial?" (2 Cor. 6:15).

The Family and the Church

Questions of the family are about much more than sexuality, but sexuality is at the root of many of the most contentious debates in this era, and indeed in most eras. Sexuality grounded in the icon of the gospel of Christ and his church means that sexual immorality has profound spiritual consequences (1 Cor. 6:17–20), ultimately leading, if not repented of, to exile from the kingdom of God (1 Cor. 6:9–10). Sexual expression isn't simply a matter of neurons firing. A Christian view of reality means that the body is a temple, set apart to be a dwelling place for the Holy Spirit. Sexual immorality, then, is not just bad for us (although it is); it's also an act of desecrating a holy place. There's little surprise then that the Jerusalem Council, while not placing the burden of the Mosaic ceremonial law on the new Gentile believers, did decree that the new believers must flee sexual immorality (Acts 15:20). In a world of concubines and temple prostitutes, a Christian sexual ethic was just as freakish and countercultural in the first-century Roman Empire as it is today, if not more so.

The family, patterned after the kingdom, is a matter of gospel priority. Salvation is not some sort of escape from the creation but instead restores the created order, directing it toward its goal. Like every other aspect of the curse, Jesus has reconciled the fallen universe to God "by the blood of his cross" (Col. 1:20). Jesus lived out a life of obedience, in the place of disobedient Adam and disobedient Israel, to every aspect of the law of God, including obedience to parents (Luke 2:51). As he dies on the cross,

Jesus did precisely what the religious leaders rebelled against in their own families: providing for his mother's care (John 19:26–27). Paul referenced Deuteronomy 21 that the sin-bearing Christ "became a curse for us" (Gal. 3:13–14), echoing the warning that the one who is hanged on a tree is cursed by God (Deut. 21:22–23). The text of that passage from Moses is about a "stubborn and rebellious son" who is charged by the elders of the city with being a "drunkard and a glutton" (Deut. 21:20). Jesus is indeed charged by the elders of Israel with being a drunkard and a glutton (Matt. 11:19). He is indeed taken outside the gates of the city where he bears the curse, not for his own rebellion (for there was none), but for that of Adam's race. And, after tasting death, Jesus is raised to announce to the women at his tomb, "Go to my brothers and say to them, 'I am ascending to my Father and your Father, to my God and your God'" (John 20:17). Jesus establishes a community, a household, a family. And as the gospel goes forward through the ages, he and his Bride are fruitful, and they multiply.

As the church moves into the future, there is no question that the culture has shifted, in some ways dramatically, on questions of the family. But the outside culture is not quite as revolutionary as they—or we—sometimes pretend. In some ways, the culture has indeed revolutionized, but even in these ways the revolution is more of a step backward, to old heresies made new by technological and economic tools rather than a move into a brave, new world. The debates over the definition of marriage, for example, and the malleability of gender are rooted in very old (and biblically mistaken) concepts of a fundamental disconnect between the self as "soul" from the body. The priority of sexual expression as essential to wholeness and well-being is similarly rooted in an almost sacral view of the orgasm as a kind of ecstatic spirituality. These concepts are present in virtually every generation, and in every generation are rejected by the Abrahamic religion.

> As the church moves into the future, there is no question that the culture has shifted, in some ways dramatically, on questions of the family.

Moreover, despite the utopian rhetoric of the language of "progress" as it relates to sexuality and gender and family, can we really pretend that the culture around us is an increasingly safe place for women or for their children? Despite the promise of women's empowerment, the Sexual Revolution has given us the reverse. Is it really an advance for women that the average adolescent male has seen a kaleidoscope of images of women sexually exploited and humiliated in pornography? Is it really empowerment to have more and more women economically at the mercy of men who leave them and their children, with no legal recourse? The adolescent girl facing the pressure to perform sex acts on her boyfriend, or else lose him, what is this but the brutal patriarchy of a Bronze Age warlord? All of these things empower men to pursue a Darwinian fantasy of the predatory alpha-male in search of nothing but power, prestige, and the next orgasm. That's not exactly a revolution.

As Countercultural as We Want to Be

At the same time, the church is accustomed to thinking of ourselves as "God's last and only hope" for a darkening Western civilization. Particularly on the issue of the family, we position our stance as out-of-step with a culture slouching toward Gomorrah. In many ways, both sides of the so-called "culture war" would agree with this characterization. But what if we are not quite the culture warriors we pretend to be? What if we instead are slow-motion Sexual Revolutionaries, accommodating to the ambient culture's concepts of the family, just a little behind the rest of the populace? Could it be that our press releases and confessions of faith say one thing, while our church directories and membership rolls say something strikingly different?

Perhaps the most immediately obvious aspect of our cultural accommodation is found in the surprisingly high numbers of those who make the trek from our baptisteries to the local divorce court. Many have already demonstrated the falseness of the claim that evangelical Christian divorce rates are higher than the outside culture, but it is true that regions of the country with high numbers of self-identified born-again Christians tend to have higher divorce rates, that the divorce dockets are fullest in those parts of the country most saturated with the Bible. On a closer look, what these studies show is not that the gospel propels a divorce culture but that an almost-gospel does. Nominal Christianity incentivizes divorce by, for example, giving social pressure to early marriage without an accompanying accountability to the church for the keeping of the vows. The ideal of a Christian marriage without a strong community of discipleship and discipline is a dangerous combination. The romantic notion of "finding a soul mate" leads to the commitment of marriage but without the communal bonds it takes to hold on to those commitments.

Again, there are economic and sociological reasons behind this, but shouldn't the "salt and light" of a Christian witness do more than this to counteract such trends? Moreover, it is true that the way we talk about divorce has changed, right along with the culture around us. This starts with the way we talk about divorce, less in terms of sin and forgiveness of sin and more in terms of recovery. We talk about the issue in our "divorce care" ministries and our "singles again" classes, but rarely in the context of prophetic preaching or congregational discipline. We often assume that this shift is one of showing "mercy" to those who have been divorced. Of course we should not be unmerciful to any sinner (John 3:17), but that does not explain why we would not warn people of a sin for which the wages of sin are death, and the consequences ruinous. It also doesn't explain why we wouldn't, as we address questions of social justice and the common good, address what is no doubt the leading cause of "widows and orphans" in our midst. Why would we speak in muted tones on divorce and in full volume, unambiguous terms on other Sexual Revolution issues that are more heated in the "culture wars" of the moment? Sometimes this is due to what the Bible calls "fear of man"—leaders afraid of angering divorced people (or their relatives) in power in their congregations. But I would suspect an even more foundational reason is the normality of divorce itself in the world around us, and in our own pews. Divorce is not a "culture war" issue, precisely because it is so common.

But notice this trajectory. The shift in our practices on divorce has come without any kind of theological reflection or conversation at all. Instead, our approach to divorce seems to have meandered just a bit behind the mainstream of American cultural patterns of acceptance of "one spouse at a time," a sad, but normal, part of life. For many within the church, divorce doesn't seem to be a "culture war" issue, because it is not shocking or disgusting. We have grown accustomed to it. New generations of the church will live in a world in which all sorts of other sexual practices and family redefinitions will seem just as "normal." Will they be more countercultural than we?

The same is true when it comes to the question of sexual immorality. Most congregations recognize the harm of what we call "premarital sex," and preach and teach regularly on this. But, even so, notice the language that is used. We speak of "premarital sex" and "abstinence" until marriage, and rightly so when we are communicating with the outside world, since these are categories the culture understands. I am not suggesting that, in and of itself, this is wrong. But notice how long it has been since you have heard the word *fornication*, even in preaching? Could it be that the loss of this word is about more than just updating our vocabulary to connect with the society around us, but that we've also lost something of our moral imagination? The word *chastity* is not the same as the word *abstinence* and the words *fornication* and *premarital sex* aren't interchangeable. This isn't merely a matter of impatience, as though the marital act misfired at the wrong time. Fornication is, both spiritually and typologically, a different sort of act from the marital act. It pictures a different reality than that of the mystery of Christ. It represents a Christ who uses the church without joining her, covenantally, to himself. It's not just "naughtiness." To use another word Christians find awkward and antiquated, it's blasphemy. That's why the consequences of such immorality are so severe. There is a real spiritual union formed, mysteriously, but one that is of a different spirit than the sanctifying Spirit of God in Christ (1 Cor. 6:15–19). Again, I'm not suggesting that we ban the language of "premarital sex" or "abstinence," especially when we're trying to explain a Christian sexual ethic to the outside world using categories already in play. I am suggesting, though, that we see how our lexicons have shifted. We speak of "extramarital sex" and of "affairs," but we still know that there is something about the word *adultery* that retains the gravity of infidelity on a home and on a conscience. Moreover, we should recognize how often our sense of marriage and morality are dictated by our ongoing quest for the normal American life. The language of "waiting" and "abstinence" are not themselves all that countercultural, if all that they mean is risk-management for those who wish not to mess up their future careers or educational plans with the "consequences" of children.

Several years ago, I was speaking in a church, preaching through the biblical book of 1 Corinthians. While expounding on 1 Corinthians 7, I noted that the apostle Paul took seriously the passion of sexual desire, and he told the church how to channel that desire. A husband and wife shouldn't have an inordinately extended time away from one another sexually "so that Satan may not tempt you because of your lack of self-control"

(1 Cor. 7:5). I spoke to the singles in the room and said that God's command to them is "if they cannot exercise self-control, they should marry. For it is better to marry than to burn with passion" (1 Cor. 7:9).

Even as I was speaking, I was struck at how the Holy Spirit understood that a naïveté about the sexual appetite doesn't lead to chastity, but rather to wantonness. I encouraged Christian parents not to pressure their sons and daughters into these long, open-ended engagements. To the unmarried in the room, I said, if you find the one you want to marry and both of you meet scriptural guidelines to be with one another, marry.

After the service, a middle-aged couple approached me with another couple, these in their mid-twenties, sheepishly behind them. The older woman spoke first. "Pastor Moore, I don't think you understand the situation here with Chad and Tiffany," she said. "Chad and Tiffany have been dating since the eighth grade, all through high school and all through college." She told me that it would be insane for Chad and Tiffany to marry, since they weren't financially ready for it. Chad was going to medical school, and needed to finish up his time there. Tiffany was finishing her graduate work in accounting. After all that, she told me, they would marry, with their blessing, but that she and her husband just wouldn't approve until after their schooling was over. It wouldn't be prudent.

I told the woman that there was an exception to every rule, and that I wasn't even giving a rule. I was simply saying what the Bible said about the way to channel sexual desire and to avoid the kind of temptation that is, almost quite literally, invincible. "Like I said, there's an exception to every situation," I continued. "I'm just glad Chad and Tiffany have been able to remain sexually pure all this time. Right, Chad?"

After several more moments of awkward silence, everyone coughed, and the middle-aged man mentioned how it was "late, honey, and we ought to be getting home." I could tell Chad was glad to be leaving. And I know I was too. What was really going on there? Now it's certainly possible that Chad and Tiffany were endowed with an unusual amount of restraint. It could be that this extended family had forgotten the power of the sexual appetite up against that kind of situation. Or it could be that these parents—like many in contemporary evangelical Christianity—found fornication a less awful possibility than financial ruin.

Pregnancy apart from marriage is indeed wrong, an act of both personal immorality and of irresponsible evasion of one's responsibilities, but the "fear" of children—right along with venereal disease or emotional distress—has awful implications, not only for the unmarried seeking to maintain fidelity but also on the way the rest of the church views children. Most of our churches actually do present sexuality as a positive joy, one that is worth saving for a lifetime of marriage. The problem is that we, often unintentionally, follow the culture in reducing the joy to simply the tingling of nerve endings and physical release only differing from the culture in restricting this pleasure to married people. Like most Protestants, I do not think that the use of (non-abortion-causing) contraceptives is a sin, but that does not mean that we should not question the way we, like the culture around us, have adjusted to view children as a threat to our freedom and our way of life.

As the father of five sons, I am constantly surprised by the way total strangers will approach us in the grocery store to say, "Do you know what's causing that?" or "What, are you Catholic or something?" Now, we are not the sort of "quiver-full" family one might think of on the fringes of American Christian life. We just happen to have five sons, and in American culture of the moment this seems strange. Some of that is due to economic shifts in American life.

There's quite a difference between perceived social and economic "cost" of a family with six children among cotton-picking sharecroppers at a revival meeting in 1926 Mississippi and that of the same family sitting in the pews of an upwardly mobile suburban Dallas megachurch. There's also a very different personal cost. The stress levels of a young mother of four children, alone with her husband in some city to which he's been transferred for his job, are quite different than those felt by her grandmother, who had an extended family and a lifelong community doors from her house. But, at the same time, I wonder how much we have conformed to a culture that sees a child as an "expense" rather than a blessing?

In short, too often we are as countercultural as we want to be, and that's not nearly enough to turn our churches, much less the world, upside down. Pastors, we have to ask ourselves honestly whether the divorce culture and family breakdown inside the churches have not been fueled in part by our own preaching and teaching. When we reduce marriage to endless sermon series on "Putting the Sizzle Back in Your Spouse" and "Ten Tips for Couples for a Hotter, Holier Romance," are we not contributing to the very same emphasis on hormonally-driven acquisitiveness as the culture,

rather than on the model of a Christ who displays not just affection but cross-carrying fidelity to his Bride? Is it any wonder, then, that so many of our men and women—to have pro-
fessed to believe the gospel—are willing to abandon their spouses and children when they find a new "soul mate"? Could it be, at least in part, because they felt the thrill of the new, the same kind of "spark" their popular music and their pastor's marriage workshops tell them they should always feel when they are in love?

> In short, too often we are as countercultural as we want to be, and that's not nearly enough to turn our churches, much less the world, upside down.

Surrendering the Culture War?

Recognizing the situation we are in is not a means to negotiated surrender on the importance of family issues, as some would suggest. Some would say that the sort of cultural accommodation I've mentioned here is reason for the church to retreat on questions of sexuality and family altogether. Since we're hypocrites on, for example, divorce and remarriage, we should shut up on such questions as the rightness or wrongness of same-sex marriage. The divorce culture is applicable in terms of warning of how we can adjust ourselves to what we know is outside a Christian sexual ethic, but not much beyond that.

There are, arguably, some circumstances where divorce and remarriage are biblically permitted. Most evangelical Christians acknowledge that sexual immorality can dissolve a marital union, and that the innocent party is then free to remarry (Matt. 5:32). The same is true, for most, for abandonment (1 Cor. 7:11–15). Now, if the church did what we ought, our divorce rates would still be dramatically lowered, since vast numbers of divorces do not fit into these categories. Still, the category of a remarried person after divorce does not, on its face, indicate sin. Moreover, the question is what repentance looks like.

Take the worst-case scenario of an unbiblically divorced and remarried couple, for example. Repentance does not mean that they compound their sin by breaking up another marriage, to attempt to reconcile the first one.

Marriages between a man and a woman, even entered into unbiblically, still meet the creation definition of marriage (John 4:18). Even if these marriages were entered into sinfully in the first place, they are marriages, signifying the Christ/church bond of the one-flesh union (Eph. 5:22–31), embedded in God's creation design of male and female together (Mark 10:6–9). Other sorts of sexual arrangements do not. In those cases, repentance means to flee immorality (1 Cor. 6:18), which means to cease such sexual activity in obedience to Christ (1 Cor. 6:11). A state, or church, decree of these relationships as marriages does not make them so.

We have much to repent for in our accommodation to some cultural patterns of family dissolution and Sexual Revolution. But our attitude should not be one that concludes, "Since many have shirked their churchly responsibilities in some things, let us now shirk our responsibilities in everything." That would be the equivalent of someone saying, "Since I had lust in my heart, which Jesus identified as root adultery, I should go ahead and have an affair" or "Since I am angry with you, which Jesus identified as springing from a spirit of murder, I should go ahead and kill you." We don't remedy our past sins by adding new ones.

The cultural shifts may be freeing the church from our captivity, even as we might cling on to such captivity for dear life. The last generation of Christian activists sometimes downplayed gospel distinctives—which the culture found strange and unfamiliar—in favor of talk about "family values," to which most Americans, the church thought, would aspire. For a long time in American culture, we could assume the words "marriage" and "family." Even people from what were once known as "broken homes" could watch stable marriages on television or movies. Boys and girls mostly assumed they had a wedding in their futures. These assumptions are changing.

> Now, the "family values" issues are the most incendiary point of difference between the conservative churches and American culture. That is not, necessarily, bad news.

Now, the "family values" issues are the most incendiary point of difference between the conservative churches and American culture. That is not, necessarily, bad news. In a world in which a Christian family ethic is strange and otherworldly, the church is forced to articulate a Christian vision of the family that is not chiefly about "moral"

issues but about gospel issues. Moreover, this can force the church to alien-
ate from American culture long enough to see what's "American" about our
families, and what's truly Christian. With that comes the opportunity to
turn back our slow-train Sexual Revolutionary ways. This means that we
have the chance, by God's grace, to take marriage and family as seriously
as the gospel does, in a way that prompts the culture around us to ask why.

The Future Renewal of the Family

The Bible Belt marrying parson who weds whosoever will show up and
rent his church; his day is over. The gelatin-spined neighborhood pastor
who hitches the cohabiting couple and hopes to see them at church when
their children are old enough for Sunday school; his time is up. In a day
when churches must fight for the cultural freedom to define marriage,
laissez-faire wedding policies, and the nominalism that goes with them
are done for, and good riddance to them. For too long, we've acted as
though the officers of Christ's church were Justices of the Peace, marrying
people who have no accountability to the church, and in many cases were
forbidden by Scripture to marry. Just because we don't have two grooms or
two brides in front of us, that doesn't mean we've been holding to biblical
marriage.

A speech on family values is more likely to get applause at a "God
and country" rally than a speech on church membership. But only transformed church communities, as outposts of the kingdom of Christ, can
provide the alternative vision of the family we so desperately need. The
Bible reveals that pastors should have well-ordered households since "if
someone does not know how to manage his own household, how will he
care for God's church?" (1 Tim. 3:5). But the reverse is also true. If one
cannot care for God's church, then how can he manage his or her own
household? The church, after all, is the "household of God," which is also
to be well-ordered (1 Tim. 3:15). How can churches castigate the outside
culture for believing the family structure is socially malleable when we fail
in our church households to maintain a consistent witness to the kingdom
of God?

What would happen if our churches, en masse, began to involve the
whole church household in shaping a new culture of family? What if this

started with weddings that are not merely "celebrations" of the love of the couple, but a gathering of the witnesses of the community, pledging to help this new family stand by their words to the glory of Christ? What would happen if rather than quietly allowing a man who abandoned his family to join a different small group Bible study with his new wife, we called him to repentance? What would happen if we, on the first word of accusation about spousal abuse, handed the unrepentant pugilist over to both the discipline of the church and over to the civil authorities? What would happen if the single mothers in our communities were treated as widows, cared for by the entire congregation spiritually, socially, and, where needed, economically? What if our foster care systems, in every one of our communities, knew that the churches are the first place willing to help families and children in crisis? Perhaps if such churches were more common, we would have a decreasing need for parachurch organizations to train our people how to love their spouses and rear their children, because our people would see such on display every Lord's Day in the assembly of Christ.

The renewal of our churches for the sake of the family would mean that we would avoid the idolatry of the family. Jesus, after all, was not married, and yet lived the alpha-and-omega point of the human life. Every Christian is not called to marriage, but every Christian is part of a family. The way of discipleship means that we need, in every generation, older men mentoring younger men and older women mentoring younger women (Titus 2:2–3). It is no accident that Paul referred repeatedly to his relationship with Timothy as that of a "father" with a "son," or that Ruth is identified with Naomi as a daughter with her mother (Ruth 4:14–17). Men in our congregations must take responsibility for the discipleship of our boys and young men, training them away from a pagan hyper-masculinity that deifies the appetites and hurts women and children. Women in our congregations must lead in training our girls and young women toward a different vision of womanhood away from submission to men in general, from seeing their worth in terms of their sexual attractiveness and availability to men.

The Family and Mission

When it comes to our mission, some things have changed, and some things haven't. Again, in a past generation, the church could assume that most people aspired to "traditional" families—meaning intact, nuclear families with both a mother and a father. Especially as this relates to same-sex unions, the cultural and legal landscape has shifted seismically. This has implications for the common good, for our social fabric, but what had changed for our witness to the gospel? In one sense, nothing. Jesus of Nazareth is alive. There is no family revolution that can get him back into Joseph of Arimathea's grave. Regardless of what happens in the culture around us, the gospel doesn't need "family values" to flourish. In fact, it often thrives when it is in sharp contrast to the cultures around it. That's why the gospel rocketed out of the first century from places such as Ephesus and Philippi and Corinth and Rome, which were hardly Mayberry.

Family issues can prompt some of the most heated "culture wars" in any society for a couple of reasons. First, they are perhaps the most personal. Conversations about family life are different from conversations about more abstract ideas, because they seem to carry with them judgment on persons as persons. That's why conversations about stay-at-home versus working mothers are so fraught with peril; it seems that one side is saying the other is either "negligent" toward her children or "wasting" her gifts and talents.

Furthermore, family issues become more heated because we, naturally, want to protect our children from forces that we believe will harm them. This can lead to a sort of seething resentment, when we compare mores we believe are going in a bad direction with the vision of the Bible, or, for that matter, just the neighborhood in which we grew up. If we believe, though, in the sovereignty of God, then we believe that we were not born at this time, and in this culture, by accident. If we belong to Christ, then this is our assigned mission field. To rail against the culture is to say to God that we are entitled to a better mission field than the one he has given us. At the same time, if we simply dissolve into the culture around us, or refuse to leave untroubled the questions the culture deems too sensitive to ask, we are not on mission at all.

We could address family issues in a new age with the airy antinomianism of those who would seek good news apart from the law and righteousness of God. But such a "gospel" is not good news, if it leaves the conscience weighted down with an expectation of judgment. There is the equally perilous temptation, though, to emphasize the righteousness of God's law without the mercy of the cross. This evidences not only a low view of the gospel but a low view of the law. The Bible tells us that "whoever keeps the whole law but fails in one point has become accountable for all of it" (James 2:10), since sin isn't a sin against a law but against the Lawgiver. We then "speak and so act as those who are to be judged under the law of liberty. For judgment is without mercy to one who has shown no mercy" (James 2:12–13). The issue isn't whether sin against God's pattern of the family is damnable; it is. All sin is. The question is whether damnation can be turned back by Golgotha Hill Blood and Garden Tomb Life. And the answer to that is "yes" and "Amen" in Christ.

We ought then to have the same sort of reaction to the family questions of the culture around us that our Lord Jesus had when he encountered the woman at the well. Jesus went through Samaria, intentionally, and encountered this woman, again, intentionally. James and John, elsewhere in the Gospel, wanted Jesus to call down fire from the heavens on Samaria, but he refused. He engaged this woman in conversation, and was neither shocked by her sin nor was he afraid of addressing the issue. Jesus said to her, remarkably, in John 4:16: "Go, call your husband, and come here." Both parts of this sentence are crucially important for our mission. "Go, call your husband"—Jesus uncovers the very thing this woman wanted to avoid: her sexual and familial sin. She wanted to talk about all sorts of other things: theology, Jewish/Samaritan relations, but, like all of us, she wanted to keep her sin hidden. Jesus addressed it—pointing out that she had had five husbands, and that the man she was living with now was not her husband at all. But he didn't stop with this. He said, "And come here." Jesus demonstrated that the gospel does not come for those who are sexually "pure" or with family "values," but to broken sinners, as every last one of us, except him, are. The people who disagree with us on family issues—whether same-sex marriage or cohabitation or monogamy or any other issue—aren't part of some conspiracy, as though they were cartoon super-villains plotting in a lair. They are, like all of us, seeking a way that seems right to them.

> We ought to love those who disagree with us, including those who see us as bigots.

We ought to love those who disagree with us, including those who see us as bigots. They are not our enemies.

This means we ought to stand for Christian conviction, and also avoid ridicule or hostility toward those who disagree. We ought to love our gay and lesbian neighbors. We ought to serve and care for our serially-divorcing or cohabiting neighbors. The loudest voices against, for example, the hounding and intimidation of gay and lesbian persons around the world should be from the wing of the church most committed to a biblical Christian sexual ethic. The people most concerned about working to end gay and lesbian homelessness, for kids who've been thrown out of their homes by parents who've rejected them, ought to be those who believe the full counsel of God on these matters. The people most willing to love and receive strippers and porn stars and prostitutes who need to be seen for more than the use of their parts, ought to be the church of Jesus Christ.

We ought also to be those who see family issues as more than merely sexual issues (though not less than this). If we care about families, rather than just protecting our families, then we will care about everything that pulls families apart. Abused women and children, for example, often stay in the shadows because they believe that our court system will not adequately protect them from further violence. They fear that reporting such behavior will fuel even worse danger later. We should work for a justice system clear and decisive enough that abusers will receive justice and the victims will be protected. Many of the families imperiled around us right now are those who are part of immigrant communities, caught in an unworkable system, prone to exploitation by employers who can threaten them not only with their jobs but with their children's futures. Whatever our disagreements on migration policies, surely we can recognize that many families are here to escape grinding poverty or violence in their home countries. These aren't seeking to "work the system" but to provide for and protect their children.

And one of the greatest threats to the family is poverty. We can argue about whether unstable families lead to poverty, or poverty to unstable families, but we ought to recognize that the two go together. Whatever our views on welfare reforms or on the right amount of the minimum wage, we should recognize how much economic hardship is present for single mothers trying to provide for their families in the absence of men who have died, or have left, or are imprisoned. These families should not be demonized to score political points. Again, we may not always agree on what economic policies will lead to family flourishing; there will not always be a clear "Thus saith the Lord." But shouldn't we at least have a church injecting a moral consideration into such debates, so that we recognize that we are not green eyeshade-wearing accountants measuring out dollars and cents, but that we must also take into consideration costs on human lives and families?

At the same time, we shouldn't pretend that our gospel ministry means simply addressing "spiritual" issues while avoiding questions of marriage and family. The gospel went forward with a call to repentance from all sin, including sexual and family sins, and the instructions for how to live in this newness of life included a word on reordering sexuality, marriage relationships, extended family, the rearing of children. We must be just as definitive, whatever the social or political or even legal cost.

And we should do so as those who recognize that, in the short-term, we have lost the culture war on sexual and family issues. Questions that previously were "wedge issues" of the "real America" against the "liberal elites" are now turned completely around on us. So be it. Long-term, though, we ought to stand by our conviction that marriage and family are resilient precisely because they are embedded into the fabric of creation and thus cannot be upended by cultural mores or by court decrees. The sexual revolution, if we're right about the universe, cannot keep its promises. Unhinged sexual utopianism can only go so far before it leaves the ground around it burned over, like every other utopianism. We need to be ready, after all that, to point a light toward older paths, toward water that can satisfy. We need to be a John 3:16 people in a John 4:16 world.

> **We need to be a John 3:16 people in a John 4:16 world.**

Sure, there will always be those who will wish to root our marriage views in nostalgia, or in caricatured pictures of masculinity or femininity or "good families." And there will always be those who ask us to capitulate on a Christian vision of the family. We won't capitulate, because we can't. To dispense with marriage and family, as God defines, them is to dispense with a mystery that points to the gospel itself. Again, this will seem freakish and nasty and bigoted, to some. Marriage may well decline, and children will be hurt, because the marginalization of marriage empowers predatory men. But the gospel flourished in places known for temple prostitutes and gladiator fights, and it still stands. As churches recover gospel-rooted marriage cultures, and contrast these with the sexually libertarian carnival around us, there will be a moment to articulate and to embody what we mean by men and women, mothers and fathers, sex and life.

And as we do, we will welcome those who are refugees from the sexual revolution, of the lonely in search of a new family. There will be those who will walk away, in search of freedom from sexual or family order. But we will be waiting, with a fatted-calf party ready to go, welcoming the wanderer home. And we will recognize that the family is a gospel issue, not a "values" issue. That means it's hard for everyone, not just for certain sorts of sinners. The path to fidelity and chastity is difficult, for everyone, and we need a great cloud of witnesses to walk in a different direction from a world that too often defines sex and sexuality as ultimate in life. Jesus isn't shocked by temptations, nor does he leave us alone to fight them.

Conclusion

The family is important to gospel Christianity, but it could be that our vision of the family will no longer be a point of contact with the world around us, and much more a point of distinction. That's not a new situation in the history of the people of God. Our convictions about the family are more immediately interesting to some people who could care less about the hypostatic union. That worked well for churches in the past, showing their neighbors they were just like them because they, too, were "family-friendly." It could be that our convictions about chastity, fidelity, discipline, sacrifice, and love will make us seem bizarre. But maybe, just maybe, this cultural strangeness will be the very thing the Spirit uses to point the culture to the Father for whom every family, in heaven and on earth, is named (Eph. 3:14–15).

And, perhaps, by recovering a vision of the family as grounded in the mystery of Christ, the church can be freed to seek the kingdom, to embody a culture, to advance a mission in a time in which it is easy to assume that a person's life consists in the abundance of his orgasms. The family is not a sentimental picture, in these times between the times. The family is a matter of spiritual warfare for everyone in this fallen wilderness. But beyond the warfare, there's a New Jerusalem, adorned as a bride for her husband (Rev. 21:2).

As I look back on my fears of "affording" marriage twenty years ago, I realize now that what I was mostly afraid of was not being a "normal American," of having what I thought we ought to have when we were expected to have it. We weren't ready to get married; that's true. But our finances were the least of our worries. I wasn't ready, at twenty-two, to know how to console a sobbing wife when she learned that her parents were divorcing. I wasn't ready to collapse into her arms when I heard that my grandfather had died. I wasn't ready for miscarriages, or for a long adoption process, or for two special-needs babies. We weren't ready to hear that we would never have children biologically, nor were we ready for the doctors to be proven wrong. We weren't ready for five sons. And I could go on and on. At least I wasn't ready for those things. But, in a very real sense, "I" didn't even exist at all. The life that I have now is defined by our life together. These aren't two separate lives, bringing our agendas together. This is two people joining together for one life, life together. One can prepare oneself to be a husband or a wife. But one can never really be "ready."

Truth is, there's no way we could have made that budget work. And there's no way we could have grown up enough to be "ready" for what providence had for us. We needed each other. We needed to grow up, together, and to know that our love for each other didn't—and doesn't—consist in having it all together. We didn't have it all together at the beginning, after all, and we still had us.

When I look back at those wedding pictures from twenty years ago, I see faces of people, some of whom are gone now. I see my grandmother's face there, and I think how right she was. I see a boy and a girl in love, though not as much in love as now. Were we ready? No. And I wouldn't have it any other way. That reality reminds me that our call to speak of the family together as a church can't be simply nostalgia for a simpler era. We must call ourselves to a different sort of stability—the sort of stability that is a sign of the kingdom. Family values aren't a means to making it in America. Family, as defined by the gospel, will make us stranger than we want to be—and it's about time.

Chapter Nine

CONVICTIONAL KINDNESS

A while back, a university study examined "road rage" to see what caused the acts of verbal outbursts or physical violence on the nation's highways. They could find no predictors along the typical lines of age, sex, ethnicity, class, or geography. They discovered though that there was one accurate predictor of road rage: the presence of bumper stickers on the vehicle of the offender.[30] The study suggested that the message on the bumper sticker was irrelevant. It's not that a "Practice Random Acts of Kindness" sticker exempts a car from susceptibility more than a "Keep Back; I'm Reloading" sticker. It doesn't matter whether a car's bumper is placarded with "Jesus Saves" or "Legalize Pot." The only factor was whether there were, in fact, bumper stickers, whatever they say. And the more bumper stickers that were on a car, the more likely the road rage.

This actually makes sense, the more I think about it. After all, a bumper sticker isn't meant to persuade. Do you actually know anyone who changed his mind about gun control because of reading a slogan on a bumper sticker, much less his beliefs about the existence of God or the meaning of life? I would guess not. The sort of person who puts bumper stickers

---

30. W. J. Szlemko, J. A. Benfield, P. A. Bell, J. L. Deffenbacher, and L. Troup, "Territorial Markings as a Predictor of Driver Aggression and Road Rage," *Journal of Applied Social Psychology*, 38 (2008): 1664–1688.

on his car is wanting to self-identify with a particular message or with a particular tribe. The person is the kind of person who wants to express his opinions to complete strangers, without the possibility of extended conversation or nuance. The person wants to be heard. This can easily tip over from self-expression into outrage.

Kindness as Warfare

This is a persistent temptation for our public witness, especially on issues of righteousness and justice: to become an ecclesial version of a bumper sticker, identifying who we are and expressing outrage at the culture around us. Nothing signals conviction and passion in this age more than the art of being theatrically offended. And it would be easy to see the vehemence of our outrage as evidence that we are "engaging the culture," when we would be doing nothing of the sort. If outrage were a sign of godliness, then the devil would be the godliest soul in the cosmos. He, after all, rages and roars "because he knows his time is short" (Rev. 12:12). Contrast that with the Lord Jesus who does not "quarrel or cry aloud" (Matt. 12:19). Why is this so? It's because the devil has no mission apart from killing and destroying and accusing and slandering. And it's because the devil is on the losing side of history. The challenge of the next generation is to cultivate a convictional kindness in our witness as we address the outside world. This kindness is not weak or passive. In fact, kindness is an act of warfare.

As the gospel advanced across the Roman Empire, the emerging congregations were faced with constant turmoil from internal and external threats, with what the gospel hymn would call "fightings within and fears without." The apostle Paul, drawing near to the end of his life and ministry, penned letters to those who would carry on the mission: to Timothy and Titus. Timothy, leading the church in Ephesus, was, from the context of the letters sent to him, plagued with a personal vulnerability to timidity and fear. Paul, imprisoned and heading for execution, was continually urging his protégé to "wage the good warfare" (1 Tim. 1:18), to "not neglect the gift you have" (1 Tim. 4:14), to "fight the good fight of the faith" (1 Tim 6:12), to "not be ashamed" (2 Tim. 1:8), but to be "a good soldier of Christ Jesus" (2 Tim. 2:3). The old apostle had to counsel Timothy through his stomach problems (1 Tim. 5:23) right after instructing him how to deal with rebuking persistent sin in the ranks (1 Tim. 5:21–23). He had to tell him to let no one despise his youth (1 Tim. 4:12). He had to remind him "God gave us a spirit not of fear but of power and love and self-control" (2 Tim. 1:7). Paul's persistent message to Timothy was the courage to fight, fight, fight. And then the apostle talks about kindness. He was not changing the subject.

The Lord's servant, Paul wrote, "must not be quarrelsome, but kind to everyone" (2 Tim. 2:24). This is perhaps easy to understand when we are talking about the internal nurture of our churches and families. Everyone, even the most hardened nihilist, understands the need to demonstrate natural affection for those in one's immediate circle, for those who are "part of us," for utilitarian reasons (if not for moral ones). The apostolic mandate, though, is not merely natural affection. Those who serve Christ must be kind to *everyone*, Paul wrote. Those who serve Christ must show honor to *everyone*, Peter wrote (1 Pet. 2:17). As

> **This is not a break from the fighting. This is how we fight.**

those who are joined to Christ, and thus anointed with his Spirit, we are to be conformed to his image (Rom. 8:29). The Spirit bears fruit in our lives, as Jesus lives out his life through us. This fruit consists of kindness and gentleness. This is not a break from the fighting. This is how we fight.

If we are on a mission, embodying the life of the kingdom in the present culture, then we should have nothing to do with "foolish, ignorant controversies" since we ought to know "they breed quarrels" (2 Tim. 2:23). In this, we express the life of Jesus. Though anointed with the Spirit of wisdom and discernment, Jesus refused to weigh in on a dispute between brothers over their inheritance (Luke 12:13–14), and often refused to answer the questions of the religious leaders seeking to trap him. And, as I discussed earlier, in the controversy in his hometown synagogue, he only engaged in controversy on his own terms, to provoke the conversation he wanted to have. When the crowds raged, he didn't answer them point-by-point, but walked forward, toward the cross. He understood his mission, and was unwilling to be distracted from it. As we grow up into Christ, we reflect the same sort of mind-set.

Years ago, when I was serving as a preaching pastor in a church, I was approached by an eleven-year-old in our congregation who wanted to introduce me to his friend, Jared. Jared was on his soccer team, and had never been to church before. After a few minutes of talking, Jared told me that he needed prayer, that his dad had left, and he didn't know what his family was going to do. He wondered if I might pray that God would "put my mom and dad back together." I prayed with him, and he turned to go back to his seat. He was wearing a shirt celebrating the inauguration of a President who was unpopular with most of the people in my mostly white, blue-collar congregation. As I watched this young man walk down his first-ever church aisle, to hear the gospel perhaps for the first time, a middle-aged man walked past him and huffed, "We need to get you a better shirt."

I was incredulous. I wanted to yell, "He's lost. He's wounded. He's hurting. He doesn't know Christ, and you're worried about this shirt!" My church member was lacking the full context, and he didn't ask. All he knew was that he didn't like the President on the boy's shirt. I wondered how often I've done the same thing. How often have I fought the fight I saw in front of me, instead of the one that was really there to be fought.

The Lord's servant is not quarrelsome, Paul commands. This is part of a more comprehensive gospel reality: as we are conformed to Christ we seek to diminish ourselves, and, by the Spirit, to live more the life of Christ within us. That's why Paul told Timothy he must "patiently enduring evil" (2 Tim. 2:24). Quarrelsomeness, the desire to fight for the sake of fighting, is a sign of pride. How often are our most bitter, sarcastic clashes with those who disagree with us less about persuading them and more about vindicating ourselves? This is especially true when we fear that those who oppose us think we're stupid or evil (or both). We want to prove to them, and to ourselves, that they are wrong about us. That's quite a different spirit from the Spirit of Christ.

One way this can show up is in the perennial temptation of Christian churches and organizations to organize boycotts of businesses who disagree with us on, for example, the definition of marriage or other family policy matters. It's not that a boycott is, in and of itself, a wrong thing. Rosa Parks and the Montgomery bus boycott demonstrate that there are times when a wise, strategically focused boycott can work. Generally, though, boycotts expose our worst tendencies. We are tempted to fight like the devil to please the Lord.

A boycott, after all, is a display of power, particularly of economic power. We seek to hurt a company by depriving it of revenue. It is a contest of who has the more buying power, and therefore who is of more value to the company. And it assumes that the "rightness" of a position is constituted by a majority with power. But isn't that precisely what the church is to be a sign to speak against? Isn't this the "Gentile" view of power that our Lord warned us against (Luke 22:25)?

We don't persuade our neighbors by mimicking their angry power protests. We don't win arguments by bringing corporations to the ground in surrender. Frankly, if we had that sort of cultural cache, corporations would already have market-tested it, and found ways to curry favor with us while keeping their immoral practices subterranean. Let others fight mammon with mammon. Let's instead offer a word of faithful witness that doesn't blink before power but doesn't seek to imitate it either.

After all, our Christ does not "cry aloud or lift up his voice," and neither does he "grow faint or be discouraged till he has established justice in the earth" (Isa. 42:2, 4). Jesus doesn't defend himself against personal offenses, and he doesn't allow injustice to stand without shining light upon it. This is because Jesus has a broader vision of what's going on. Jesus doesn't blink before Pilate because he knows, ultimately, he is setting the agenda, not Pilate (John 18:36–37). This is not because Jesus doesn't see the fight before him, but because he sees a bigger, more seemingly intractable, fight in the distance. Kindness and gentleness grow, not when we downplay warfare, but when we emphasize it. For Paul, kindness is not politeness. It's a weapon in spiritual warfare. We teach and rebuke with kindness and gentleness, so that "God may perhaps grant them repentance leading to a knowledge of the truth, and they may . . . escape from the snare of the devil, after being captured by him to his will" (2 Tim. 2:25–26).

Marching as to War

This sort of talk provokes squeamishness, even in the most conservative and orthodox Christians among us. The first reason is because such talk of the demonic is viewed as strange, indeed insane, in our cultural context. The Scriptures, we know, present a picture of the universe as a war zone, with the present age a satanic empire being invaded by the rival kingdom of Jesus. Talk of such realities rise and fall in the history of the church, oscillating between preoccupation and embarrassment. The church around the world—especially in what sociologist Philip Jenkins calls the Global South—grasps the kind of demon-haunted universe presented in the

Scriptures. But many North American and Western European Christians wince at the "spiritual warfare" novels of the previous generation, with invisible angels and demons duking it out over small-town America.[31] We cringe at the latest television faith healer describing the demons that were persecuting him right around the time he was caught with the cocaine and the prostitutes.

Many liberal Protestant churches excised "Onward Christian Soldiers" and other such "martial" hymns years ago. They are not the only ones. When was the last time you heard an evangelical praise chorus speaking of the war against the satanic powers?

Despite all that, the softening of apocalyptic language hasn't led to a more "peaceful" church. Listen to Christian media or attend a "faith and values" rally, and you'll hear plenty of warfare speech. Unlike past "crusades," however, such language is directed primarily at people perceived to be cultural and political enemies. If we are too afraid of seeming inordinately Pentecostal to talk about the devil, we will find ourselves declaring war against mere concepts, like "evil" or "sin." When we don't oppose demons, we demonize opponents. And without a clear vision of the concrete forces we as the church are supposed to be aligned against, we find it very difficult to differentiate between enemy combatants and their hostages.

We also grow uncomfortable at that point. The Pauline spiritual language sounds as though we are suggesting that those who reject the gospel are "demon-possessed." Many use that sort of language to mean just that. "Devil" and "Satan" are essentially metaphors for their enemies. What's implied when a fiery speaker refers to an ideology or a religion as "of the devil" or "satanic" can easily fit this description. The assumption is that there is a "light versus darkness" contest, and that our side is on the Lord's side, the other side is on the devil's side.

That's not what Paul argues for here, nor does the rest of Scripture. As a matter of fact, the gospel tells us a very different story about ourselves and about those who oppose us.

The "capture" of which Paul speaks isn't possession, and it doesn't mean that unbelievers are any more evil or more irrational than anyone

---

31. Philip Jenkins, *The Next Christendom: The Coming of Global Christianity* (New York, NY: Oxford University Press, 2011).

else. Unbelievers are often kinder, gentler, more rational, and more intelligent than Christians. The work of the devil isn't typically a supernatural display of evil. The work of the devil typically is simply to distract us from the supernatural altogether, to keep us walking in the path in which we're already walking (Eph. 2:1–3), focused on what seems right to us (Prov. 14:12). That's why the gospel doesn't simply address the warning of "devilishness" to unbelievers.

James wrote to the churches, made up of believers, to watch out for a kind of "wisdom" that is "earthly, unspiritual, demonic" that is characterized by "jealousy and selfish ambition" (James 3:15–16), which can look awfully spiritual or at least like good leadership skills, with the right spin-doctoring. After Simon Peter confessed Jesus as Christ, through the power of the Spirit (Matt. 16:16–17), Jesus said to him, "Get behind me, Satan! You are a hindrance to me" (16:23). This does not mean that Peter was a plotting satanist fifth column within the disciples' ranks. What Peter said to provoke this eruption from Jesus seems perfectly reasonable. Peter was assuring Jesus that he would not face the awful fate Jesus was speaking of: arrest and crucifixion. Wouldn't any of us expect any of our friends to comfort us if we said, "You know, it's a nice night but I'm probably going to end up murdered and tossed into an unmarked grave." Peter here was just, well, normal. And that's the point. The hindrance Jesus identified was a "mind" set on "the things of man" rather than the "things of God" (16:23).

The devil is normal. The ways of the devil are not what witch-hunters suppose, some preternatural and recognizably dark power. The devil's power is to leave us where we are, under the sentence of accusation, hiding behind whatever we can find—ideology, philosophy, religion, morality, pleasure, success, or whatever—to keep us from paying attention to where we are going. The devil's way is the "course of this world" (Eph. 2:1–2). In this fallen world, the devil is normal; it's the gospel that's strange

Believers are no longer "captured" by the devil, meaning that his accusing power is defanged by the forgiveness of sins that comes through the gospel. And yet, we are consistently wrestling with our inner satanist, as we struggle to submit ourselves to the lordship of Christ, which still seems strange even to us. The line between light and darkness doesn't line up by party affiliation or by moral values, but right through every one of our hearts and souls.

The Scriptures command us to be gentle and kind to unbelievers, not because we are not at war, but because we're not at war *with them* (2 Tim. 2:26). When we see that we are warring against principalities and powers in the heavenly places, we can see that we're not wrestling against flesh and blood (Eph. 6:12). The path to peace isn't through bellicosity or surrender, but through fighting the right war (Rom. 16:20). We rage against the Reptile, not against his prey.

> The Scriptures command us to be gentle and kind to unbelievers, not because we are not at war, but because we're not at war *with them*.

We hear many calls, from across the religious and political spectrum, for civility. But civility is not enough. Civility is a neutral ground, a sort of mutual nonaggression pact, where we agree to respect one another and not to belittle one another. That's important, and a good start, but that's not enough. Just as we are not for "toleration" of those who religiously disagree with us but for "liberty," so we should not be for mere civility, but for, from our end, kindness. Civility is passive; kindness is active and strategic.

This sort of kindness is directly related to our Christianly bleak view of human nature. We know what was (and is) wrong with us, and that ought to keep us from a superficial view of the motives of those who oppose us. Fallen humanity responds to the light of Christ not just with cognitive rejection but with moral revulsion (John 3:19–20).

Ambassadors for the Kingdom

How is this broken? The apostle Paul said that his conversion was a model for the grace of God shown to others (1 Tim. 1:16). How did this convinced anti-Christian change his mind? Though he was an intellectual, trained at the feet of the scholar Gamaliel, he was not turned around by arguments. He was instead stopped in his tracks, where he heard a voice that spoke to him, person to person. In his encounter on the way to arrest the church in Syria, Saul/Paul experienced exactly what he would later explain as, in some sense, the experience of every convert. "For God, who said, 'Let light shine out of darkness,' has shone in our hearts to give the light of the knowledge of the glory of God in the face of Jesus Christ," he wrote (2 Cor. 4:6). How do we encounter this? It is through the "open statement of the truth," which addresses "everyone's conscience in the sight of God" (2 Cor. 4:2). People change their minds because they recognize a voice, the voice of Jesus of Nazareth, speaking "Come, follow me."

That's why we speak with kindness. We are ambassadors who are charged to deliver a message from the One who has sent us. We speak not only what he said, but also how he says it. That's because we are not only seeking transformation with "content," but with Christ himself. Authority resides in his voice, and when he speaks, things happen. Tone isn't a matter of public relations, but of accurate representation. One could read the 23rd Psalm accurately at a graveside service by screaming it with an arm extended in a Hitler Youth salute. All the words would be there, but the meaning would change dramatically from a word of comfort, as intended, to a word of threat and bedlam. In our message, people are to hear the Galilean accent of Jesus of Nazareth.

After all, Paul wrote that the goal for all of us is "repentance," the "come to their senses" (2 Tim. 2:25–26). How does this happen? The Bible tells us that "God's kindness is meant to lead you to repentance" (Rom. 2:4). God led Israel through the wilderness with "cords of kindness," as One who "bent down to them and fed them" (Hos. 11:4). Jesus taught that God shows kindness and patience, even in the rising of the sun and the coming of the rains, even on both the just and the unjust, and that we are to model such in our own witness (Matt. 5:43–47).

This kindness, though, is not the grinning, syrupy nonconfrontation we often see in some sectors of Christianity, especially the more therapeutic, market-driven forms. Paul did not mean "kindness" to mean an avoidance of controversy, because he immediately spoke of such kindness as "correcting his opponents with gentleness" (2 Tim. 2:25) through a teaching that doesn't back down. Jesus, after all, confronts those he encounters, repeatedly, with whatever it is that they are holding to as idols in the place of his lordship. This continues in his confrontation with Paul himself: "I am Jesus of Nazareth, whom you are persecuting" (Acts 22:8). Jesus, though, did not confront with the purpose of personal catharsis, and he certainly did not do so as a means of shoring up his "base" among like-minded religionists. In every case, Jesus confronted with the goal of creating a crisis—the sort of crisis that brings the person face-to-face with the call to repentance, to faith, to the possibility of a new creation.

I remember several years ago reading the account of a man who, while yet an unbeliever, started visiting the Sunday evening services at London's Westminster Chapel. This was after World War II, in the ascendancy there of the famed preacher D. Martyn Lloyd-Jones. The seeker said that he was in awe of the authority of the Word preached there. He said that Lloyd-Jones was "a steamroller" of biblical truth. But, he said, he was "a very gentle steamroller." At first, I laughed at what seemed to me to be a mixed metaphor. How can a steamroller, of all things, be "gentle"?

But the more I have thought about it, the more I realize that this is precisely what Jesus was, and is—a gentle steamroller. Because he is not in bondage to fear of man, Jesus rebukes and exposes that which is wrong. But, also because he is not in bondage to fear of man, Jesus seeks to save, not to condemn, and he is unafraid to be in conversation with those the rest of society would see as "immoral" or "not our kind of people." He wrecks lives, pulling us away from our chosen paths, and strapping on our backs a cross. At the same time, he doesn't break a bruised reed, doesn't snuff out a wavering wick. That is our calling too.

The Cost of Convictional Kindness

This sort of convictional kindness, though, is not merely a change in tone, and it does not mean a lessening of controversy, but a heightening of it. Sometimes church leaders will ask me to tell them how they can engage on controversial issues, usually related to the Sexual Revolution, without appearing mean or evil. I always respond that I can't do that. If they stand for biblical principles, and if they call people to repentance, they will indeed seem to be mean, and bigoted, and evil. Jesus told us to expect this. "A disciple is not above his teacher, nor a servant above his master," he said. "If they have called the master of the house Beelzebub, how much more will they malign those of his household" (Matt. 10:24–25). The issue is whether we actually *are* mean or evil. That's what we can control.

Moreover, a convictional kindness means a doubling of one's potential criticizers. Those who don't like the gospel call to repentance will resent the conviction, and those who don't like the gospel drive to mission will resent the kindness. When Jesus went to Zacchaeus the tax collector's house, he no doubt incurred the wrath of those who would argue that the morality of their embezzling and defrauding for the Roman government was none of his business. But he also caused the grumbling of those who said, "He has gone in to be the guest of a man who is a sinner" (Luke 19:7). They wondered what sort of "signal" Jesus was sending. Jesus seems placidly unperturbed by such things.

If you are not drawing fire from both Pharisees and Sadducees, you are probably saying something other than what Jesus said. And if your message is not drawing both tax collectors (Roman collaborators) and zealots (anti-Roman insurrectionists) to repentance, you are probably speaking with a different voice than does he. Jesus wasn't inconsistent. He saw the Roman Empire, despite all its pretensions to preeminence both in its own mind and in the mind of its opponents, as a temporary obstacle, not the defining point of his agenda. We stand and we speak, with reconciliation in view. We see, therefore, even our most passionate critic not as an argument to be vaporized but as a neighbor to be evangelized. This doesn't mean that we back down one iota from the truth. But we proclaim the whole gospel of truth and grace, never backing down from either. That means taking seriously the arguments of our opponents, not merely caricatures of those arguments.

> We see, therefore, even our most passionate critic not as an argument to be vaporized but as a neighbor to be evangelized.

Preaching, Not Preachiness

I once clicked off a television program I normally love because it just became too preachy to watch. The program drew me in with fresh and creative writing, along with a talented ensemble cast of likable characters. This particular episode, though, was about preventing sexually transmitted diseases. A cartoonish, stereotypical Religious Right activist insisting on abstinence education frustrated the task of educating persons about proper condom use. The story line enabled a series of coarse jokes, sprinkled with ongoing messages that abstinence doesn't work and hurts people, and that government officials need the courage to fight the ideologues and to do what is best for public health.

I, of course, am a conservative evangelical Christian who believes, with the entire historic Christian church of every wing, that chastity until marriage is God's design and is necessary for human flourishing. I also think many efforts at sex education—those built merely around disease and pregnancy prevention rather than human dignity—have hurt people and diminish civil society. But that's not why I turned off the television. I don't mind hearing other viewpoints, and I'm not afraid of them. I turned it off, not because I was outraged, but because I was bored. This program was presenting a viewpoint with the kind of smug assurance of rightness that simply caricatured, unfairly, the views I hold. My point is not that this was rude to me. The point is that they weren't talking to me at all. The story line wasn't intended to engage an alternative position, and to show why it fails to measure up. Instead, the program was meant to cause people who already held such views to nod their heads in affirmation at the morons who oppose good common sense, and to feel much better about their moral and intellectual superiority to the Neanderthals out there. Now, in this case, that's fine. There are more people who hold to the view articulated on this program than those who hold to my views, and the program wasn't trying to win an argument anyway. They were reveling in an argument already won.

I'm not worried about televised comedies. I didn't want a boycott or a campaign against them. I was provoked, though, to think about how often we, as the Body of Christ, do the same thing. We can caricature our detractors' positions in the grossest terms, in order to help reassure us that those who oppose us out there are particularly stupid of peculiarly wicked, and we can get "Amens" from our side. But that's preachiness, not preaching, and there's a difference.

Jesus' preaching took clear stands, with sharp edges. But Jesus never turned the sword of the Spirit into a security blanket for the already convinced. With the Samaritan woman at the well, for example, it would have been easy for Jesus simply to tell his disciples how Samaritans are sexually licentious because they reject the authority of the prophetic and wisdom books of the Bible. He could even have ridiculed her about her self-delusion about her many failed marriages, and her current cohabitation. He could have asked her how she was qualified to have theological debates about the right place of worship, or about the right amount of reverence for the dead patriarch Jacob, when she couldn't even interpret whether a man was a loser or not. Instead, though, he spoke to her, not about her. He uncovered how (even) she had to acknowledge the barrenness of the spiritual water she'd been lapping up.

Jesus, in continuity with the prophets before him and the apostles after him, didn't shy away from moral confrontation. But he refused to leave it at the kind of superficiality we all crave. The disciples weren't allowed to congratulate themselves for being free from adultery or murder, because Jesus in his preaching drove the law deeper and deeper into their consciences, exposing the roots of the kind of internal adultery and murder it is much harder to identify much less to wash away. The apostle Paul, likewise, demonstrated the moral degeneracy of the Gentile nations (Rom. 1:18–2:16), but he didn't allow the Jewish believers to step back and applaud him for his calling sin "sin." He asked whether they, too, were guilty of the same things they censured in their foes (Rom. 2:17–29). The point of this apostolic preaching wasn't to evoke smug grins from the audience, but to shut every mouth with the law and to drive every heart to the gospel (Rom. 3:9–31).

Many of the ideologies and practices and policies we must confront are indeed deadly. But we aren't preaching to those in bondage to such dangers if we simply repeat slogans. We must ask why such things are appealing, and why arguments for them can seem plausible. Our opponents, after all, are not cartoon super villains in a lair somewhere, conspiratorially plotting the downfall of the good and the true. They believe themselves to be following the right way. Only when we speak to their consciences can we get to where people are, as we all once were, hiding from God.

Reductive Darwinism, which rules out divine intervention in the universe, cannot adequately explain the mystery of the universe of humanity. But when we laugh and say, "My grandpa wasn't a chimpanzee," we are not taking seriously the claims of those who hold such views. In fact, we're not speaking to them at all, just to ourselves. When unbelievers hear a canned, caricatured picture of their views, they recognize what I recognized in that television show. They conclude that we don't wish to convince them or even to talk to them, simply to soothe the psychologies of our partisans. Preachy propaganda doesn't arrest the conscience. We, as ambassadors of Christ, are dealing with the aroma of life and the stench of death (2 Cor. 2:15–16). We must appeal to the depths of accused consciences that already know God, but shrink back from him in fear.

Convictional kindness means loving people enough to tell them the truth, and to tell ourselves the truth about them. Those who oppose us aren't (necessarily) stupid. They're not any more hell-deserving than we are, apart from our rescue by the grace of God in Christ. So we don't just talk about them; we talk to them. And we don't just talk to them; we plead with them. We seek to persuade. Preachiness never changed anybody's mind. Preaching, on the other hand, can change everything.

Grace, Not Enabling

The conviction in convictional kindness likewise recognizes the different modes of discourse used for sin on the "outside" and sin on the "inside" of the community of God. Paul seems to be inconsistent in his letter to Timothy, writing about kindness and gentleness and then immediately pivoting to warn about those who are "lovers of self, lovers of money, proud, arrogant, abusive, disobedient to their parents, ungrateful, unholy, heartless, unappeasable, slanderous, without self-control, brutal, not loving good, treacherous, reckless, swollen with conceit, lovers of pleasure rather than lovers of God" (2 Tim. 3:2–4). This is not a contradiction. First of all, remember that kindness is not "niceness." Kindness does not avoid conflict; kindness engages conflict, but with a goal of reconciliation. But, moreover, those against whom Paul wrote with such fury are those who have the "appearance of godliness" while "denying its power" (2 Tim. 3:5). They are those who "creep into households," exploiting vulnerable women all the while purporting to represent Christ and the gospel (2 Tim. 3:6).

> **Kindness does not avoid conflict; kindness engages conflict, but with a goal of reconciliation.**

The Bible everywhere warns us about the reality of spiritual imposters. Sometimes these "wolves" are there to introduce, subtly, false doctrine that undermines the gospel. Paul's letter to the Galatians is a strong antidote to such false teaching. But often these spiritual carnivores seem to hold to true doctrine, but they use this doctrine and service for predatory ends. The sons of Eli, for example, used their priestly calling to co-opt the fat of the offering and to have sex with women at the altar (1 Sam. 2:12–17, 22). Virtually every New Testament letter warns us about the same phenomenon. There is something about the church that draws those who wish to deceive and to harm.

Deception, after all, can look a lot like discipleship. A disciple is like a son learning from his father; the student resembles his teacher, Jesus tells us. That's good and right. But darkness can turn all good things toward evil. A spiritual imposter can mimic such discipleship when he's, in fact, just "casing the joint," watching the mores, learning the phrases, mimicking the convictions. It can seem like the passing down of the faith when, in reality, it's a vampiric taking on of another identity, all for the sake of some appetite or other.

Moreover, many of these impostors are looking for something they cannot find in bars and strip clubs. Many of them "feed" off of innocence itself. That's why Paul warned against those who take captive "weak women, burdened with sins" (2 Tim. 3:6). They gain power over the weak not only by deceiving them with plausible-seeming teaching but also by morally compromising them. The impostor mimics spiritual authority, sometimes with a precision almost to the point of identity theft, but uses it to destroy rather than to build up.

Impostors can find a welcome home within the church because of a perversion of the Christian doctrine of grace. The gospel offers a complete forgiveness of sin, and not only that, a fresh start as a new creation. But both Jesus and the apostles warn us this can easily be twisted into a kind of license. Faith is not real without repentance, and faith is not like that of the demons, simply assenting to true claims. Faith works itself out in love. Faith takes up a cross and follows Christ. A notion of "grace" apart from lordship can provide cover for all sorts of wickedness. The immoral leader always compares himself to King David, and those who seek to hold such leadership accountable are presented as unmercifully unwilling to help the one who is "struggling." Ignoring such evil in our ranks is not kindness, and it is not mercy. We lose the merciful ministry of Christ if we do not tend the flock of God, which includes fighting off doctrinal or moral predators hiding behind the veneer of spiritual authority. This is entirely consistent with the approach of Jesus himself. Jesus is harsh with those who claim God's authority and use it to twist revelation and to condemn. But he is gentle to those who are "sheep without a shepherd." Too often, we do the exact reverse.

Confidence, Not Hand-Wringing

One final, indispensable, aspect of our call to kindness in our engagement is that of confidence. Paul warned about the awful deceivers of these "last days," but he did so without hand-wringing or resignation. As I was writing this, I was simultaneously watching a number of discouraging fissures within churches and ministries. Some of them involved leaders falling. Some involved petty disputes between Christians that resemble Hollywood actors in grudge-matches over whose dressing room is bigger. I told a friend that this made me all the more in awe of the ministry of Paul. After all, we have two thousand years of history behind us. He was battling external threats of arrest, and internal wrestling in the churches with heresy and immorality. And all he had to go on was a career wrecked by a light and a voice. Paul said that the false teachers were the equivalent of Jannes and Jambres, the Egyptian magicians who mimicked Moses' and Aaron's signs from God with their own occultist power (Exod. 7:11–12). God's servants authenticated their sending from God by transforming a staff into a writhing, living serpent. But Pharaoh's court magicians turned back their argument by doing the same thing. Exodus tells us simply, "But Aaron's staff swallowed up their staffs" (Exod. 7:12). That's the point. Paul concluded a section of horrifying pessimism with the words, "But they will not get very far" (2 Tim. 3:9). This is crucial.

"This country is spiritually in decline," or "If God doesn't judge this country, he will have to apologize to Sodom and Gomorrah." Writer Marilynne Robinson notes that those who speak in such a way rarely include themselves, or their circles of friends, in this assessment. It becomes another form of "us" versus "them" demarcation. Moreover, it feeds into a sort of apocalypticism that feels invigorating, like, she says, a panic attack—with a jolt of adrenaline to fire up the passions. Behind that, Robinson speculates, is a deep prejudice against Christianity, by the very Christians who are lamenting the mess we're in. We assume, she writes, that Europe is the wave of the future, and that the gospel cannot withstand such cultural and intellectual sophistication.[32] She's right. Pessimism is for losers.

32. Marilynne Robinson, *When I Was a Child I Read Books* (New York, NY: Farrar, Straus and Giroux, 2012), 30, 134–36.

The opponents of the gospel often picture the onward advance of secularization and of moral "freedom" as the inevitable march of historical progress. Christian orthodoxy is on the "wrong side of history." They believe this, but, too often, so do we. The culture around us knows what it means when they see a church in perpetual outrage and bluster. They know that we are scared. How different this is from the mind-set of Jesus himself.

The kindness of Jesus toward sinners is not that startling—at least on the surface. We know, after all, that Jesus was on a redemptive mission, even when it's hard to see how we fit into that mission. But what is remarkable to me is Jesus' kindness, at least on one occasion, to the devils themselves. When Jesus encountered the man of the graves, filled with unclean spirits, the Bible tells us the demons "begged him not to command them to depart into the abyss" (Luke 8:31). The Scripture says that these spirits begged to be sent into a herd of pigs. My response would have been one of fear, I'm quite sure. These are, after all, terrifyingly dark beings, normally shielded from our perception. Jesus doesn't panic. He exhibits as he does in all sorts of terrifying situations a calm tranquility. The Bible says, simply, "So he gave them permission" (Luke 8:32). Why? Jesus obviously was not seeking to redeem these spirits; the Bible says they are unredeemable, not even included in the atonement of Christ (Heb. 2:16). Jesus responded this way because he was not afraid. He was confident in his Father's mission for him, and thus was free from the need, rooted in insecurity, to constantly prove himself.

If all we have to go on is what we see around us, then, of course, we will become scared and outraged, and our public witness will turn into an ongoing temper tantrum, designed just to prove to our opponents, and to ourselves, that we are still here. And in so doing we would employ the rhetorical tricks of other insecure movements: sarcasm, vitriol, ridicule. But we are not the voice of the past, of the Bible Belt to a post-Christian culture of how good things used to be. We are the voice of the future, of the coming kingdom of God. The message of the kingdom isn't "You kids, get off our lawn." The message of the kingdom is, "Make way for the coming of the Lord."

A gloomy view of culture leads to meanness. If we believe we are on the losing side of history, we slide into the rage of those who know their time is short. We have no reason to be fearful or sullen or mean. We're not

> The message of the kingdom isn't "You kids, get off our lawn." The message of the kingdom is, "Make way for the coming of the Lord."

the losers of history. We are not slouching toward Gomorrah; we are marching to Zion. The worst thing that can possibly happen to us has already happened: we're dead. We were crucified at Skull Place, under the wrath of God. And the best thing that could happen to us has already happened; we're alive, in Christ, and our future is seated at the right hand of God, and he's feeling just fine. Jesus is marching onward, with us or without us, and if the gates of hell cannot hold him back, why on earth would he be panicked by Hollywood or Capitol Hill? Times may grow dark indeed, but times have always been dark, since the insurrection of Eden. Nonetheless, the light shines in the darkness and the darkness has not, the darkness will not, the darkness cannot overcome it. The arc of history is long, but it bends toward Jesus.

Conclusion

We speak with kindness and gentleness and with conviction and with clarity because we are targeting the right enemy. Anger is sometimes right. God in his holiness displays wrath. But God's anger is slow to kindle, rooted in the patience of the One who is "not wishing that any should perish but that all should reach repentance" (2 Pet. 3:9). God's anger is not a means of catharsis, and it certainly isn't the theatrical display of a temper out of control. That's why the Bible warns us that "the anger of man does not produce the righteousness of God" (James 1:20).

We overcome, not because we're a moral majority or a righteous remnant, but because we're blood-covered sinners who know that if the gospel can change us, it can change anyone. We speak with kindness and persuasion not because we're weak but because the gospel is strong. We speak the truth, with conviction and with gentleness, as those who have nothing to prove.

The gospel commands us to speak, and that speech is often forceful. But a prophetic witness in the new covenant era never stops with "You brood of vipers!" It always continues on to say, "Behold the Lamb of God who takes away the sins of the world." We make arguments, even as we understand that arguments are merely the equivalent of brush-clearing, to get to the main point: a personal connection with the voice that rings down through the ages from Nazareth. We want not simply to convey truth claims, but to do so with the northern Galilean accent that makes demons squeal and chains fall. Kindness isn't surrender. Gentleness isn't passivity. Kindness and gentleness, when rooted in gospel conviction, that's war.

Chapter Ten

A GOSPEL COUNTER-REVOLUTION

The next Billy Graham might be drunk right now. That's a sentence I remind myself of almost every day, every time I feel myself growing discouraged about the future. It all goes back to a conversation I had years ago with an elderly theologian. This was a conversation in which, even though I was in my mid-twenties and he in his mid-eighties, I was the curmudgeon. Carl F. H. Henry, then nearing the end of his life, was on the campus of the seminary where I was working on my doctoral degree. It turned out to be the last time I ever saw him. And that one conversation changed my life.

Several of us were lamenting the miserable shape of the church, and about the downward slide of the culture. We were giving example after example of doctrinal vacuity, vapid preaching, nonexistent discipleship, clergy scandals, and on and on. Henry seemed not the least bit unnerved by it all. Then he cleared his throat and offered up the rebuke I needed. It was right after I had asked, rhetorically, whether there was any hope for the future of Christian witness in the public square.

"Why, you speak as though Christianity were genetic," the old theologian said. "Of course, there is hope for the next generation of the church. But the leaders of the next generation might not be coming from the current Christian subculture. They are probably still pagans."

"Who knew that Saul of Tarsus was to be the great apostle to the Gentiles?" he asked. "Who knew that God would raise up a C. S. Lewis, once an agnostic professor, or a Charles Colson, once Richard Nixon's hatchet man, to lead the twentieth-century church? They were unbelievers who, once saved by the grace of God, were mighty warriors of the faith."

Of course, he knew what he was talking about, because the same principle applied to Henry himself. Who knew that God would raise up a nonreligious newspaperman from a nominally Lutheran family, save him, and then equip him to defend the truthfulness of the Scriptures and the necessity of Christian social witness for generations of evangelical Christians? But that's precisely what happened. And I was too ignorant to see it because, he was right, I implicitly assumed that somehow the Christian gospel was just a matter of genetic passing along of the faith. This is something we must remember as we seek to cultivate a renewed Christian moral witness for the next generation.

Generationally Connected

In Matthew 21:28–32, Jesus told us a story—one of the parables that illuminate the meaning of the kingdom. Unlike some others, the Prodigal Son, for example, or the sower and the soils, this parable is not reflected on nearly enough. The chief priests had challenged Jesus on where he had obtained his authority. And that was a fair enough question. They, after all, had trained in the Scriptures and were set apart by the structures of the people of God. Jesus, on the other hand, seemed to be a self-ordained Rabbi, wandering about saying explosively provocative things. The implied question is, "Who do you think you are?" Keeping with his usual practice, our Lord turned the questions back around on them. He asked them about John the Baptist, whether his baptism was from God or from human imagination. In this, Jesus demonstrated, again, his wisdom in knowing human nature, including the nature of political machination. He knew if they said "from God," they would immediately be asked why they didn't then submit to John's teaching. And if they said his baptism wasn't from God, they would lose a segment of their base, those who accepted John as a genuine prophet. So they dodged the question altogether. Jesus then told a story of two sons.

A father asked his two sons to work in the vineyard. This was, like the prodigal son story, a tale of inheritance. The vineyard, after all, was not merely the father's property. It was, rather, the family's property. He had probably received it from his father. He would work the ground, tend the vines, and then turn it over to the next generation who would do the same. The father asked the first son to work and the son said no, but then, changes direction, and agreed to do so. The second son immediately agreed to go, but then later turned and said, "I will not." Which of these sons, Jesus asked, is faithful to the will of his father? The answer to that question is essential if we are to reframe our witness.

Thinking about that second son is difficult, for a family, for a church, for a movement. After all, we have all seen this exact trajectory—someone or some group who start off faithful and obedient and then turn and walk away. And there's a great deal of fear among American Christians, as they face the headwinds of a secularizing (and sexualizing) American culture, that this is where the church is headed. Some of them are, and that's true in every generation. No one is exempt from the possibility of prodigal children. But Jesus' point was even more intrusive than that. Persistence itself, he revealed, is no sign of fidelity, if that persistence doesn't persist in obedience. The church is fearful the cultural shifts around us will lead to a falling away of the next generation: from the church, from the ethical truths of Scripture, from the gospel itself. Every generation fears that. Jesus tells us, though, that there's something far more dangerous to fear: those who walk away from the gospel but don't know it. Jesus identified the religious establishment of the nation of Israel as persistent in observance and in structure. But they had so lost their way that they couldn't recognize the kingdom of God, standing before them in flesh and bone. That's our warning too.

The same elderly theologian I mentioned before, around the same time as the conversation I referenced, also memorably attended with a friend of mine the Sunday service of a booming evangelical megachurch. After the service, my friend asked him, "Sir, what did you think?" The theologian sat for a moment, silently, and said, "I think that service represents the success of the American evangelical movement." My friend smiled, knowing how this man had himself been one of the founding fathers of that movement, creating institution after institution after World War II, reshaping the American religious landscape. But then the old man said, "We were so successful with our youth rallies that our teenagers grew up and want to repeat them, and call them worship." For him, I should add, this was not a good thing.

This elderly man knew that the very things that helped this Christian movement flourish—entrepreneurialism and freedom from long-standing institutions—could easily, when unmoored from doctrinal orthodoxy and church rootedness, become the undoing of the movement. The size of the crowds, the amounts of the budgets, the influence of the voting blocs—none of these things signal success. All of that can be initiated, and can be maintained, without the presence of the Spirit, without the power of the gospel. Success means a gospel-anchored engagement that is transmitted from one generation to the next.

As I mentioned earlier in this book, a newer generation of evangelical Christians are often suspicious of the sort of engagement that characterized their parents' and grandparents' generations. In many ways, this is short-sighted. Many assume that somehow by disengaging, they will be better able to carry out the mission of the church, without recognizing that they have already surrendered part of their mission, and that total cultural disengagement doesn't end culture wars but rather provokes them. But, with that, there's a recognition of something true and right: that previous generations have sometimes engaged morality without gospel, argument without invitation. As with so many other aspects of ministry and mission, the question is whether we will have a generationally connected church or a church at war with itself.

> Many assume that somehow by disengaging, they will be better able to carry out the mission of the church, without recognizing that they have already surrendered part of their mission, and that total cultural disengagement doesn't end culture wars but rather provokes them.

The warhorses of the past (not all of them, but some) can be tempted to resent and to seek to block newer generations, with different emphases and different strategies. Some of that has to do with theological and ideological differences, slight as they may be. But much of it has to do simply with egos that refuse to be crucified. I can count on one, maybe two, hands the number of megachurches who have had pastoral transitions from one generation to another, without some sort of private or public trench warfare in the pews. The same dynamic is at work in institutions of public engagement. For some, let's be honest, there's a Culture War Industrial Complex to protect. Those who do things in a different way are seen as competitors to be snuffed out. For others, there's a sense of personal pique. Those who do things differently are somehow a repudiation, personally, of them and their own efforts and labors. This is a temptation for the older generation now, and will be for the younger generations later. James warned us of this: "For where jealousy and selfish ambition exist, there will be disorder and every vile practice. But the wisdom from above is first pure, then peaceable, gentle, open to reason, full or mercy and good fruits, impartial and sincere" (James 3:16–17).

The truth is, many in the younger generation, though doing things differently than their forebears in many ways, are awakening to the need for a robust Christian witness in the social arenas. To kindle this, we need an older generation able to take "yes" for an answer, and to cultivate rather than to combat.

In 1964, the Republican Party signed up a leader to argue its principles around the country. Many were suspicious of this new leader, and understandably so, because he was, until very recently, not a Republican but a Democrat. He had campaigned for and raised money for Democratic candidates over Republican ones. He was even a labor union activist, advocating for the New Deal and for collective bargaining. The Republicans could have punished this leader for supporting Roosevelt over Landon and Truman over Dewey. They could have punished him for sounding different from the typical Republican brand of the time—with his futuristic optimism and youth-oriented style. They could have punished him by not allowing him to carry their banner, choosing instead someone who had "paid his dues." But, shrewdly, the Party understood that this wouldn't punish Ronald Reagan but the Party. Reagan resonated with the principles of the Party, and he knew how to speak to people who, like himself, didn't think of themselves as Republicans because they were connected with the legacy of Roosevelt and Truman and Kennedy. The Christian church is not a political party, and we're not defined by a partisan program. So it's a very imperfect analogy. But a similar situation is at work. We can expect uniformity across the generations, or we can expect God to address a changed cultural landscape in a different way, anchored to the same revelation.

The older generations in the church, in every era, must decide if they will respond to their successors as Saul to David or as Paul did with Timothy. In David, Saul saw his own mortality, and seethed with jealousy and envy, ending in the throwing of the spear. Instead, he should have seen God's goodness, in keeping his promises to Abraham. Paul, on the other hand, spent his final moments shepherding and mentoring his successors: Timothy and Titus and others. Every generation has a choice: to go out like Saul or to go out like Paul.

Once I was speaking at a conference in Minneapolis, and had with me a young seminary student. The conference organizers knew that I like bluegrass music so they surprised me, right before I preached, with a rousing rendition of "Brethren, We Have Met to Worship," complete with a mandolin and a fiddle (not a violin, a fiddle). I loved it, both because I liked the way they did it, and because the old hymn brought back memories of singing it as a boy in my home church. The student with me though grew up in a very different context, led to Christ as an adult by a very contemporary campus ministry. After the service, he exclaimed how "awesome" that "new song" was the band had played.

Many assume that newer generations are hell-bent on throwing out all the old patterns and structures in order to start all over again with the new. That's just not true. Young musicians are writing not only new hymns and songs, but they are also reworking for a new day some really old songs, some so old that they would prompt tears of recognition from those who remember them and some that wouldn't even be recognized by a senior-adult Sunday school class because they're older than they are. Just in recent days, I heard one of the youngest, most innovative bands in the country belting out a version of "Trust and Obey." No one in their audience would have known that that's a gospel song beloved by older generations. They didn't sing it because it's in the hymnal. They don't even know what a hymnal is. But when they hear it, the song resonates authentically with what they've found to be true in the gospel. I think there's a parable there for our social witness. But that requires a mentoring of the next generation, as well as a learning of what they see that previous generations missed. That means connecting ethics to the gospel, to the kingdom, to the mission. Persistence itself is no sign of fidelity.

But then there's that first son of Jesus' story. The first son said he would not go, he would not work. This sort of arrogant indolence would have provoked anger in the father, and indeed in anyone in the ancient Near Eastern context who heard this tale. The temptation would be to give up on this son, to move on to the next. But Jesus said that the son then changed his mind, and decided to work the vineyard. Is he not, Jesus asked, the more faithful son?

Not "Yet"

As a child, I remember seeing a man sitting in front of me, with his arm resting on the pew. The arm was covered with a large tattoo of a woman who was, well, let's just say she didn't fit what we would consider biblical standards of modesty in her attire. This was not in a "relevant" urban church, mind you, but in the most stereotypically "hellfire and brimstone," King James-quoting, gospel hymn-singing Southern revivalist church you could imagine. I couldn't believe I was seeing this, in my church. I was simultaneously thrilled (when else does one get to see naked women in church?) and outraged (how dare anyone do that in my church?). So I nudged my grandmother and pointed, as if to say, "Can you believe this?"

My grandmother leaned down and whispered. I expected her to share my outrage (though not my secret titillation). She was, after all, a pastor's widow with strict moral standards who had once washed my mouth out with soap because I had said "Gosh," which was, of course, to her just a rebranded way to take the Lord's name in vain. But that side of her didn't show up in that moment. She whispered, "Yes, honey, he doesn't know the Lord yet, and he's had a hard life, with drink and drugs and all. But his wife had been trying to get him to come to church for a long time, and we've all been praying for him. He's not trying to be ugly to anybody. He just doesn't know Jesus yet."

I'll never forget that word "yet." With that one word she turned my imagination on its head. She put before me the possibility that this hardened ex-military man with the naked woman tattoo might one day be my brother-in-Christ. And, in time, he was. I suppose as time went on this new Christian started to see that his tattoo was potentially a stumbling block to others, because I started to see it less and less as he started to wear long sleeves to church. Some of the other kids in the church said (since tattoo removal technology wasn't much of a thing then) that he had added a bikini to her, and then later a one-piece bathing suit. For all I know, he may have died with her in a plaid pantsuit and a briefcase. I guess this man started to see that tattoo as emblematic of an old life he'd left behind. He didn't need a tattooed pastor (and in that church, he never had one). But he did need a church that didn't see his tattoo as evidence of a life gone too far, of someone too rowdy to be loved with the call to repentance and faith.

I don't like tattoos, and I can't emphasize this enough (especially if you're one of my children, one day, reading this). But if the Spirit starts moving with velocity in this country, our churches will see more people in our pews and in our pulpits with tattoos, and that ought to change our public witness. Now, what I do not mean by this is that we need more Christians to tattoo crosses or the Apostles' Creed or the sinner's prayer across their arms and necks. That's not a sign of gospel awakening. It's just, at best, personal fashion, and, at worst, more marketing in an already over-marketed American Christian subculture.

Tattoos don't mean what they used to. In previous generations tattoos carried with them a clear kind of "tough" image. Granted, there are still some rough images out there—markings of blood-drenched skulls, or of profane sexual boasts or threats to violence, some even pagan or occult. And as I see them in the streets around me, I am chastened by how rarely my first thoughts are rooted in my grandmother's wisdom. Not everyone with tattoos is an unbeliever or has lived a hard life.

But I wonder how many people don't listen to our gospel message because they assume they don't "look" like the kind of people who would be Christians—namely shiny, happy Republicans. And, shamefully, how many times do we filter out our gospel preaching and our social witness to people who would, upon baptism, be able to pose nicely for our ministry advertisements? How often do we assume the good news of Christ is a message just like a political campaign or a commercial brand, targeted toward a demographic of a certain kind of buyer?

That was precisely Jesus' point in his story of the two sons. He turned to the religious establishment and said, shockingly, "Truly, I say to you, the tax collectors and the prostitutes go into the kingdom of God before you" (Matt. 21:31). That was Jesus' point from his sermon in his hometown synagogue in Nazareth, throughout his public ministry, and right to his dying moments, pardoning a repentant terrorist. Jesus was building his church with those who seemed to have wrecked their lives forever: prostitutes, Roman collaborators, outcasts with infectious diseases, demon-possessed grave-dwellers, and on and on. If we're really carrying forward his message, this means there are going to be people listening whose very bodies may carry messages contradictory of the Word of God. So did our hearts and psyches. The young woman with the "Legal Abortion Without Apology" tattoo or the old man with the Hell's Angel marking, they may wonder, as they feel the pull of the gospel, "How can I enter with this visible reminder on me of my past?" That's not a new question. That's the question we all had to ask, regardless of how "respectable" we looked when we came to Christ: "Deep is the stain that we cannot hide. What can avail to wash it away?"

Sharing the Mission

Jesus will build his church, with us or without us. But if we are going to be faithful to him, we must share his mission. This means we don't just talk about lost people; we talk to them. And we don't talk to them as enlightened life-coaches promising an improved future, but as crucified sinners offering a new birth. The hope for the future is not that Christianity will be seen as more respectable or more influential in the sectors of American power. The hope for the future is churches filled with people who never thought they fit the image of "Christian." We'll see that the markings on the flesh, whatever they are, count for nothing, but that what counts is a new creation (Gal. 6:15). We've come not to call just those who look like whatever Christians are supposed to look like, but the whole world. If the church is powered by the gospel, then the Body of Christ has tattoos.

That reality ought to crucify our dour, gloomy, curmudgeonly pessimism. Our fretfulness is evidence of defeatism, a sign of wavering belief in the promises of Jesus himself. That's what the elderly theologian taught me, as I stood there and wrung my hands over the pragmatism, the hucksterism, the liberalizing tendencies I saw in the Christianity around me, and wondered, "Does gospel Christianity have a future in this country at all?" He looked at me as though I were crazy. Of course gospel Christianity had, and has, a future. But the gospel Christians who will lead it may well still be pagans. He was right. Christianity is not like politics, rife with the dynasties of ruling families. God builds his church a different way.

The next Jonathan Edwards might be the man driving in front of you with the Darwin Fish bumper decal. The next Charles Wesley might be a misogynistic, profanity-spewing hip-hop artist right now. The next Charles Spurgeon might be managing an abortion clinic right now. The next Mother Teresa might be a heroin-addicted porn star right now. The next Augustine of Hippo might be a sexually promiscuous cult member right now, just like, come to think of it, the first Augustine of Hippo was.

But the Spirit of God can turn all that around, and seems to delight to do so. The new birth doesn't just transform lives, creating repentance and faith; it also provides new leadership to the church, and fulfills Jesus' promise to gift his church with everything needed for her onward march through space and time (Eph. 4:8–16). After all, while Phillip was leading the Ethiopian eunuch to Christ, Saul of Tarsus was still a murderer. And that happens over and over again, as God raises up leaders who seem to come out of nowhere, with shady pasts and uncertain futures. And none of us would be here, apart from them.

> The new birth doesn't just transform lives, creating repentance and faith; it also provides new leadership to the church, and fulfills Jesus' promise to gift his church with everything needed for her onward march through space and time (Eph. 4:8–16).

Most of the church, in any generation, comes along through the slow, patient discipleship of the next generation. But, just to keep us from thinking Christianity is evolutionary and "natural," Jesus shocks his church with leadership that seems to come, like a Big Bang, out of nowhere. Whenever we are tempted to despair about the shape of American Christianity, we should remember that Jesus never promised the triumph of the American church. He promised the triumph of *the church*. Most of the church, in heaven and on earth, isn't American. Maybe the hope of the American church is right now in Nigeria or Laos or Indonesia or Argentina. Jesus will be King, and his church will flourish. And he'll do it in the way he chooses, by exalting the humble and humbling the exalted, and by transforming cowards and thieves and murderers into the cornerstone of his New City. That atheist on the highway in front of you, the one who just shot you an obscene gesture, he just might be the one who evangelizes your grandchildren.

Our public witness ought never to back down in confronting injustice, especially when so much is at stake: the lives of unborn children, the freedom of the conscience, the structure of the family. But we ought to always recognize that those we are arguing with, including sometimes the most vitriolic of our opponents, just may be our future brother and sister in Christ. This doesn't mute our argumentation, but it sees that these are not just arguments but persons. And this recognition means that we open ourselves to those Nicodemus-like conversations that often happen under cover of darkness when those who disagree with us are haunted by the pangs of conscience or by the fear of death. We must fight for culture, yes, but we should never be such culture warriors that we cannot be evangelists first. That's not just for the sake of the lost; that's for our sake too.

An Almost-Gospel Won't Do

We must equip a new generation for different days. They must know how to fight for doctrinal orthodoxy and for public justice. An almost-gospel won't do;, a cut-rate righteousness won't either. This advocacy is an act of love, equipping the church to push back the arguments behind which guilty consciences hide, in order that they may hear the voice we once heard, the voice that calls, "Adam, where are you?"

> **An almost-gospel won't do; a cut-rate righteousness won't either.**

Yes, we face difficult times, every generation of the church does. But we also face unprecedented opportunities, as cultural Christianity falls all around us. Many of our neighbors around us will be burned over by the unkept, and unkeepable, promises of the sexual revolution and of Faustian individualism. Short term, these things will ravage communities and families and churches. But long-term, they will leave people wanting. And so we need to be ready for those who—like the woman at the well in Samaria—need to hear of living water that can alone satisfy. We must labor to preserve something ancient, something ever new, not just for us, and not just for our children, but for our future brothers and sisters in Christ, many of whom hate us right now. Many of them may one day lead us by the power of the Spirit that calls to life that which was dead. In that, we are no different from any other era.

God's promise to Abraham came to us, in the first place, through a child named "Isaac." He, of course, was the son of promise, given to the old and childless Abraham. The name came about because Sarah, the mother of all those who live by faith, was incredulous when God promised blessing (Gen. 18:10–14). She laughed, and thus the child was named "Isaac," for "laughter." But, as in Jesus' story, Abraham had two sons. The other was Ishmael, delivered when Abraham sought to accomplish God's work on his own, by taking in a concubine to impregnate. Ishmael is a son of exile, the son of the "will of the flesh." And yet, even though Isaac represents God's grace and God's freedom, his story is tragic too.

In order for Abraham to receive God's blessing, he had to lay on the altar every hope that he could see of being blessed—including God's promise of this son. He offered up Isaac, believing the Scripture tells us that God's promise is stronger even than death. God didn't allow that sacrifice to go forward, as we know. But Isaac ultimately died, and so did all of his children. And in the biblical story, erased also was the very Land of Promise itself. The people of God were left without patriarchs, without kings, and without even the security of home.

The Bible Belt was no Promised Land. "Christian America" was no nation of Israel. And yet, many of us too are nervous about the future, about losing the security of a culture hospitable to Christian ethics, and to Christianity itself. We wonder what more will be erased and forgotten. But that's kind of the point. Our faith isn't "safe" because of a lack of threat. It isn't "safe" because of some illusion of permanence. Isaac is offered up, and, eventually, Isaac died. But God is not, Jesus told us, the God of the dead but of the living. And he identifies himself, even now, as the God of Abraham, of Isaac, and of Jacob (Mark 12:26–27). All of our security, all of our sense of "at-homeness" in the culture and in this cosmos, will eventually be submerged beneath the fire of God's righteous judgment. But, out of that, springs a new creation that started in a promise God made thousands of years ago to a Middle Eastern wanderer, when he was still a pagan, without a people, without a hope, without God in the world.

Conclusion

Many who are now standing will fall away, unable to bear the scandal that comes with following Christ in a culture that sees such as superstition or hatred. Some who started out well will change their minds. And, at the same time, many who we now see as enemies will see their own lives in the cross of Christ. To them, we say, with our Lord, "When you have turned again, strengthen your brothers" (Luke 22:32). We will face struggle and loss and disappointment and the dust of death itself. But there's a promise out there that took on flesh in a virgin's uterus somewhere in Nazareth. If we could see the kind of inheritance, the kind of restoration of home, that he has waiting for us, well, we'd probably laugh in wonder at it all. It may be that America is not "post-Christian" at all. It may be that America is instead pre-Christian, a land that though often Christ-haunted has never known the power of the gospel, yet.

In the meantime, we stand and we speak, and we pray that through our witness we see not only a more just, more righteous public order but that we also see the church filled with those who were prostitutes, with those who were tax collectors, with those who were without hope and without God in the world. God will raise up leaders, as he always does, but we probably can't see them yet. They just might be drunk right now.

CONCLUSION

Next to me on my desk, as I write this, is a shard of glass, small, jagged, rugged. If you were to see it, your first instinct might be to sweep it up and toss it into the trash. But it's been with me for most of my life now, and it means almost everything to me. I picked it up off the pavement outside my home church, back in Biloxi, Mississippi. A group of us kids were playing ball in front of the church before a Sunday evening service. Somebody threw a ball too close to the building. It hit the window, and the glass rained down all around us. Something in me moved me to kneel down and pick up this remnant, and it's been with me through every stage of my life, and every once in a while I'll pull it out of a drawer and hold it in my hand, in order to remind myself of the past, and to point myself to the future.

Seeing the window at the front of that church shatter disoriented me. And not just because I was afraid that we were going to be called into a swarm of angry deacons. It was also that this sanctuary seemed to me to be the most permanent thing I could imagine—a doorway to the transcendent. Every summer I would march, with the other children, through those same front doors for the opening ceremonies of Vacation Bible School. It was the closest thing we low-church Baptists had to a liturgy or a calendar of the Christian year. And the gravity, at least for us, was akin to a presidential inauguration, except with stale cookies and watery punch afterward. At the front of the line would stand one of us, chosen to carry the American flag. Close behind him, would stand another, carrying the

Christian flag. We would march in to the sanctuary as the piano and organ streamed the majestic march, "Onward, Christian Soldiers."

The flag-bearers would plant their flags on either side of the pulpit, and we would stand, waiting to be led in the pledges to them. But that little Mississippi congregation pictured something to me, even without words, something that has lingered to this moment. Hanging over the American flag, hanging over the Christian flag, hanging over all of us, up there above the baptistery, was a cross. That pinewood cross pictured an ancient truth that no government, no emperor, no court, no army, no church could stand above or beside, the kingship of the crucified and resurrected Jesus of Nazareth.

That cross stood over us, all the time, and I saw it and heard it reflected, imperfectly to be sure, in the lives of those people. Even now, I tend to mentally translate any Bible passage into the King James Version because that's what they taught me—not out of some sort of theological claim to KJV superiority but because, honestly, I don't think we knew there were any other translations out there. They taught me to sing with them, "Rescue the Perishing, Care for the Dying," and "There Is a Fountain, Filled with Blood." Subjects and verbs didn't always agree, and sometimes Sunday school lessons were delivered through a mouthful of Levi Garrett chewing tobacco. But behind all those south Mississippi accents, I heard a northern Galilean accent, saying what he has said in countless dialects for 2,000 years now, "Come, follow me." That shard of glass reminds me of who I am, and that whatever that is, it's because of who they were.

As I write this, I sit a block from the United States Capitol in a city gleaming with marble, signifying the greatest political and military power the world has ever known. It all seems so permanent. The shard of glass in my hand reminds me that nothing this side of the New Jerusalem is as unshakable as we think. One day, perhaps in a thousand or in 5,000 years, the shining Capitol building over there may stand in ruins. The Washington Monument may be the equivalent of the pyramids now, a symbol of a once-great civilization. The Jefferson Memorial may be covered over in vines, picked through by antiquities dealers. I don't know, but I know this: the kingdom of God will stand.

The days ahead will probably be quite different than those faced by our parents and grandparents. We will be forced to articulate things we once could assume. That is nothing to wring our hands over. That is no call to retreat or to surrender, and it's also no call to keep doing it the way we've been doing it, except at a louder volume. We may be seen as strange in American culture. If so, onward Christian strangers. Our message will be seen as increasingly freakish to American culture. Let's embrace the freakishness, knowing that such freakishness is the power of God unto salvation.

In the public square, orthodox, evangelical Christianity has articulated a vision of human dignity, of religious liberty, of family stability, sometimes heroically, though never consistently enough. In that, these Christians sought to remind the church that we are to be the sort of people who recognize justice and righteousness. We should continue the best of that tradition. We should push back against the fallenness and injustice around us, and within us. We live in a world where too many children are disposed of as medical waste, and where too many languish in orphanages and in group homes. We live in a world where too many persons are trafficked and molested, too many are ravaged by divorce and poverty, too many are placed in shallow graves as a result of famine or disease or genocide. Too many are dehumanized because of their ethnicity or their immigration status or their stage of development. Too many are harassed for their deepest convictions by tyrants or armies or bureaucrats. We ought to stand then with conviction and contend, as the prophets and apostles did before us, against injustice. But we must do so with voices shaped by the gospel, with a convictional kindness that recognizes that winning arguments is not enough if one is in a cosmic struggle with unseen principalities and powers in the air around us.

At the same time, we must recognize that this is a different day. The Bible Belt will not long be a safe haven for "traditional moral values." Increasingly, the church is recognizing that more and more Americans do not greet us as liberators, but indeed see the idea of a "Christian America" as more of a threat than an ideal. If we ever were a moral majority, it's hard to make the case that we are anymore. Let's not seek to resuscitate the old civil religions. Let's work instead for something new, and for something old: the kingdom of God, on earth as it is in heaven, gathered in churches of transformed people, reconciled to one another, on mission with one another, holding together the authentic gospel of Jesus Christ. Let's avoid the temptation to keep saying the same thing we've always said, except louder and angrier. And let's avoid the temptation of retreating into our subculture, or of disentangling the gospel from our concern for human well-being. If we do not surrender to the spirit of the age—and we must not—we will be thought to be culture-warriors. So be it. Let's be Christ-shaped, kingdom-first culture warriors.

> Let's work instead for something new, and for something old: the kingdom of God, on earth as it is in heaven, gathered in churches of transformed people, reconciled to one another, on mission with one another, holding together the authentic gospel of Jesus Christ.

We all see, the Bible tells us, "through a glass darkly," but I find myself looking, more and more, at the world through that little shard of shattered stained glass. It reminds me of who I am, where I come from, and who found me there. But it also reminds me of brokenness, of loss, of what it means to live in a universe at war. It reminds me that no matter how rooted we are, we are strangers and aliens still. We are all broken shards of glass, rejected building stones, being fitted into a temple we cannot fully even imagine. The gospel we've received isn't just strange to the culture around us; it's strange to us too. That's what makes it good news.

It's our turn to march into the future. And we do so not as a moral majority or a righteous remnant but just as crucified sinners, with nothing to offer the world but a broken body and spilled blood and unceasing witness. We are strangers and exiles, on our best days, but we are not orphans and wanderers. Our strangeness is only hopeful if it is freakishly clinging to the strange, strange mission of Christ crucified and risen. The pursuit of righteousness and justice is of no purpose if it doesn't flow from seeking the kingdom first. Beside us, there may be flags, and we'll pledge allegiance where we ought and where we can. But over, always over us, there's a cross. We may not always see where we are going, but we know the Way.

Onward.

ACKNOWLEDGMENTS

In some sense, I've been writing this book all of my life, seeking to articulate what I believe about the relationship between the kingdom of God and the cultures of this present era. There are more people to thank in the span of all these years than I could possibly note here.

First, I wish to thank Woolmarket Baptist Church in Biloxi, Mississippi. John Calvin rightly said that no one has God for his Father who does not have the church for his mother. My mother congregation taught me well. Thanks to that church, I can confidently say, before and after everything else, "Jesus loves me; this I know."

Thank you to two very different men, one who worked mostly in the City of God and the other in the City of Man, who shaped my thinking and intuitions from very early on. Carl F. H. Henry, now with the Lord, spent time with me near the end of his life, answering questions and spurring me on. His little book, *The Uneasy Conscience of Modern Fundamentalism*, influenced me more than anything in print not inspired by the Holy Spirit. And United States Congressman Gene Taylor, my old boss, mentored me as a man who served in public life with integrity and skill.

I am grateful to my band of happy warriors here at the Ethics and Religious Liberty Commission, especially my cabinet members Phillip Bethancourt, Daniel Patterson, Barrett Duke, Daniel Darling, and Andrew Walker, and my assistant Sam Dahl. These friends and colleagues encouraged me along and asked the sorts of questions that helped sharpen my arguments. More than that, they make my life joyful because I not only respect each of them, I love them, and look forward to seeing each of them every day.

B&H Publishing Group, my publisher, has been excellent, every step of the way. I am especially grateful to Jennifer Lyell, director of trade publishing, and my editor, Devin Maddox. The two of them are creative geniuses with theological and publishing brilliance.

Many of the ideas in this book were started in embryonic form in pieces I wrote in *Christianity Today, First Things, Touchstone,* and elsewhere, as well as in lectures at Boston College, the American Enterprise Institute, the Vatican, and the Faith Angle Forum. I am grateful for all who interacted with me as I spoke and wrote about these issues in all those venues.

Of course, it is not enough to say "thank you" to my beautiful wife Maria, and our five sons, Benjamin, Timothy, Samuel, Jonah, and Taylor. They all adjusted to a major life-change as I took my "dream job" this year. Cheerfully, they've lived with a husband and dad who works in two cities at once. Sometimes that means doing Latin homework prep via computer video uplink. On top of all of that, they helped me as I scribbled away on this book. I look forward to moving onward into the future with them.

This book is dedicated to Jonah, our fourth son. In some ways, that's because it is "his turn." But it is also because he represents for me much of what this book is about. He bears a prophet's name with kindness and gentleness and quiet conviction. He is brimming with grounded hope. Jonah, you are my beloved son and with you I am well pleased.

6-WEEK BIBLE STUDY

ONWARD

·RUSSELL·
MOORE

ENGAGING THE CULTURE
WITHOUT
LOSING THE GOSPEL

SHARE THE ONWARD BIBLE STUDY IN YOUR SMALL GROUP AND HELP OTHERS
RECLAIM THE WEIRDNESS OF THE CHRISTIAN FAITH THAT SETS IT APART.